Foreword

This book is the result of several months spent in various places of Apulia in southern Italy as well as on Google Maps.

While the exceptional architectural heritage of the region is nowadays well known, this attempt highlights sacred places that have never really won the local population over.

It is a story of accidents.

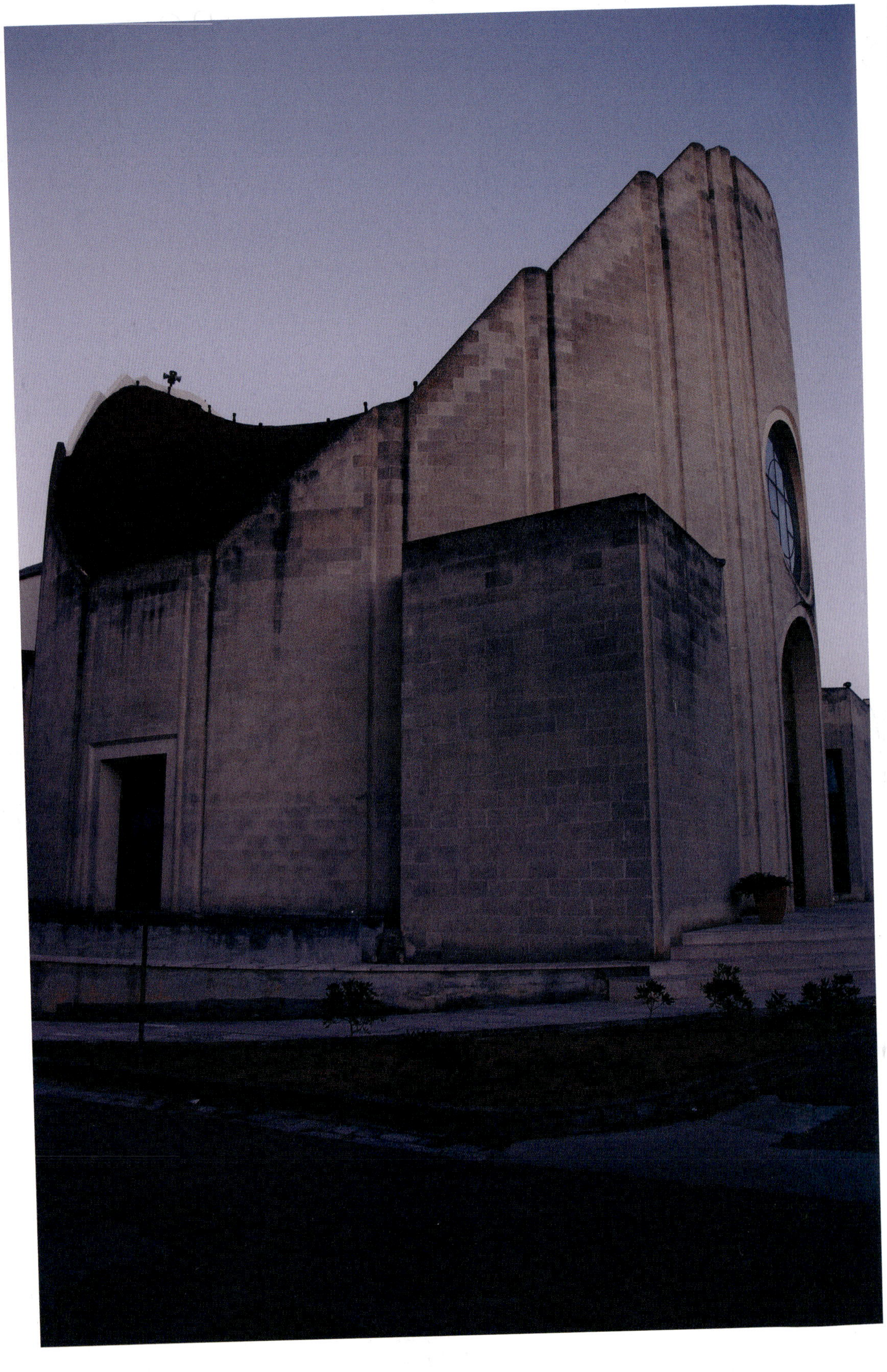

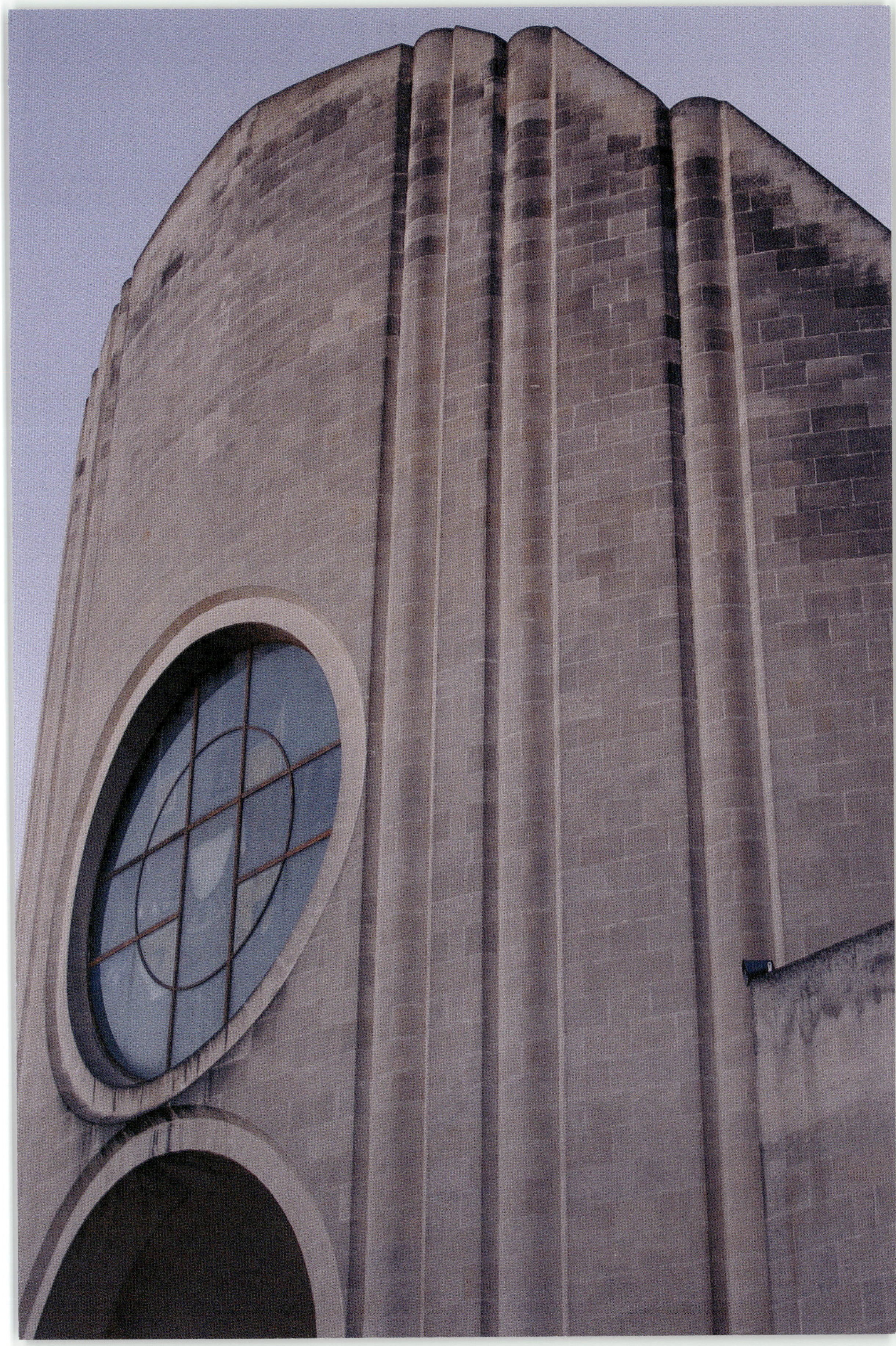

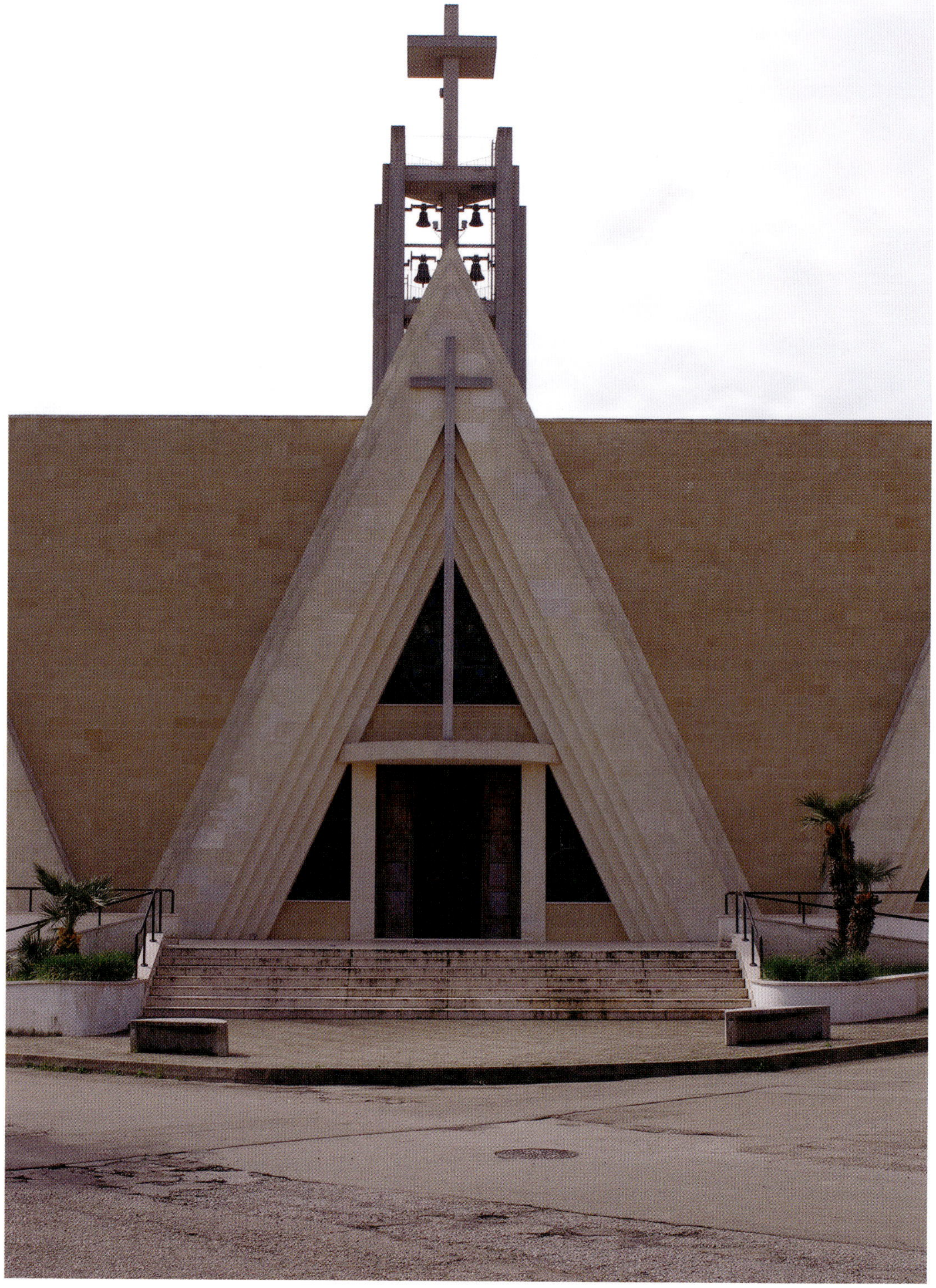

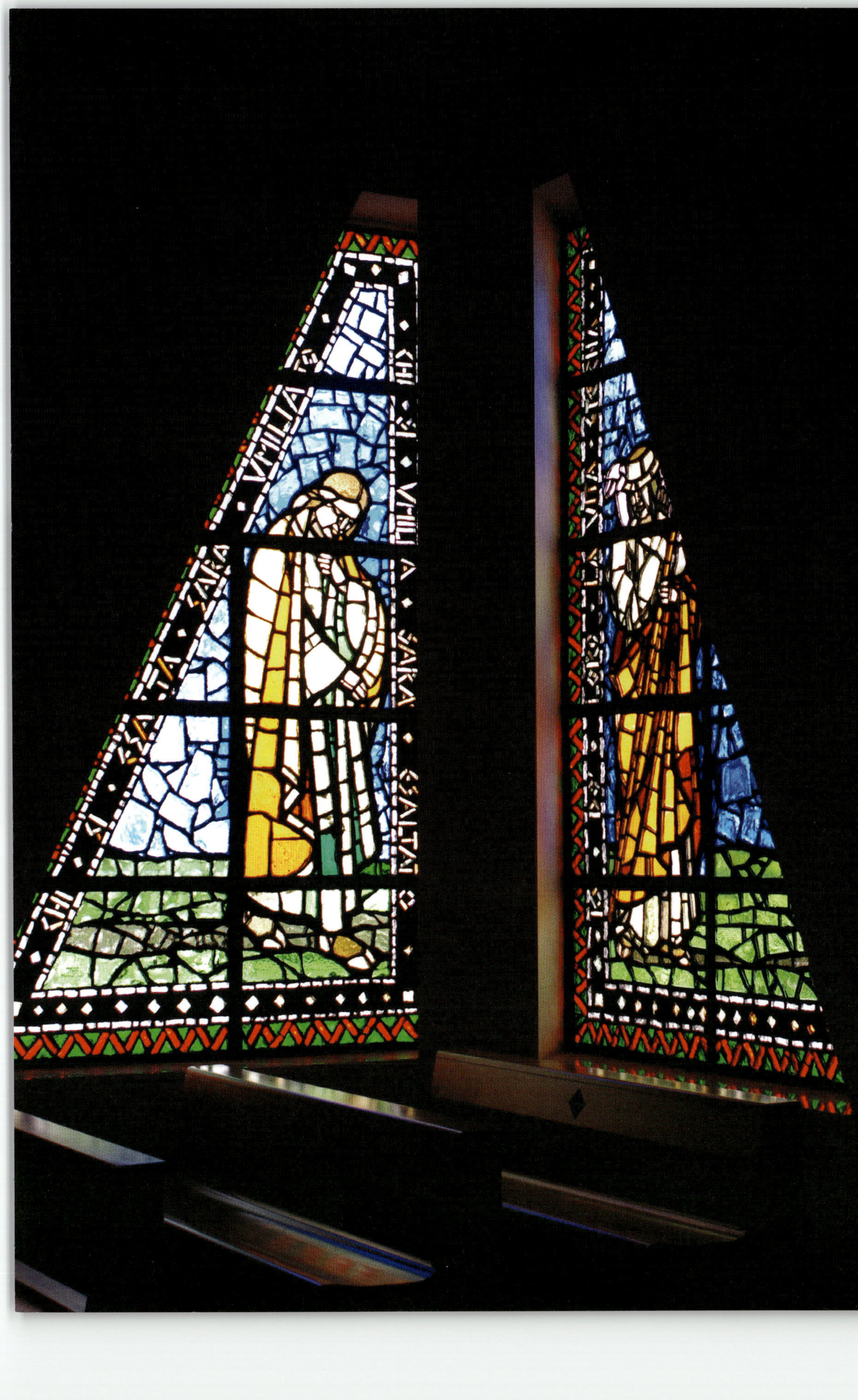

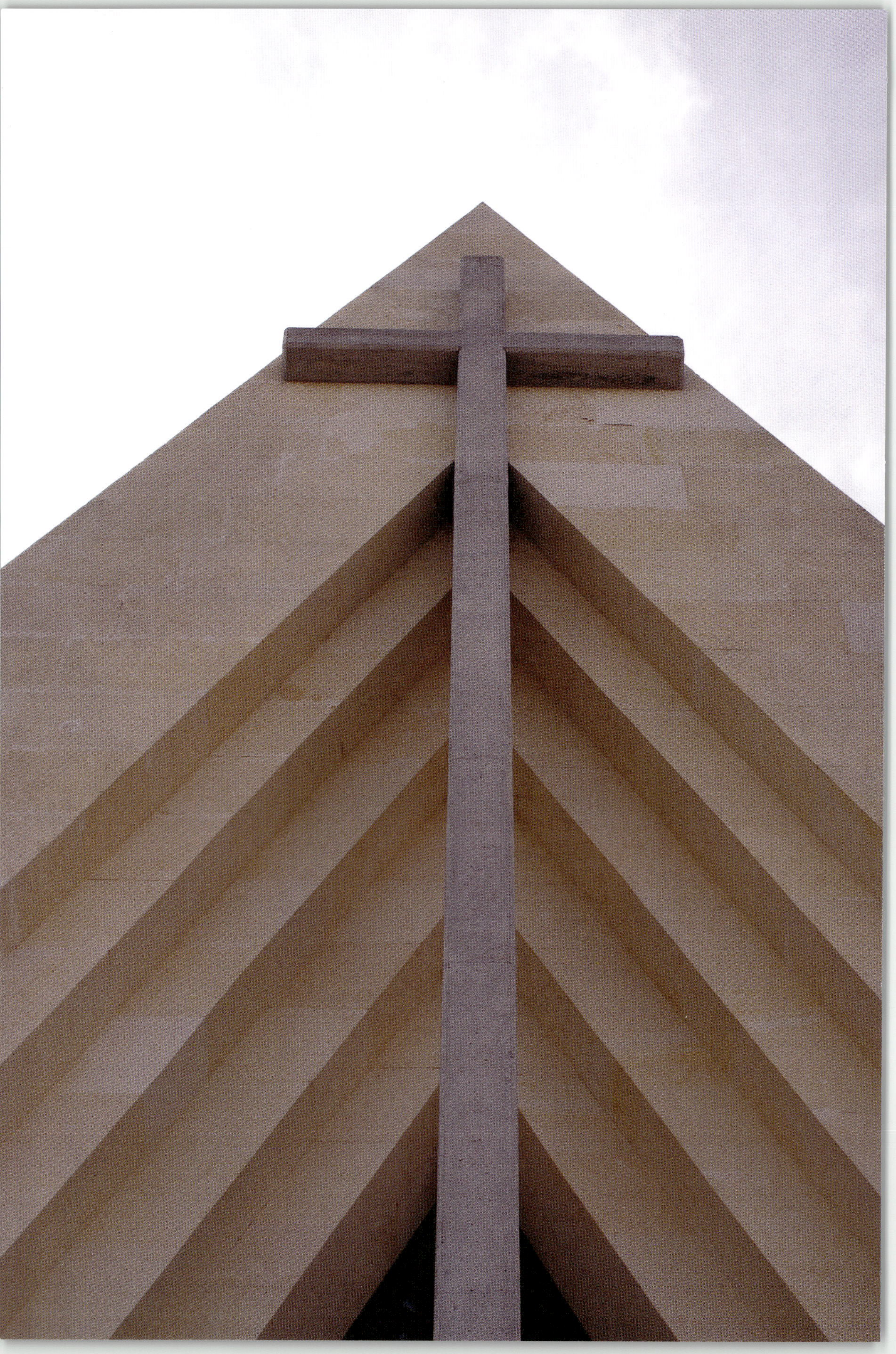

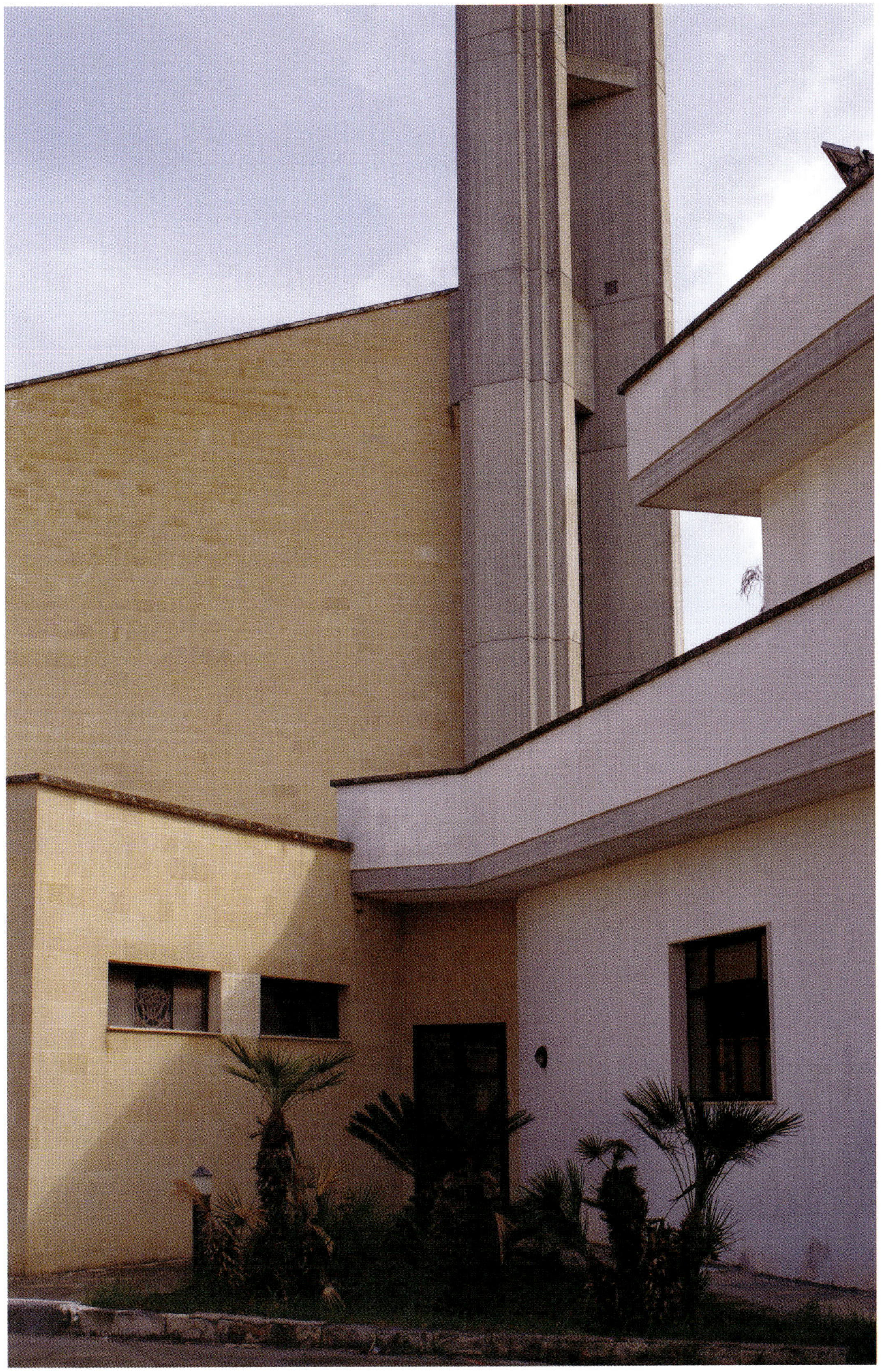

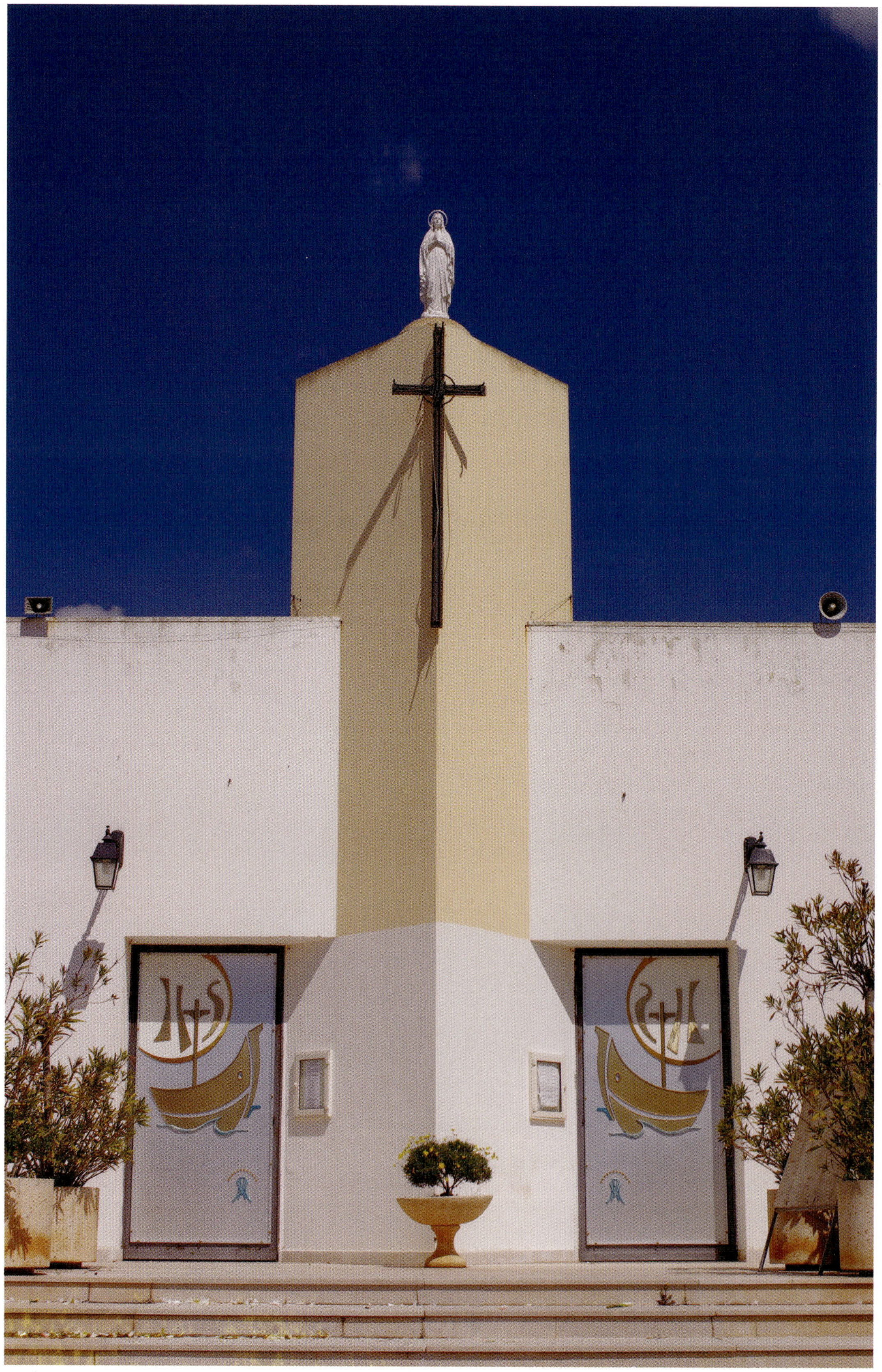

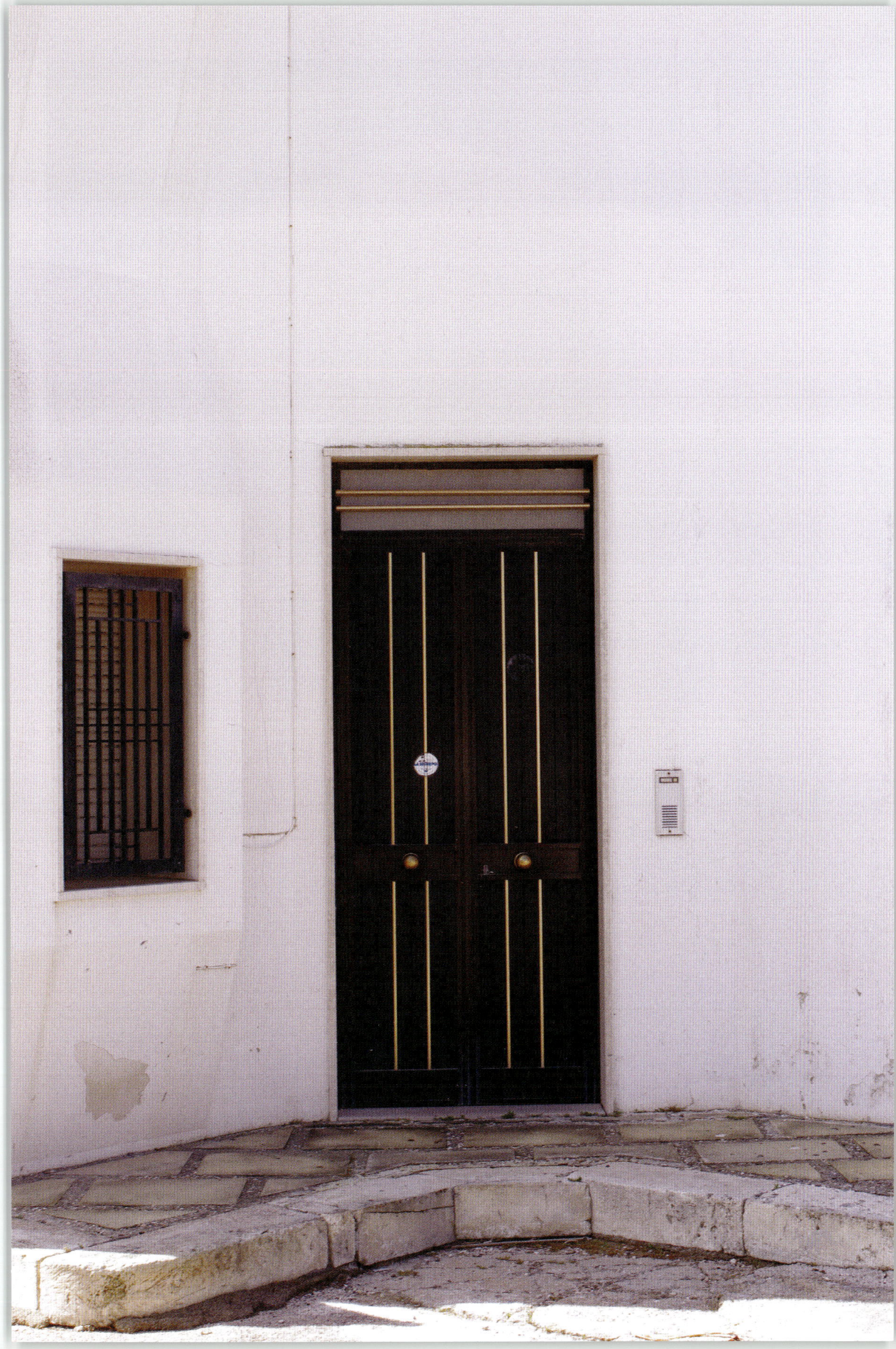

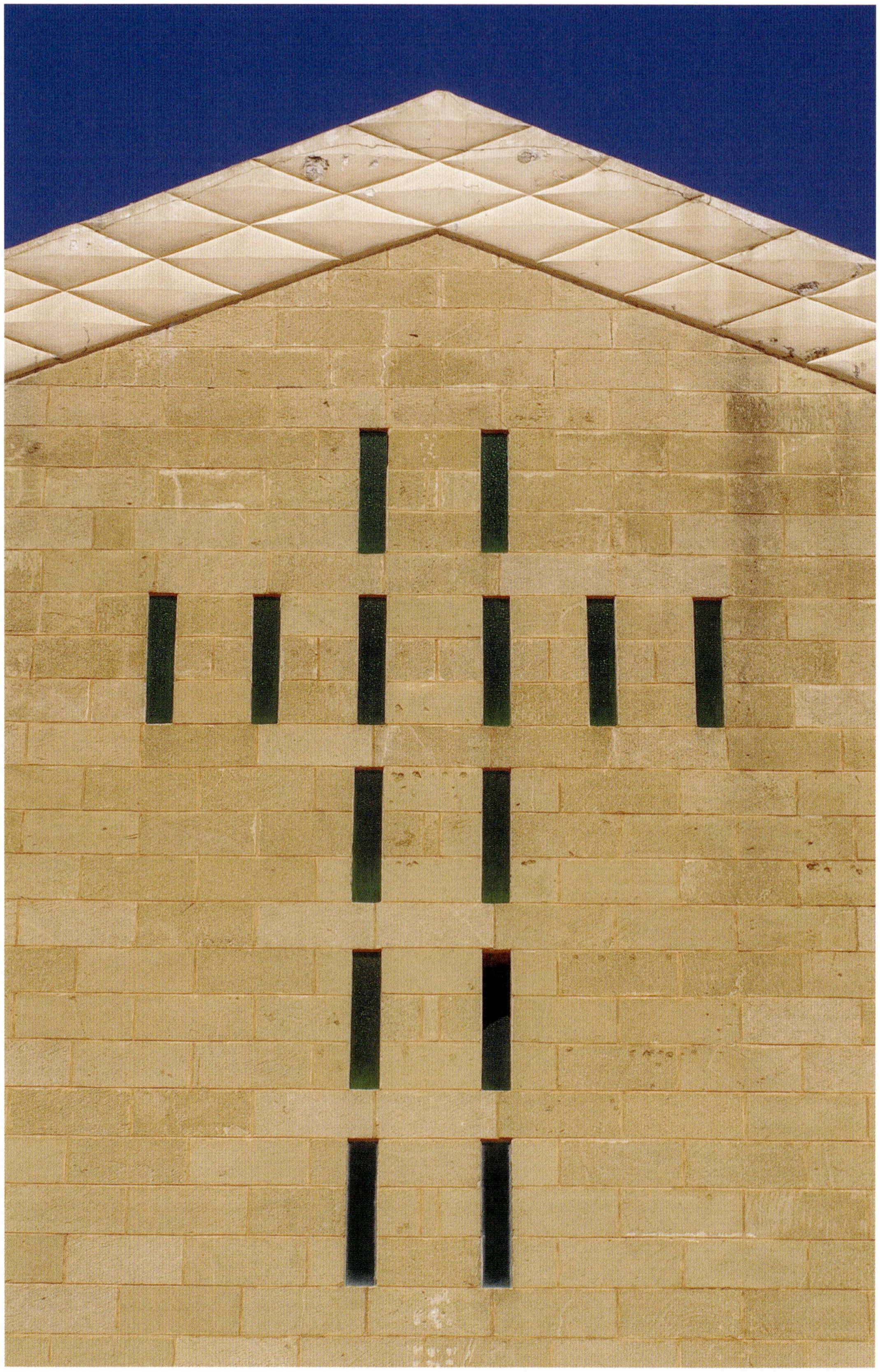

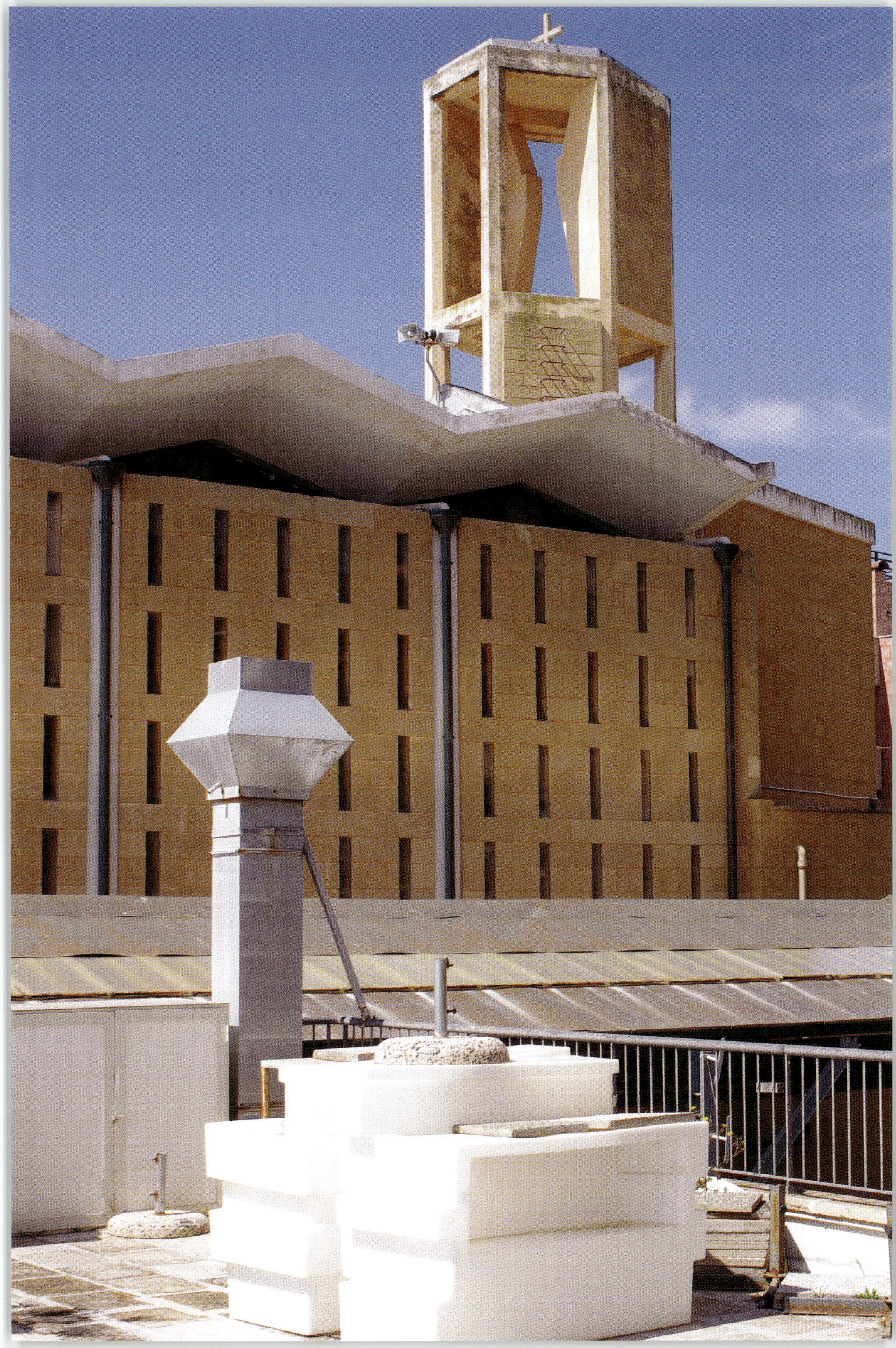

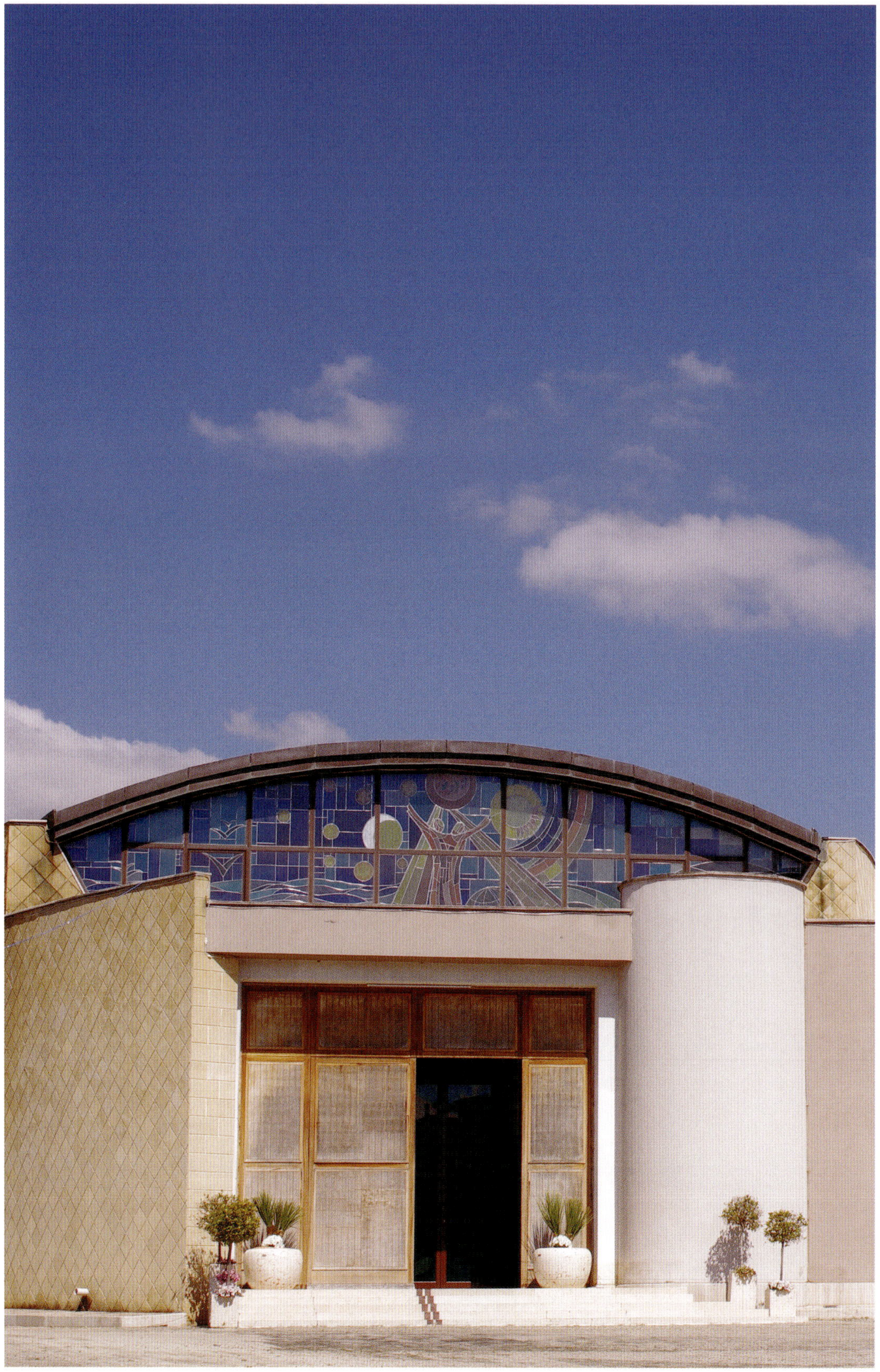

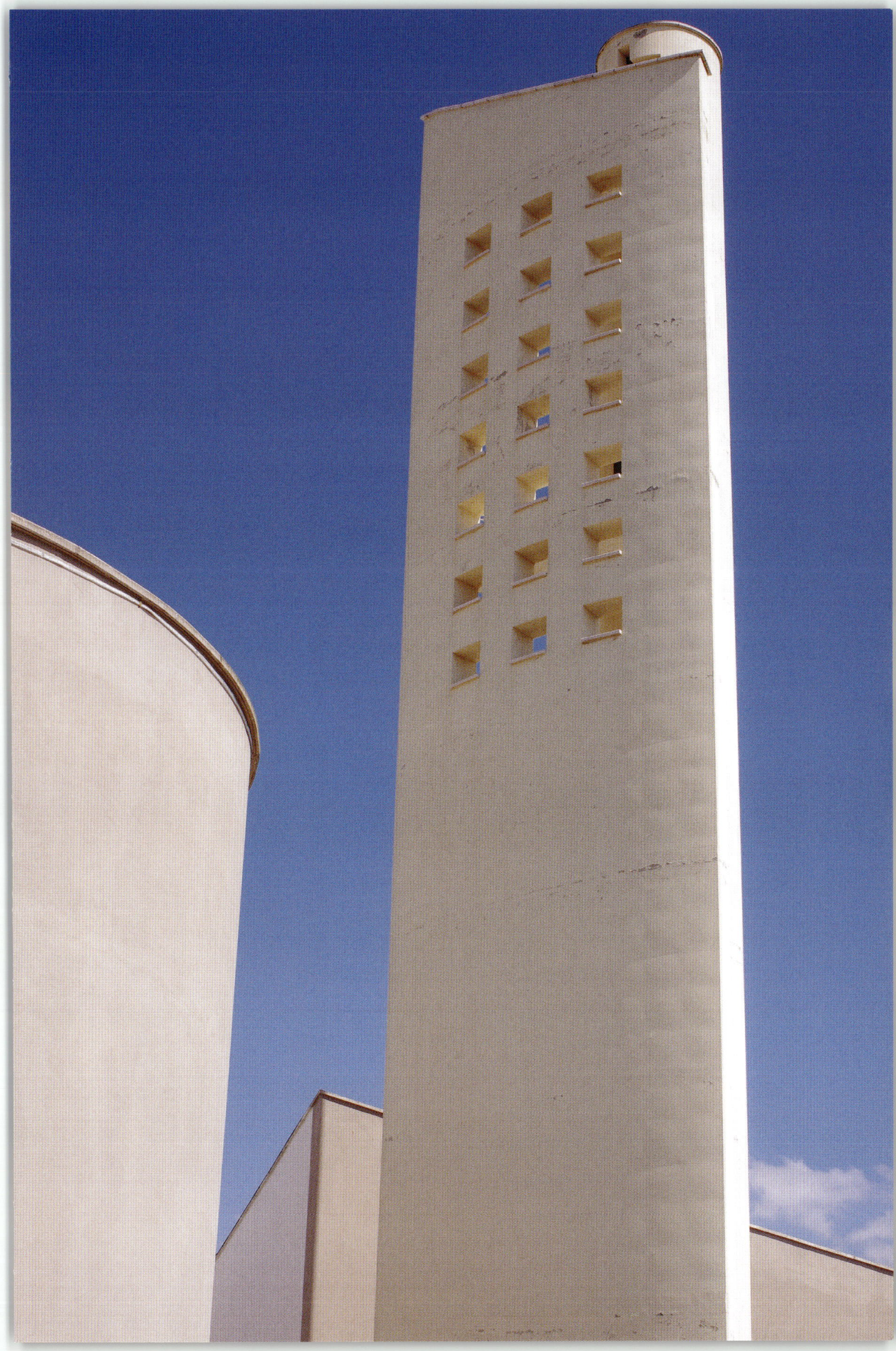

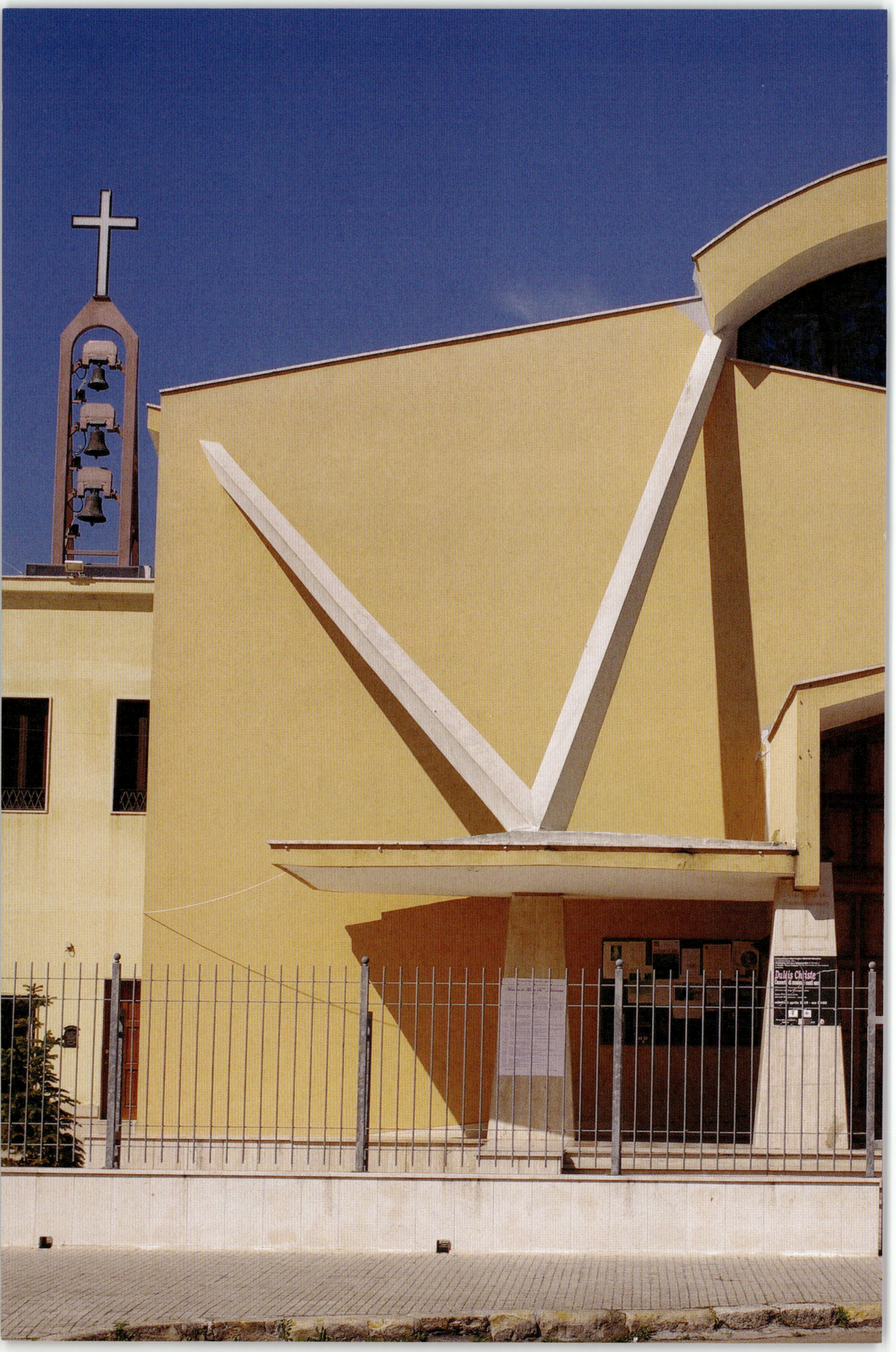

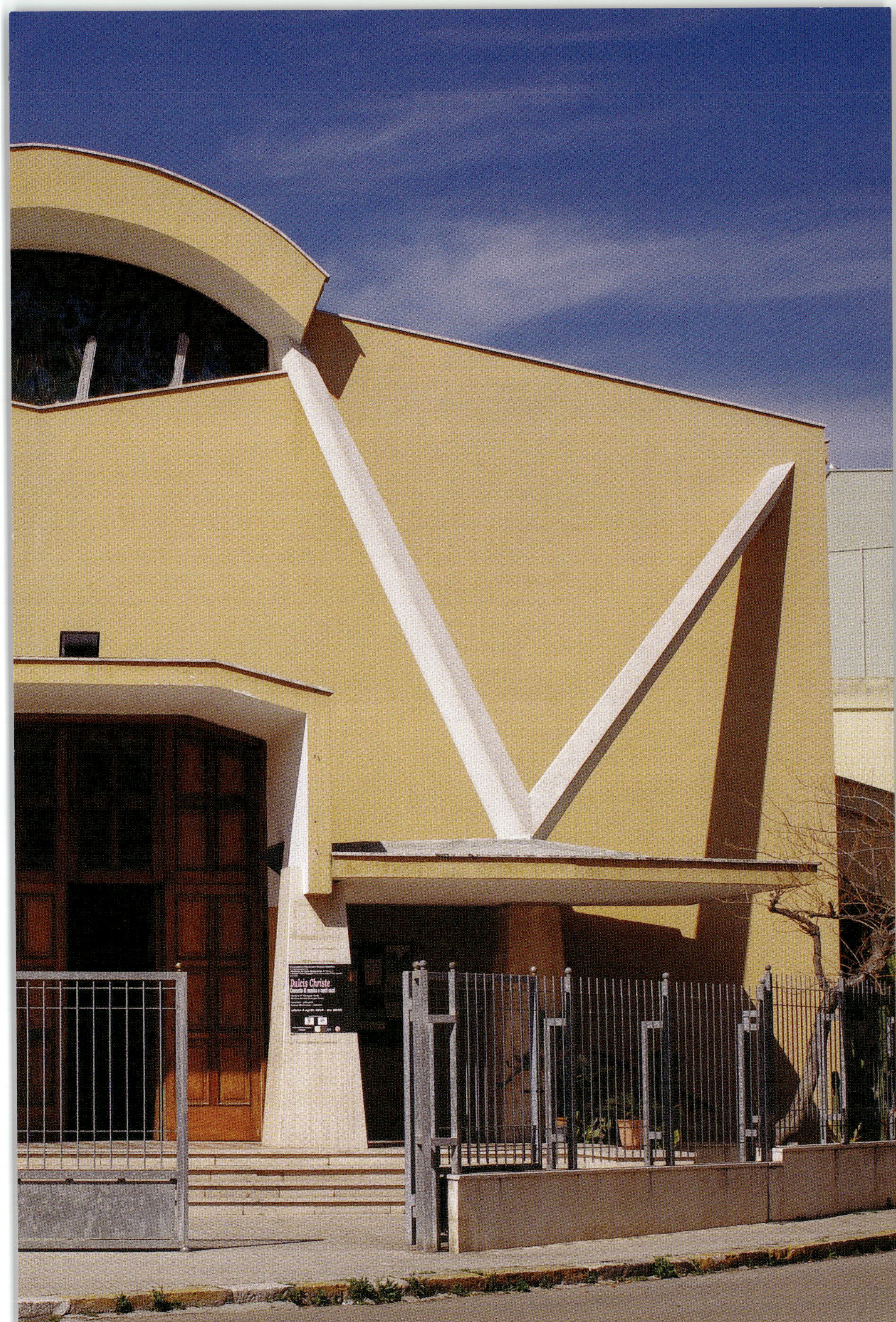
Dulcis Christe

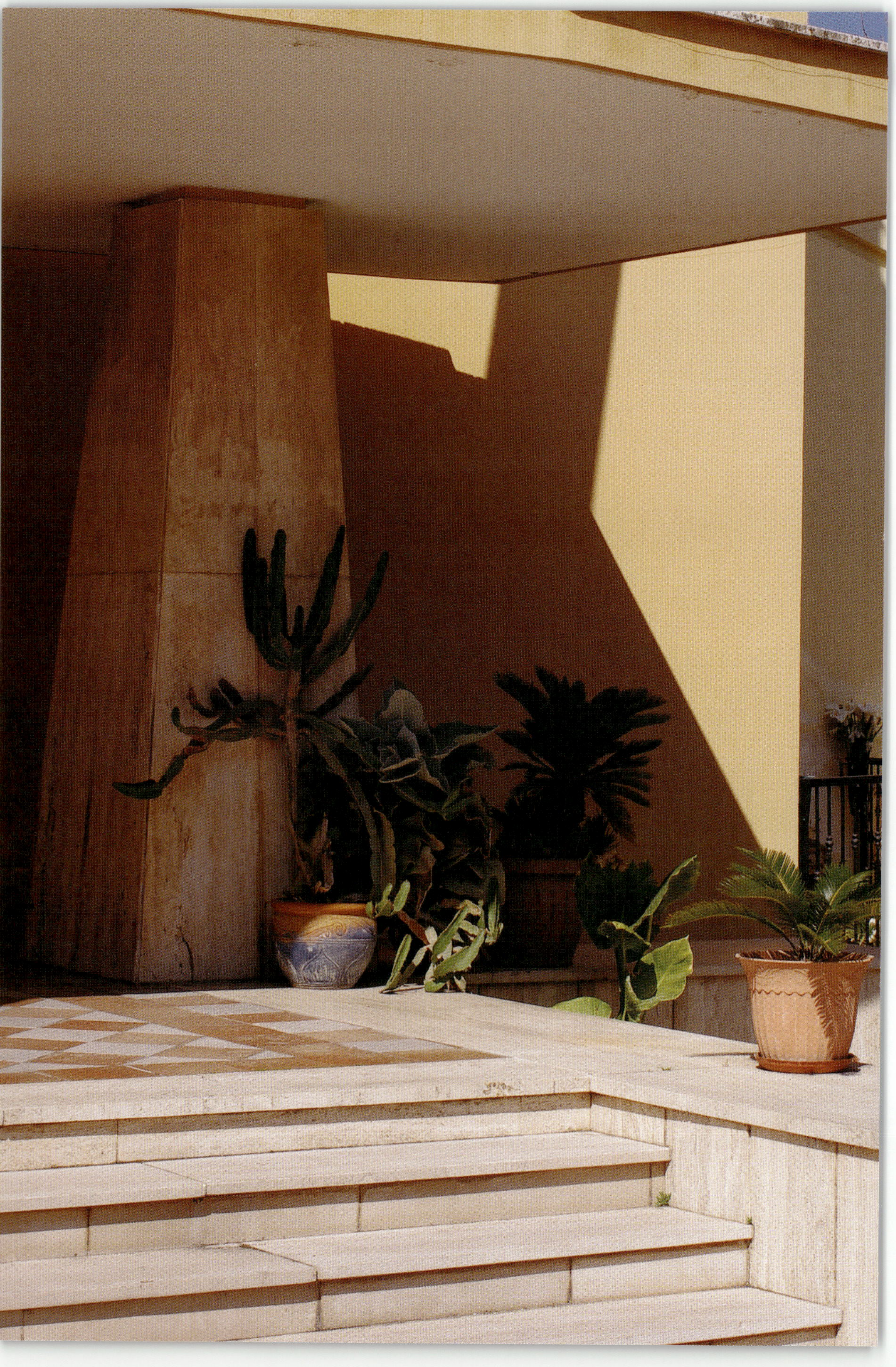

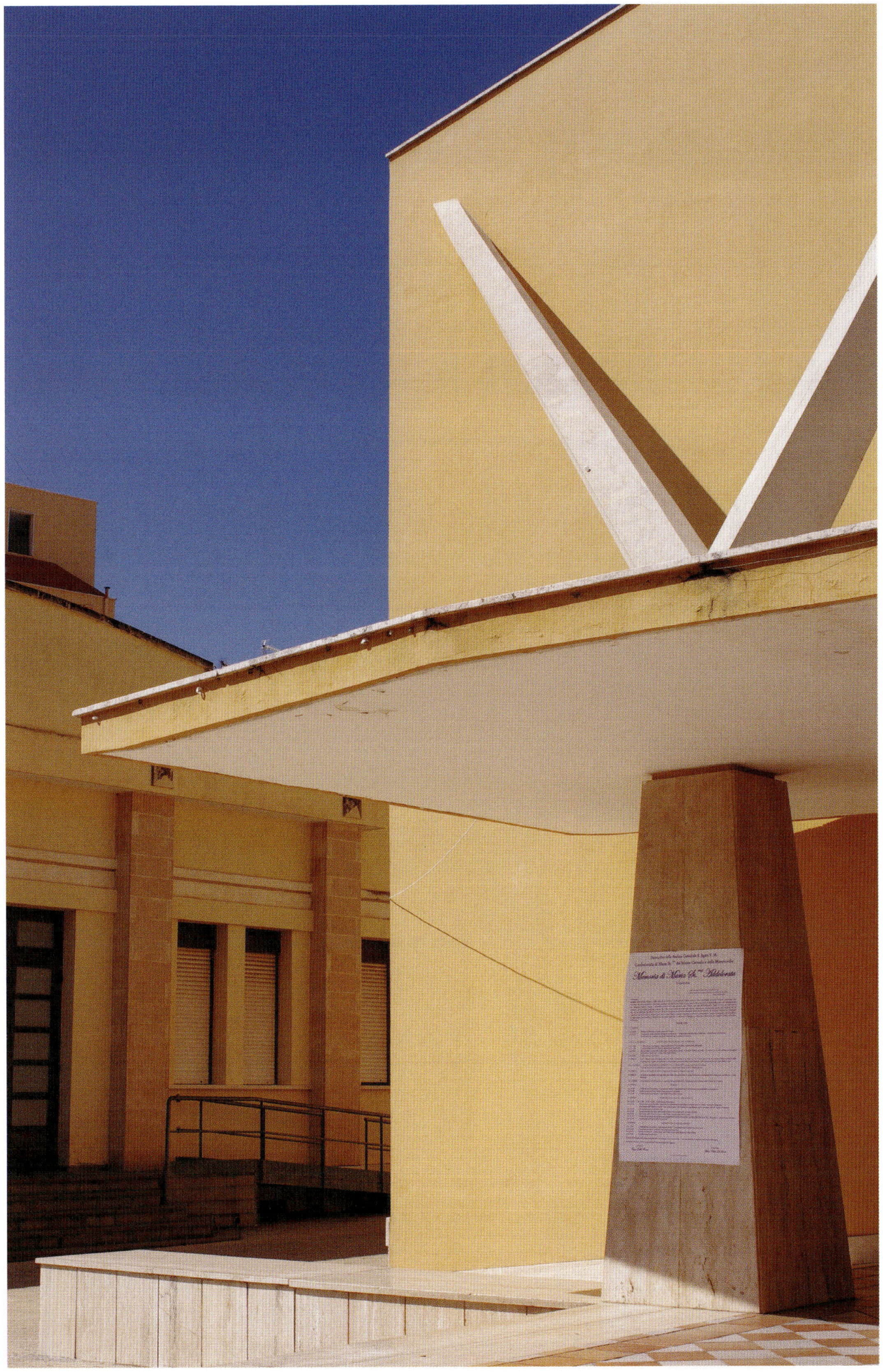

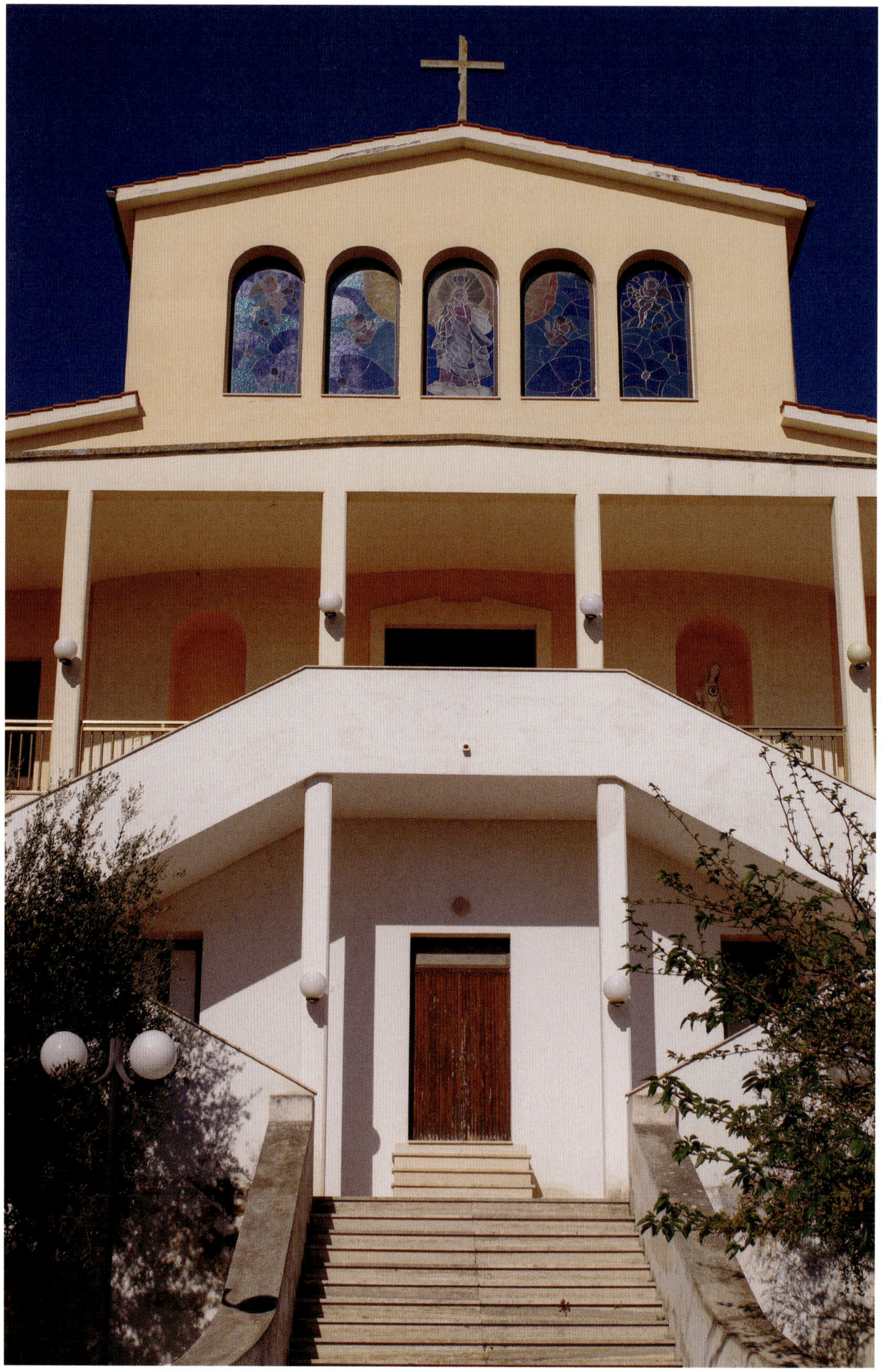

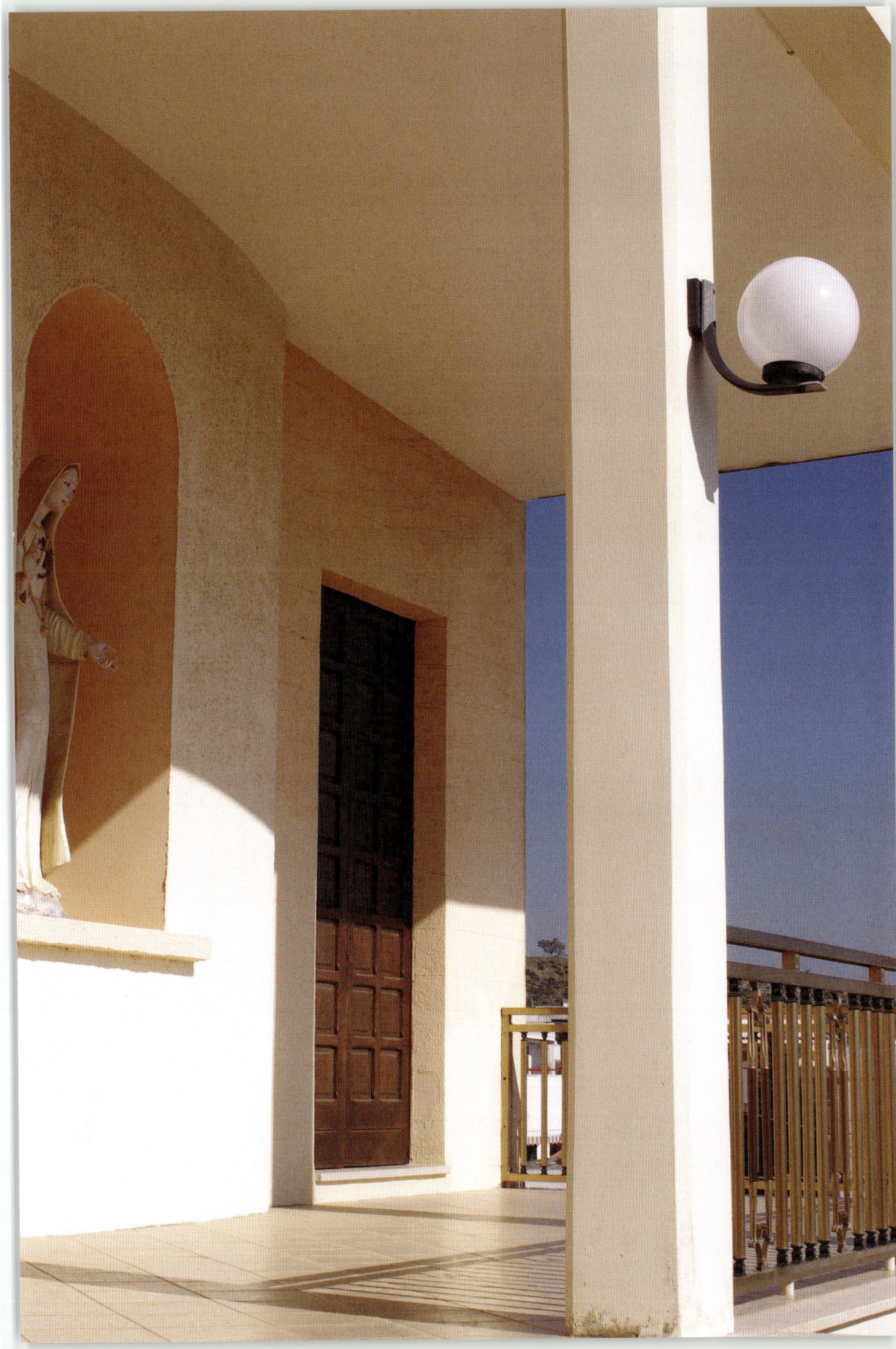

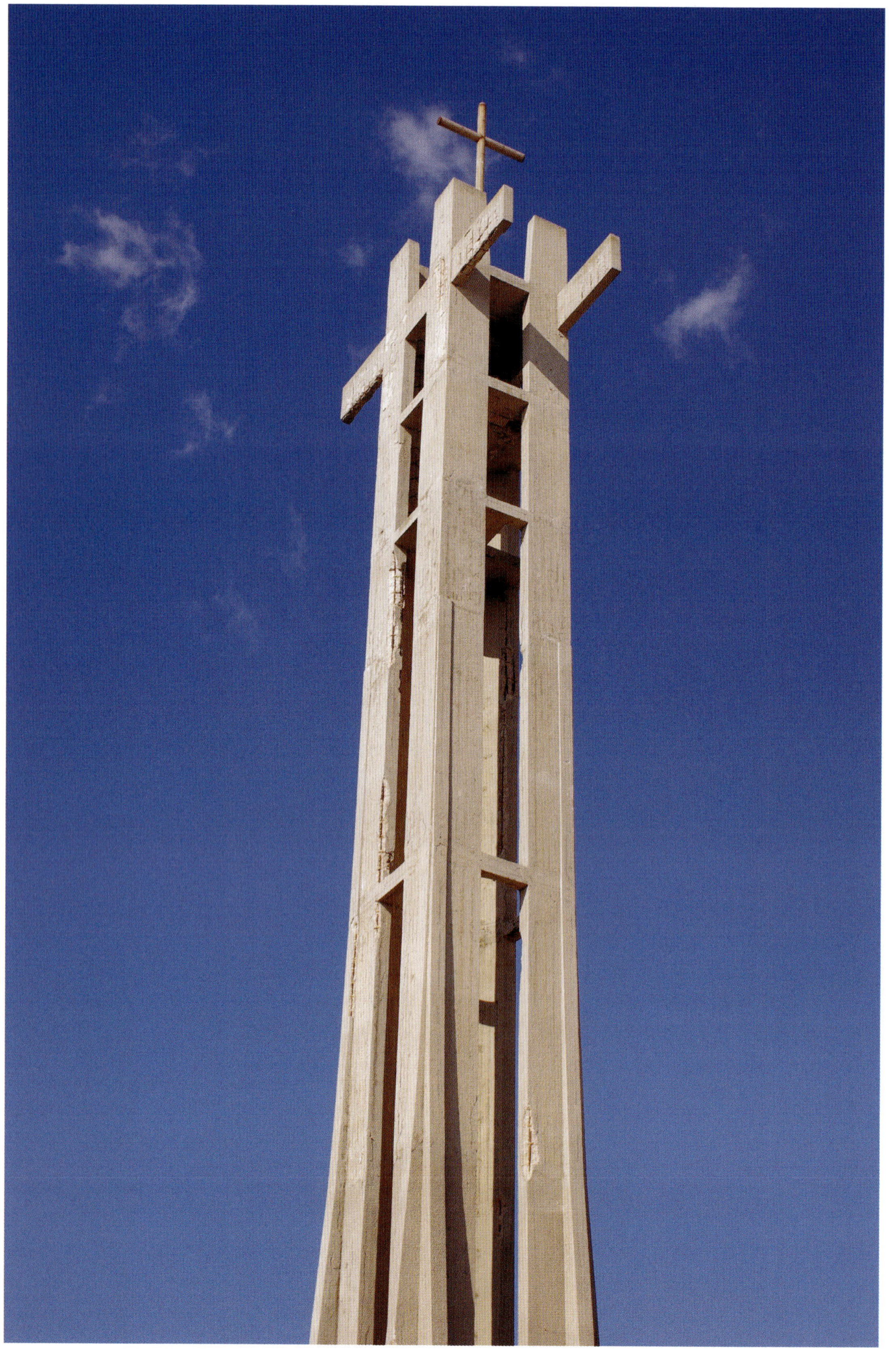

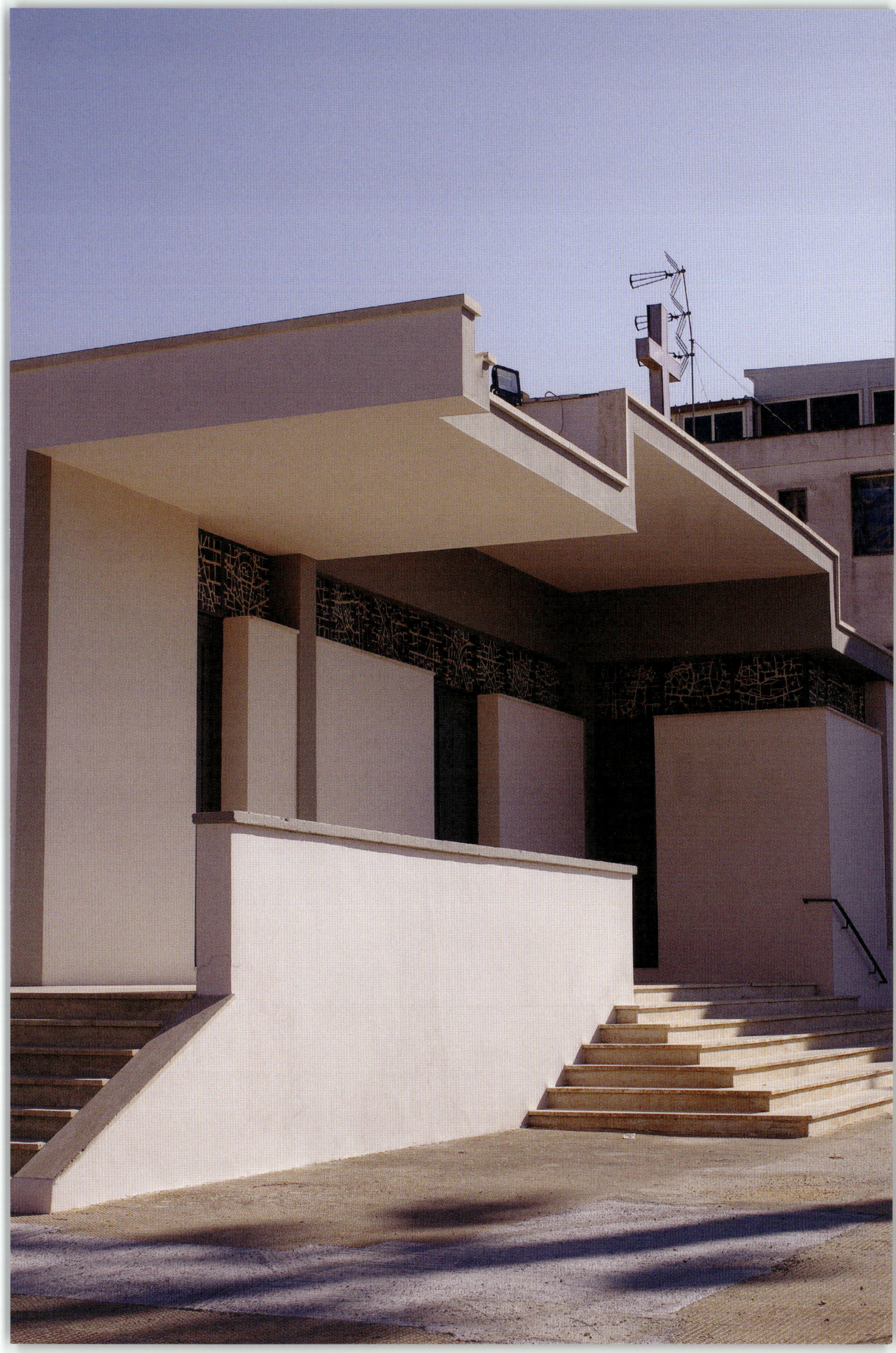

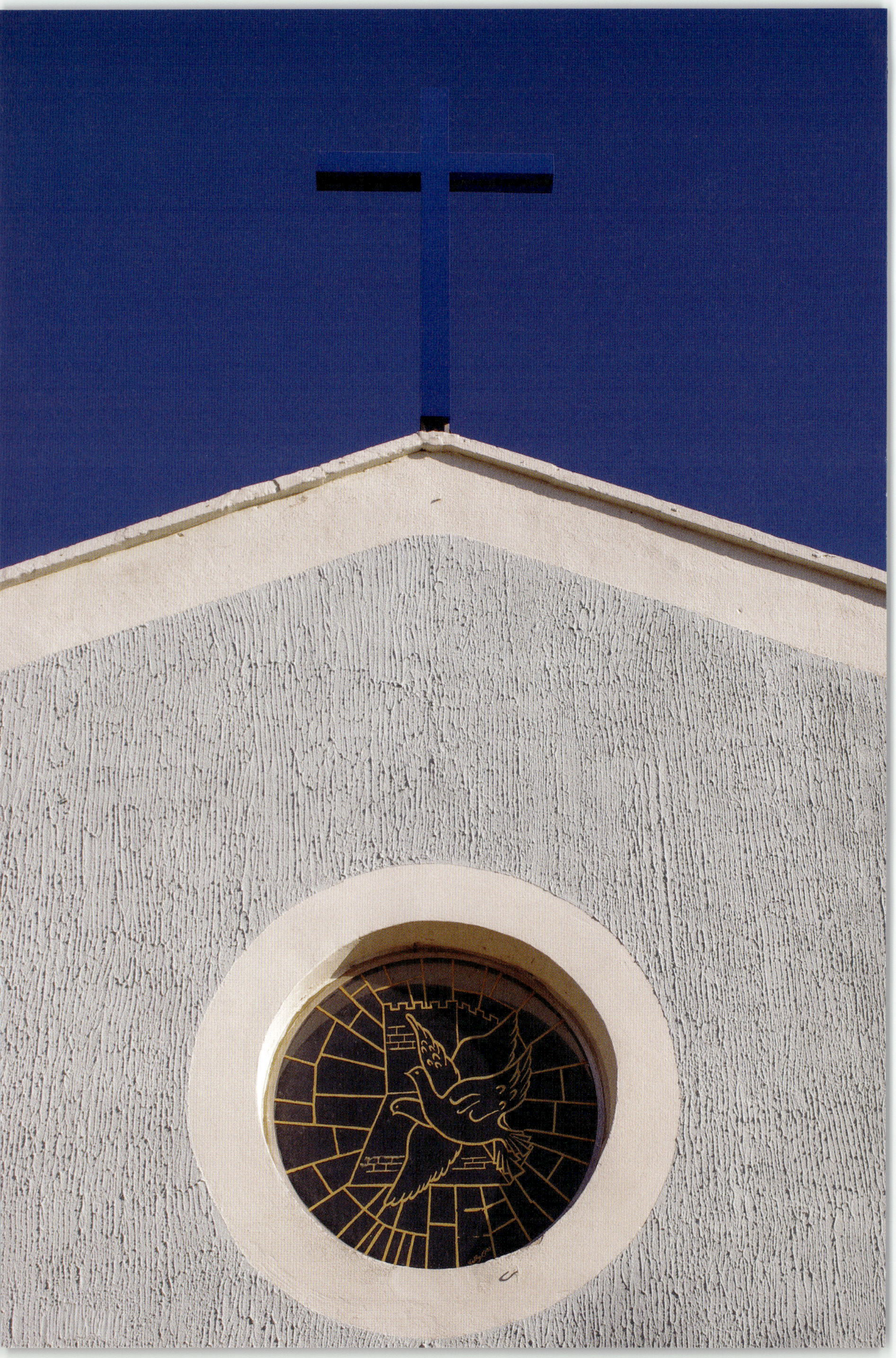

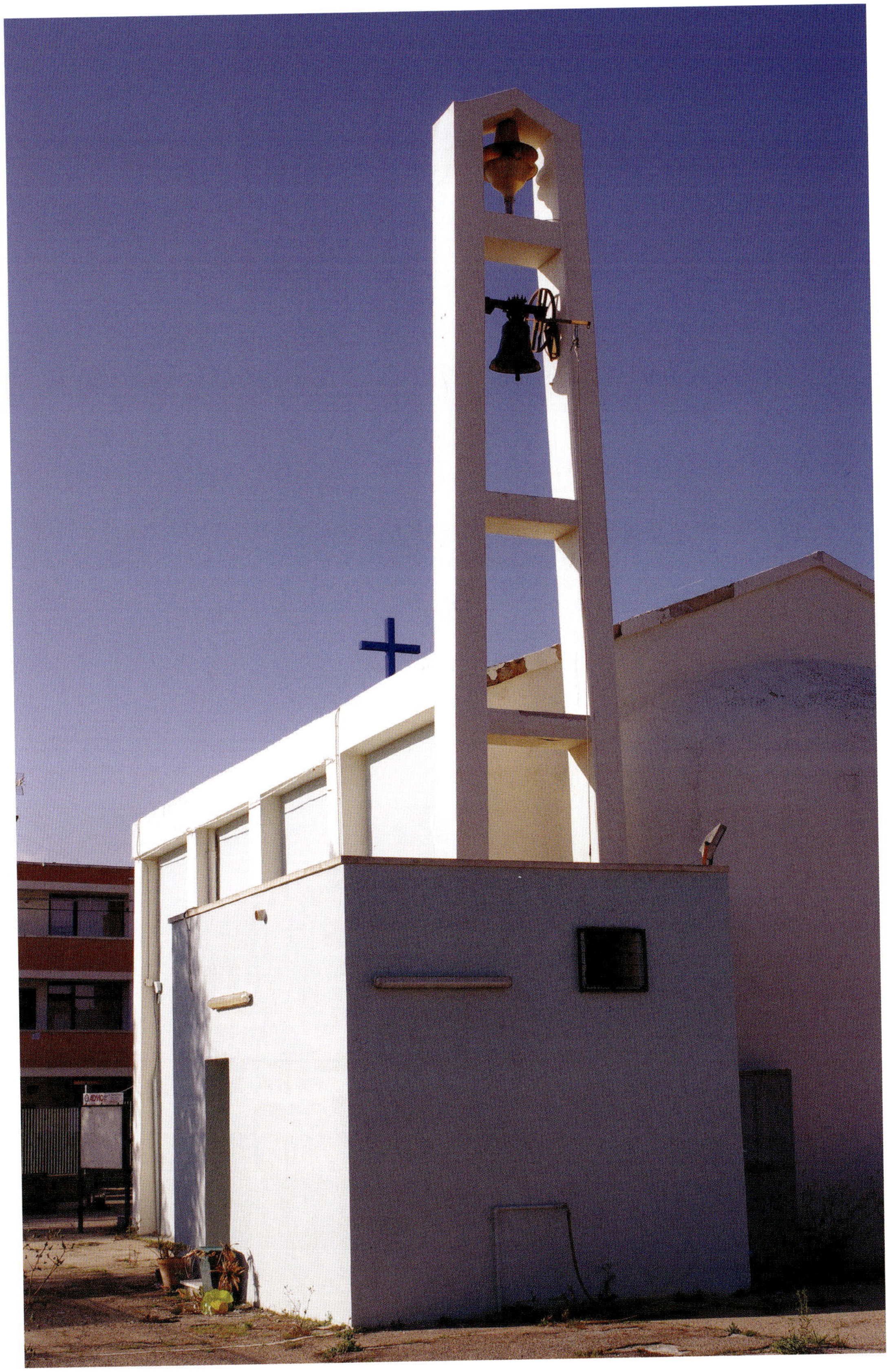

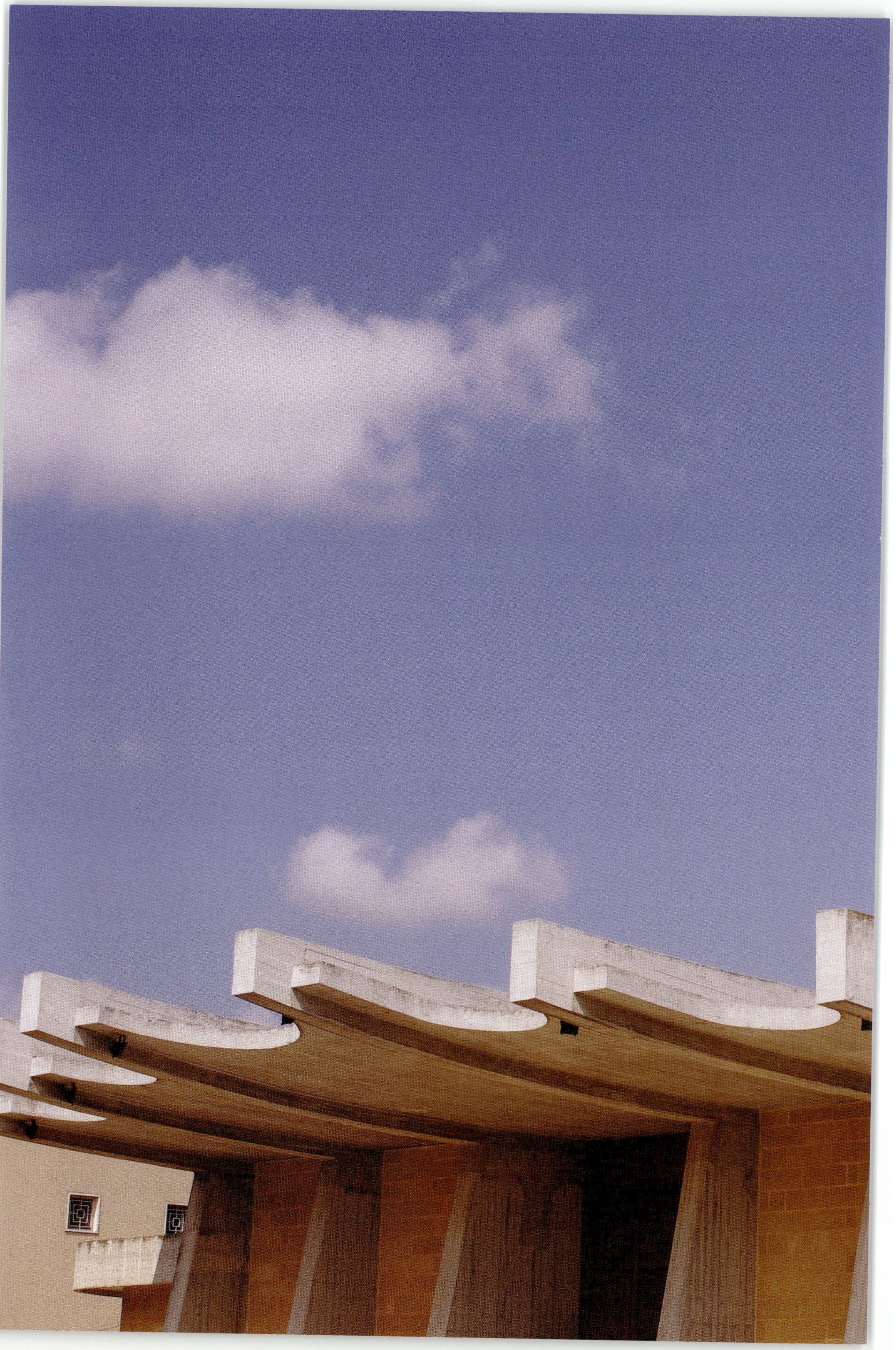

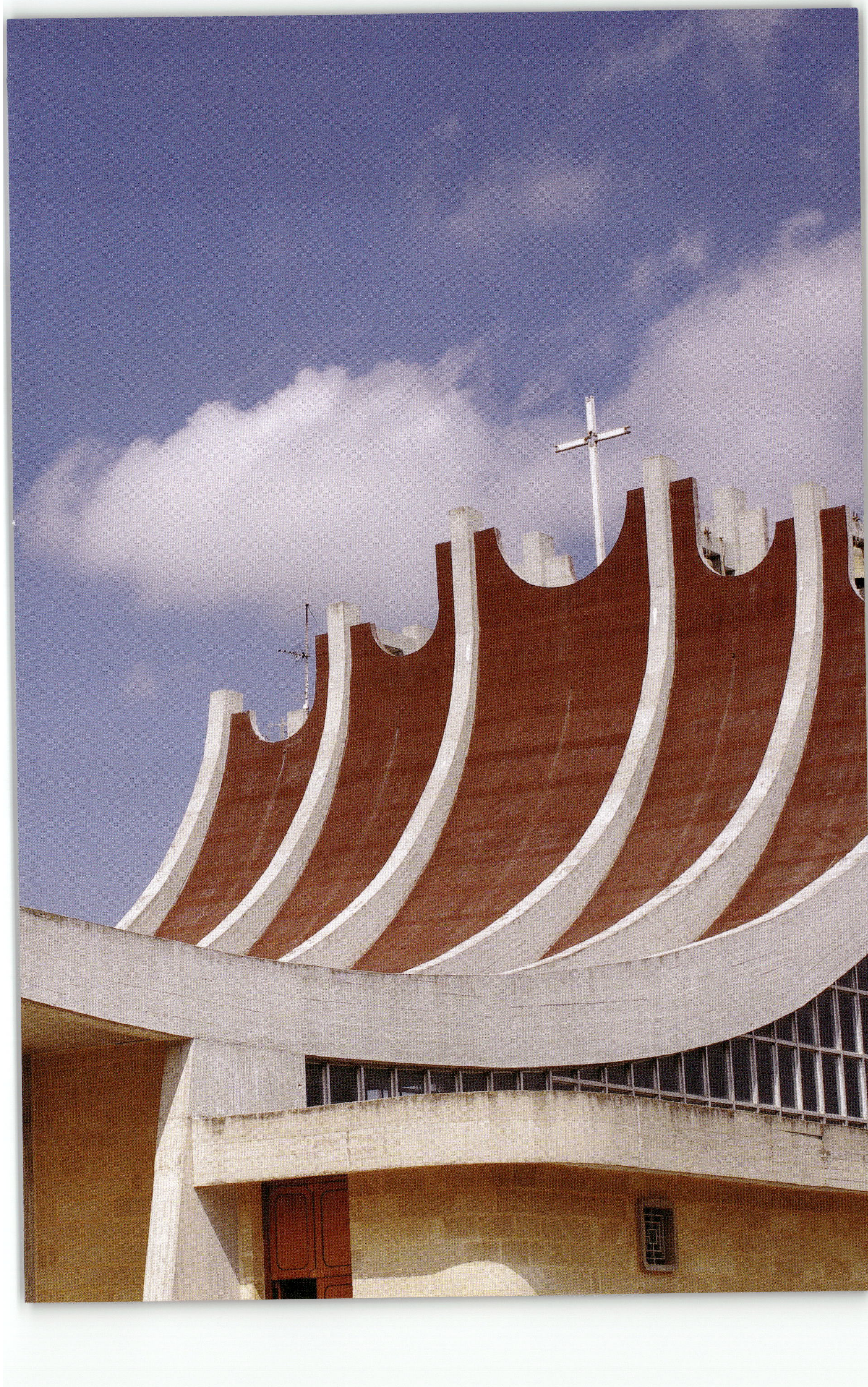

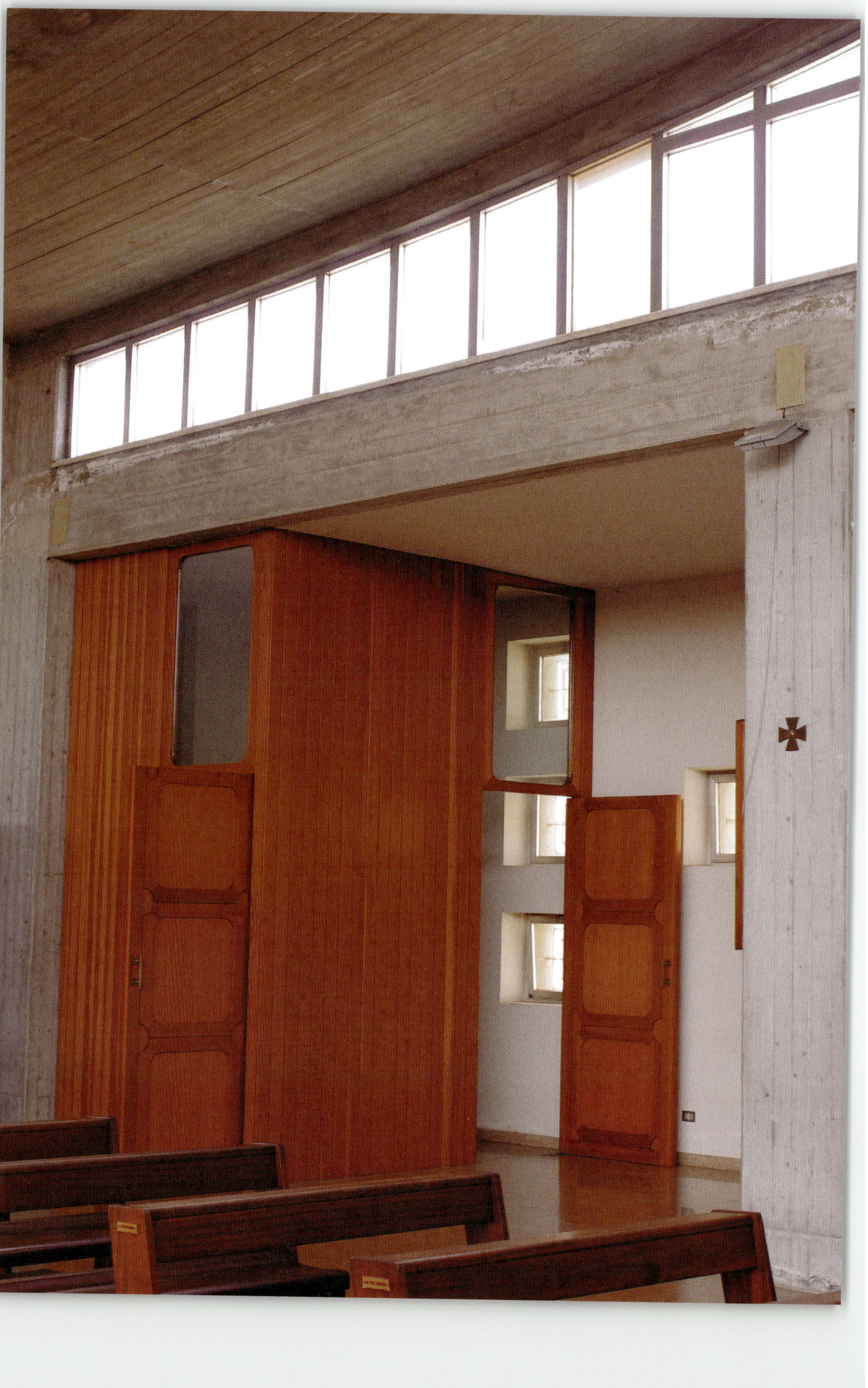

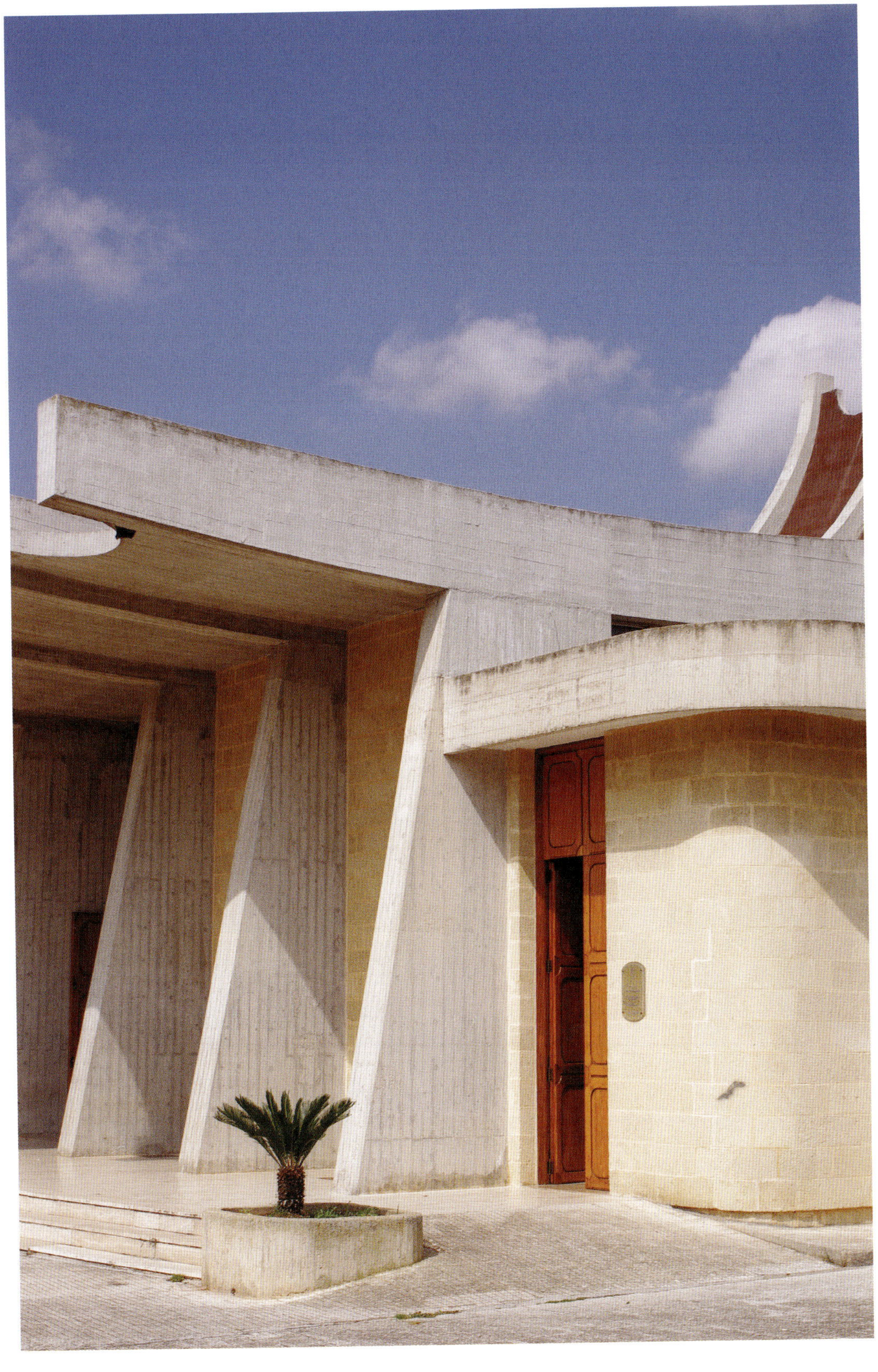

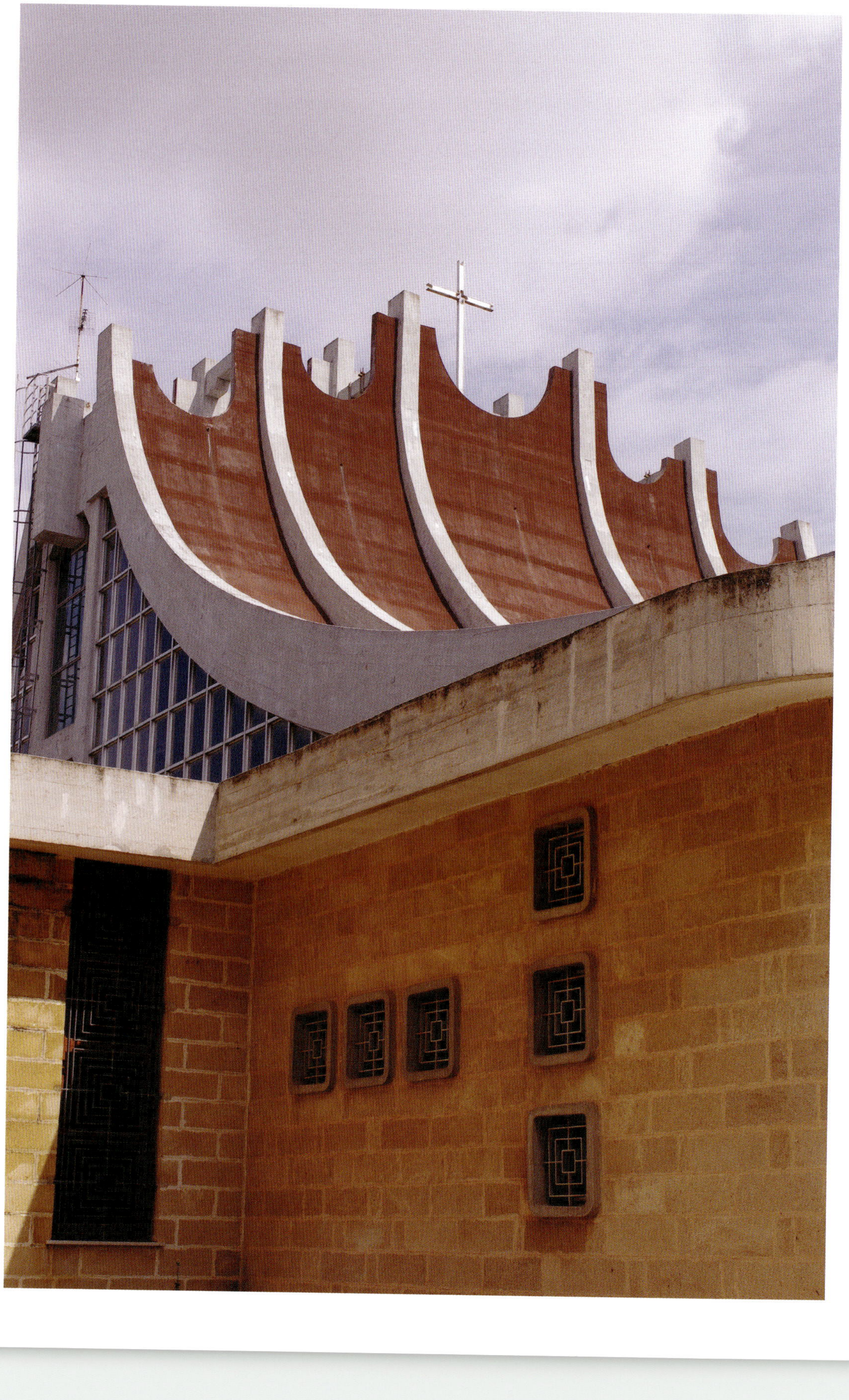

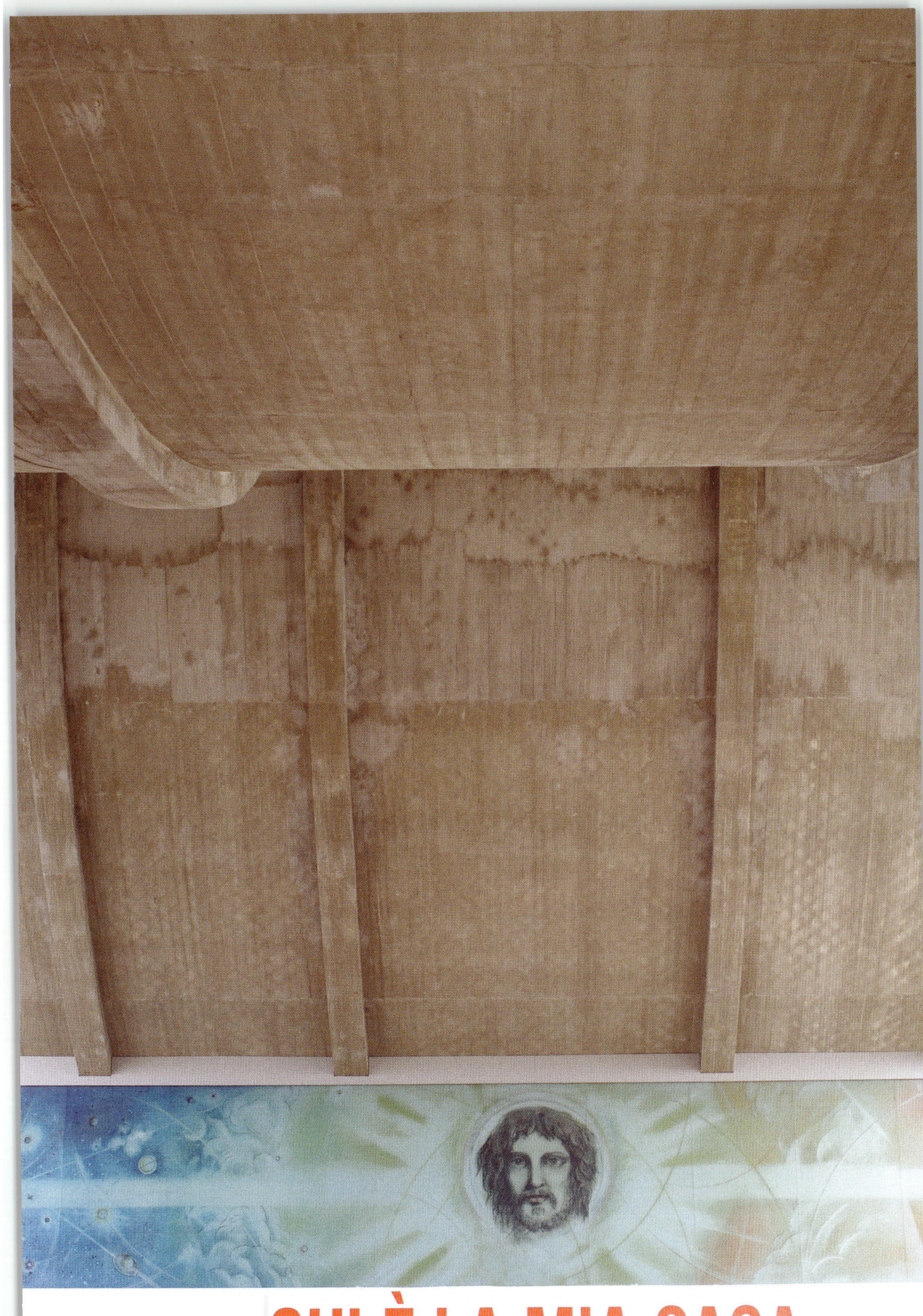

QUI È LA MIA CASA

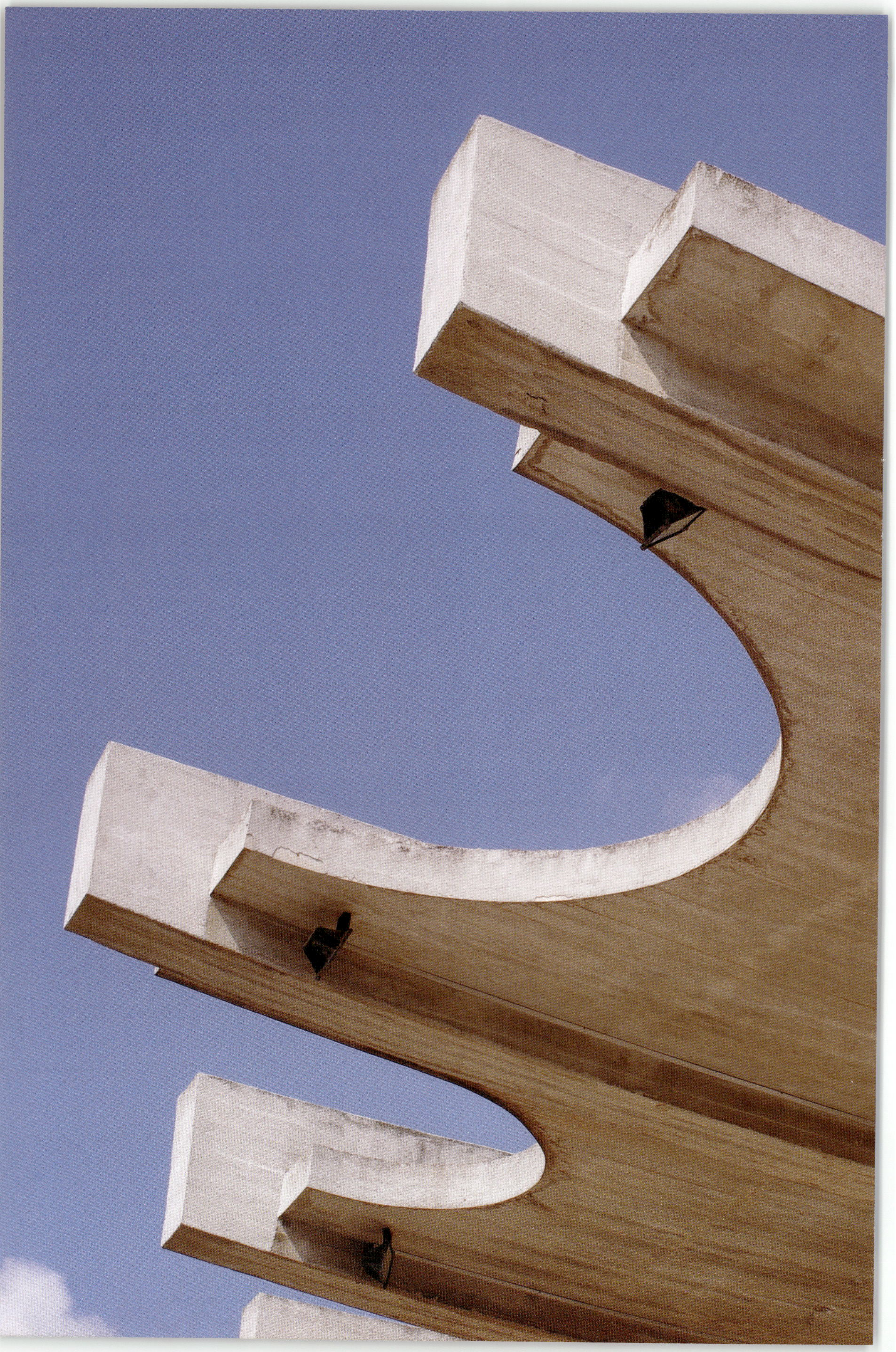

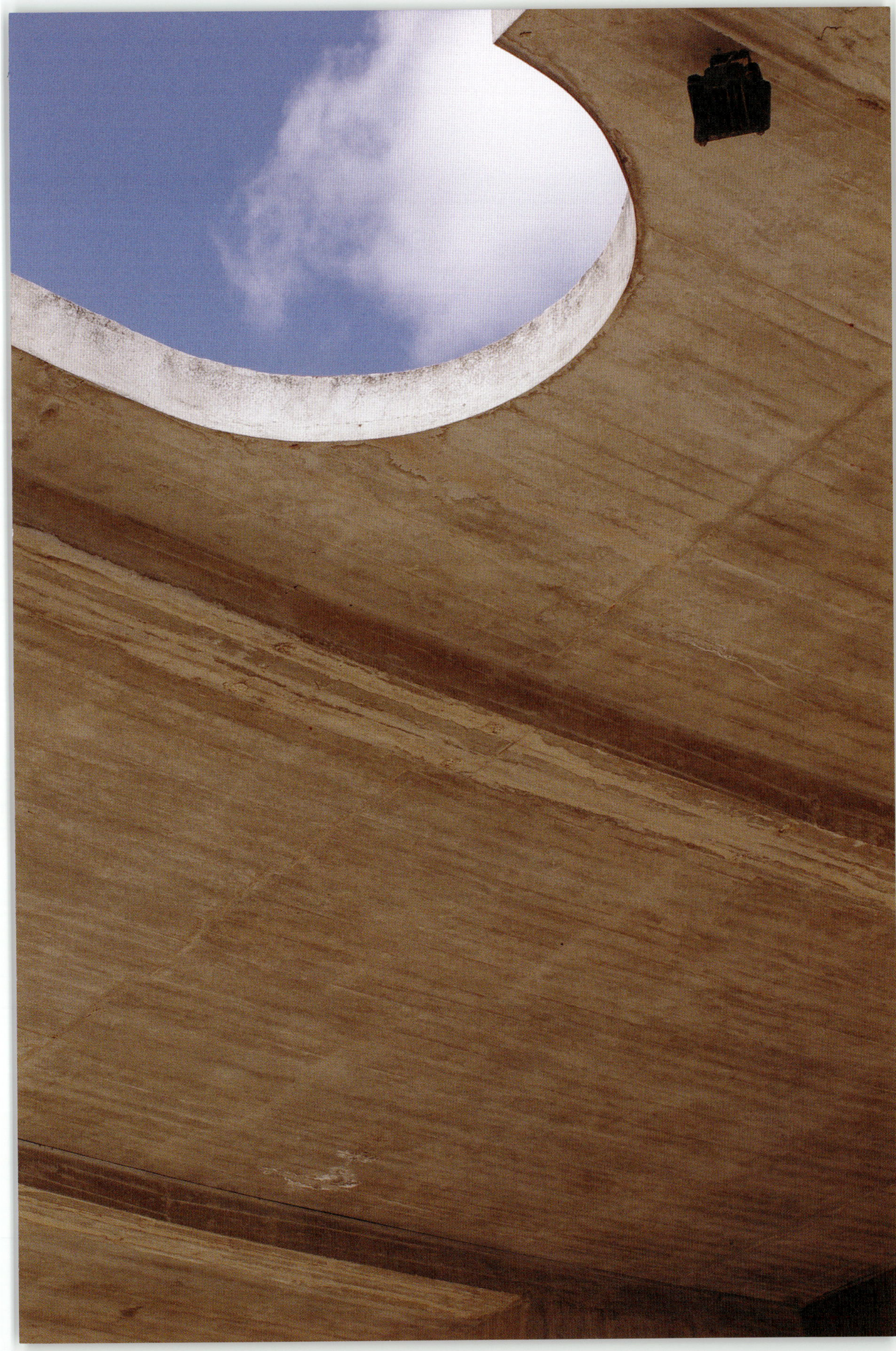

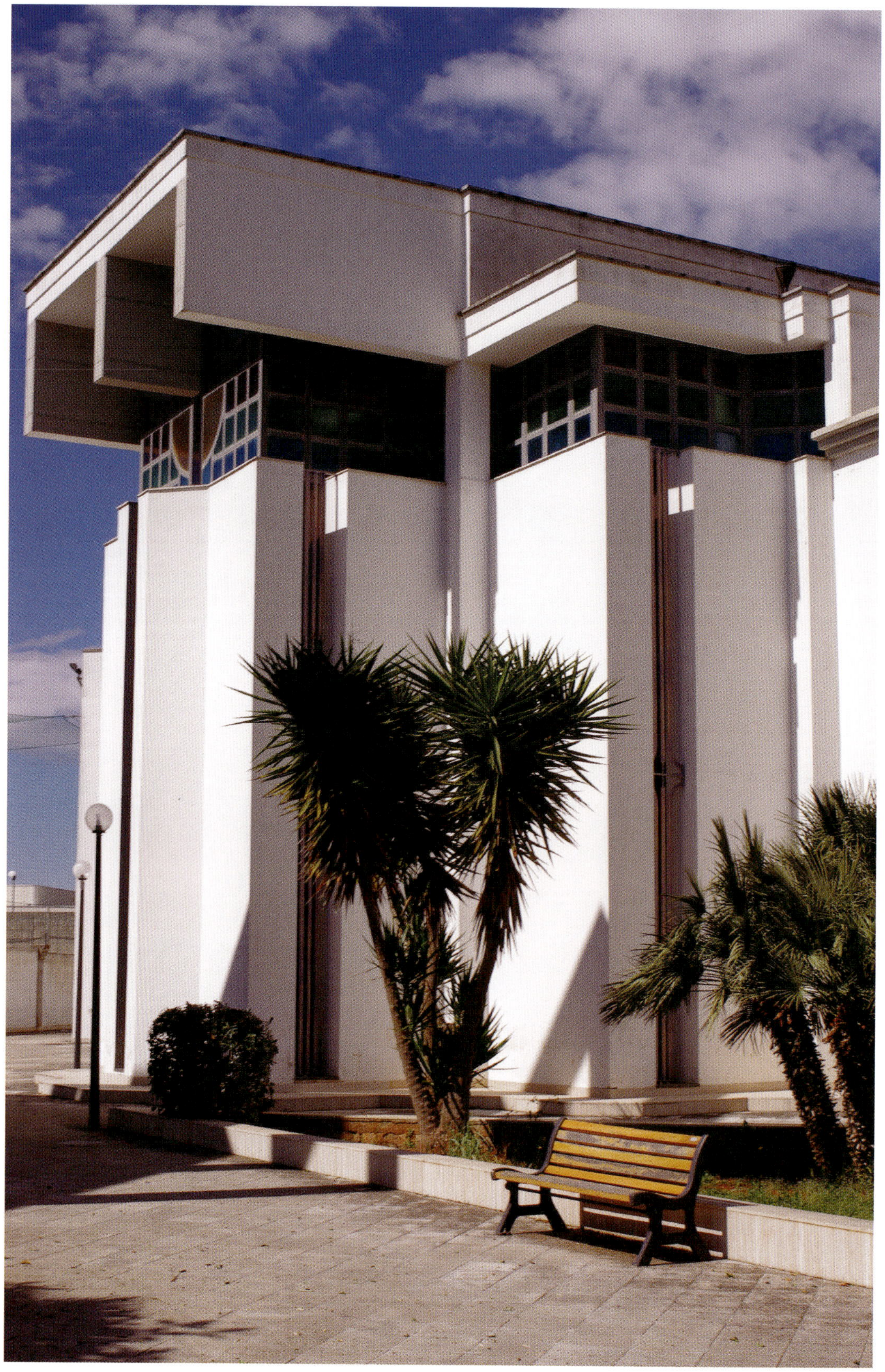

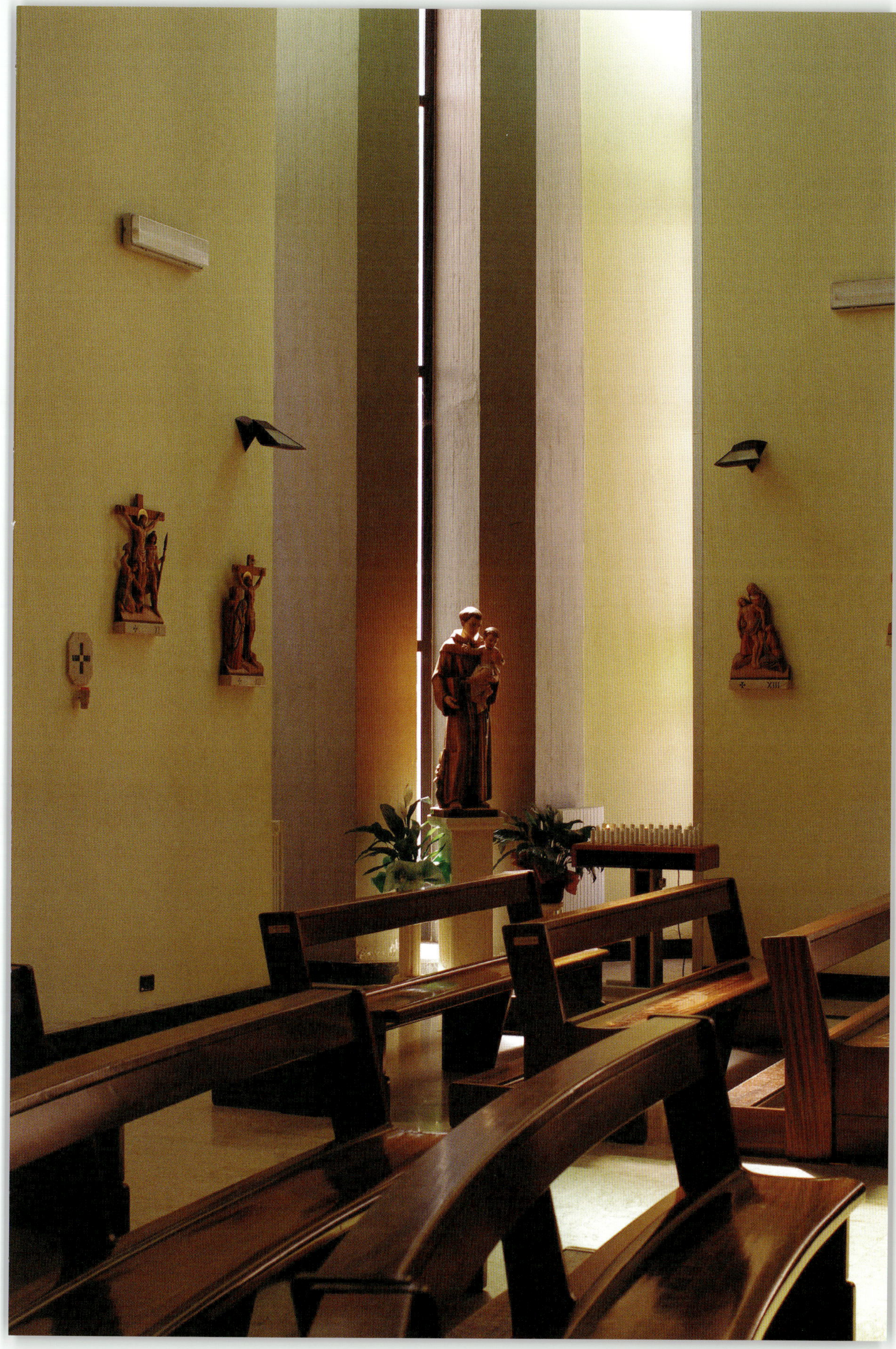

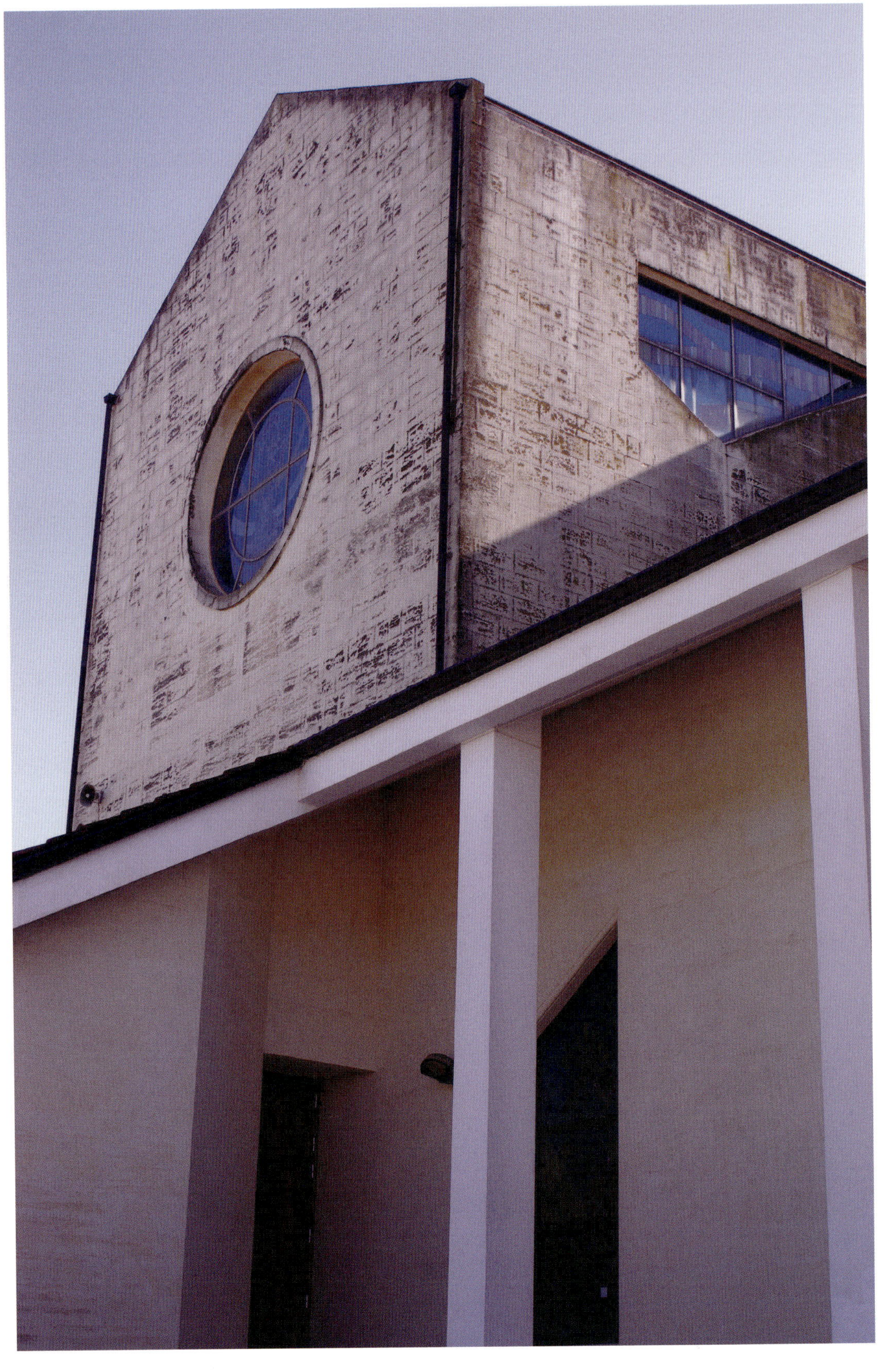

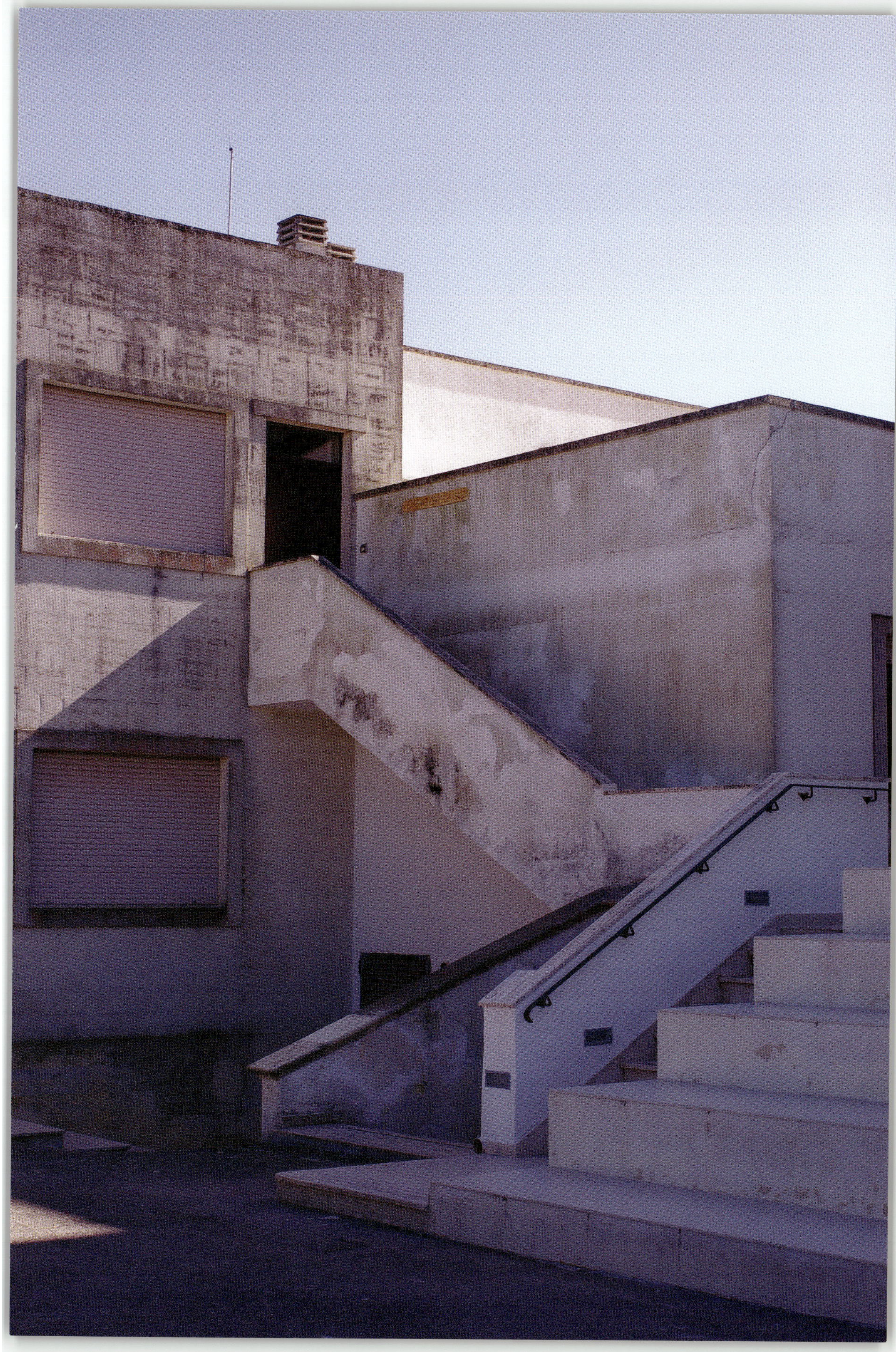

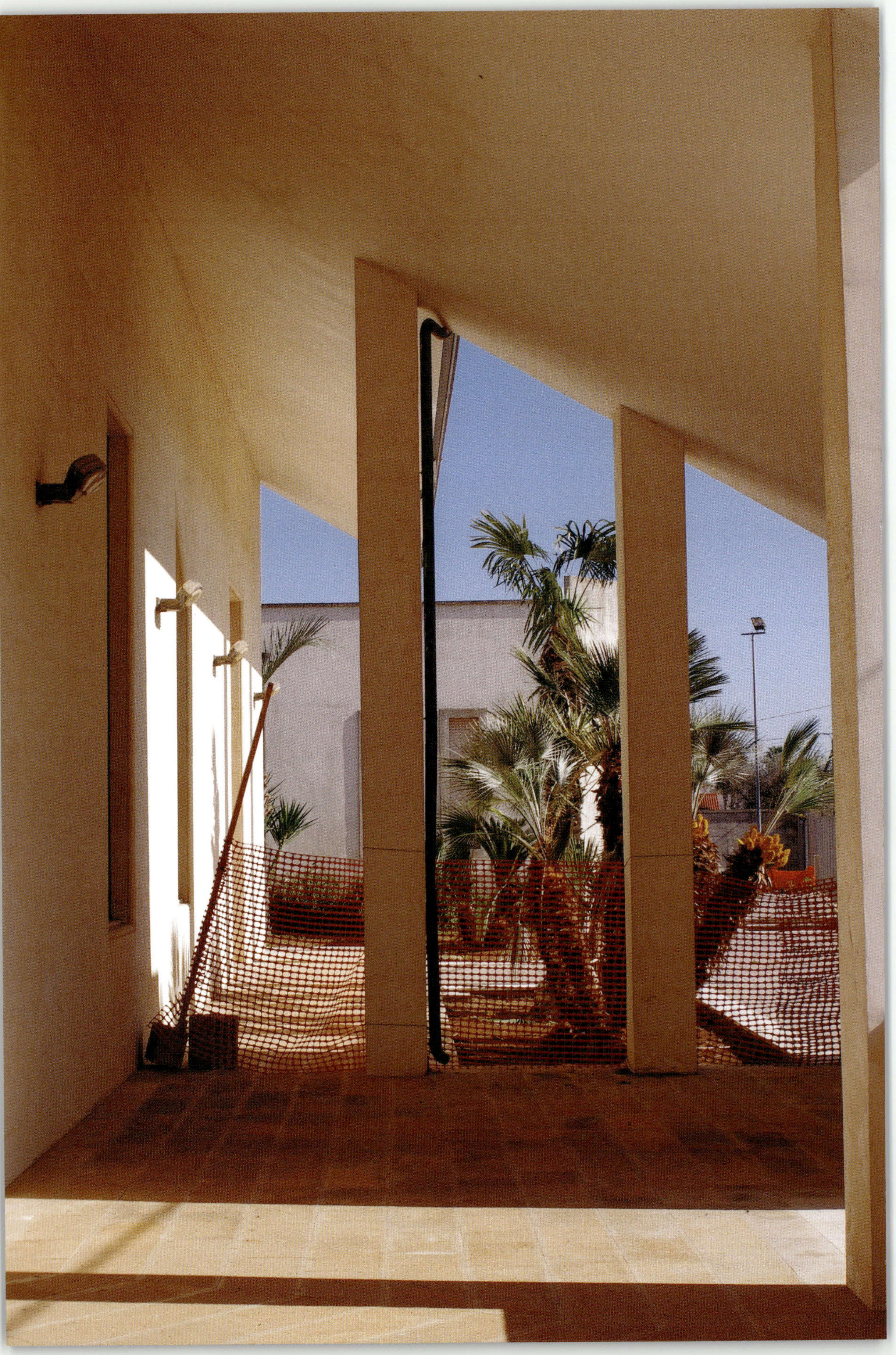

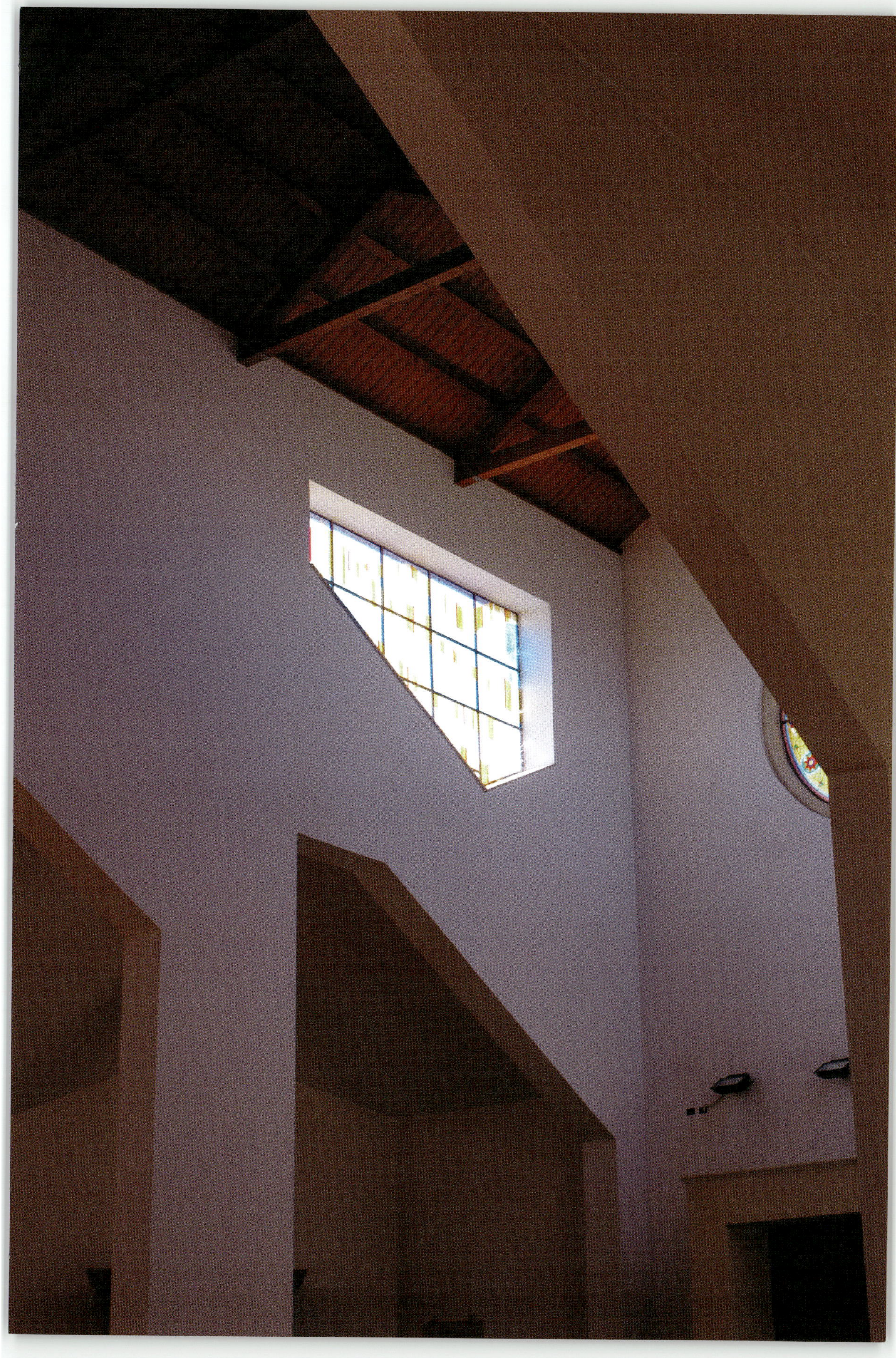

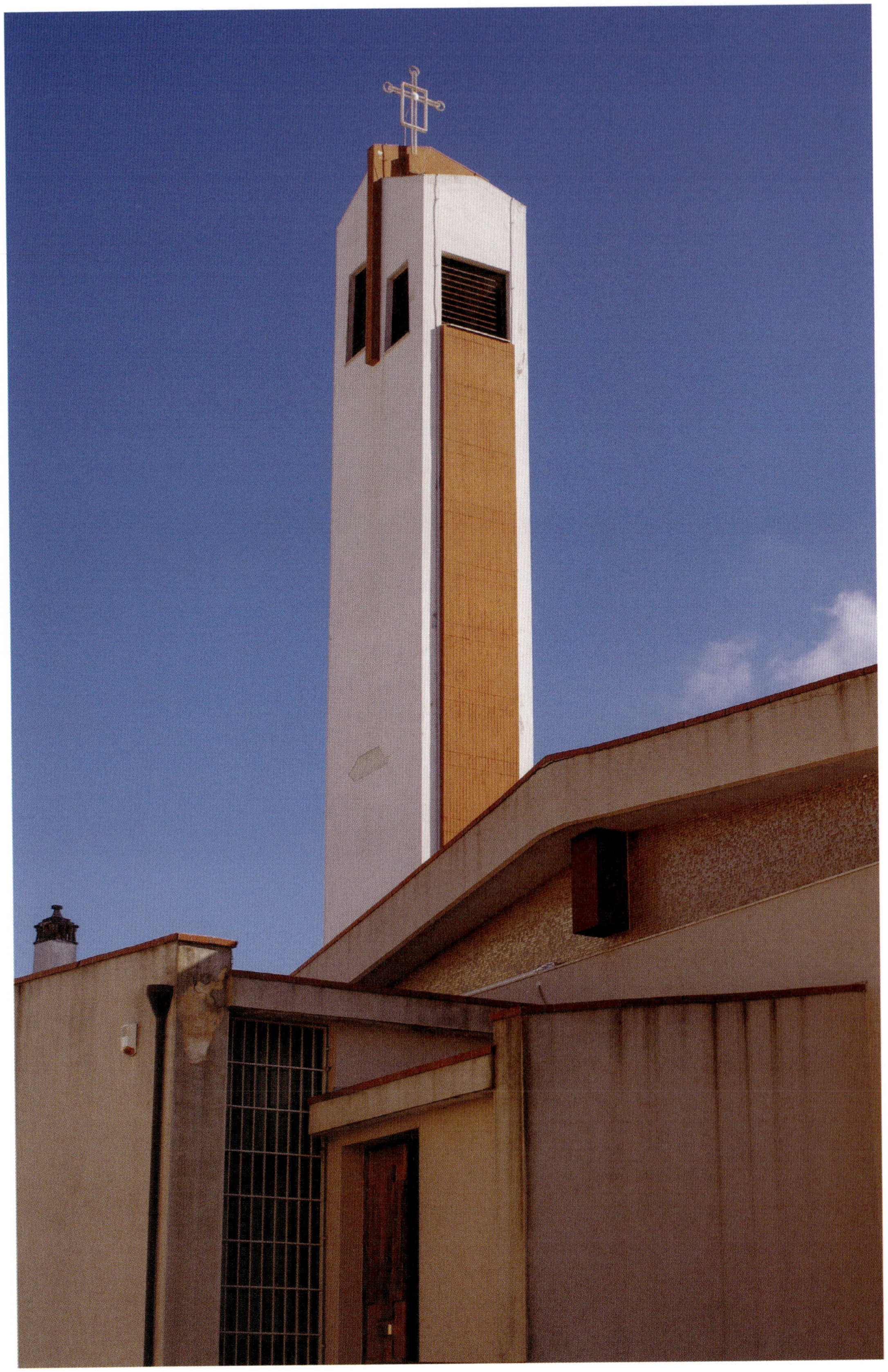

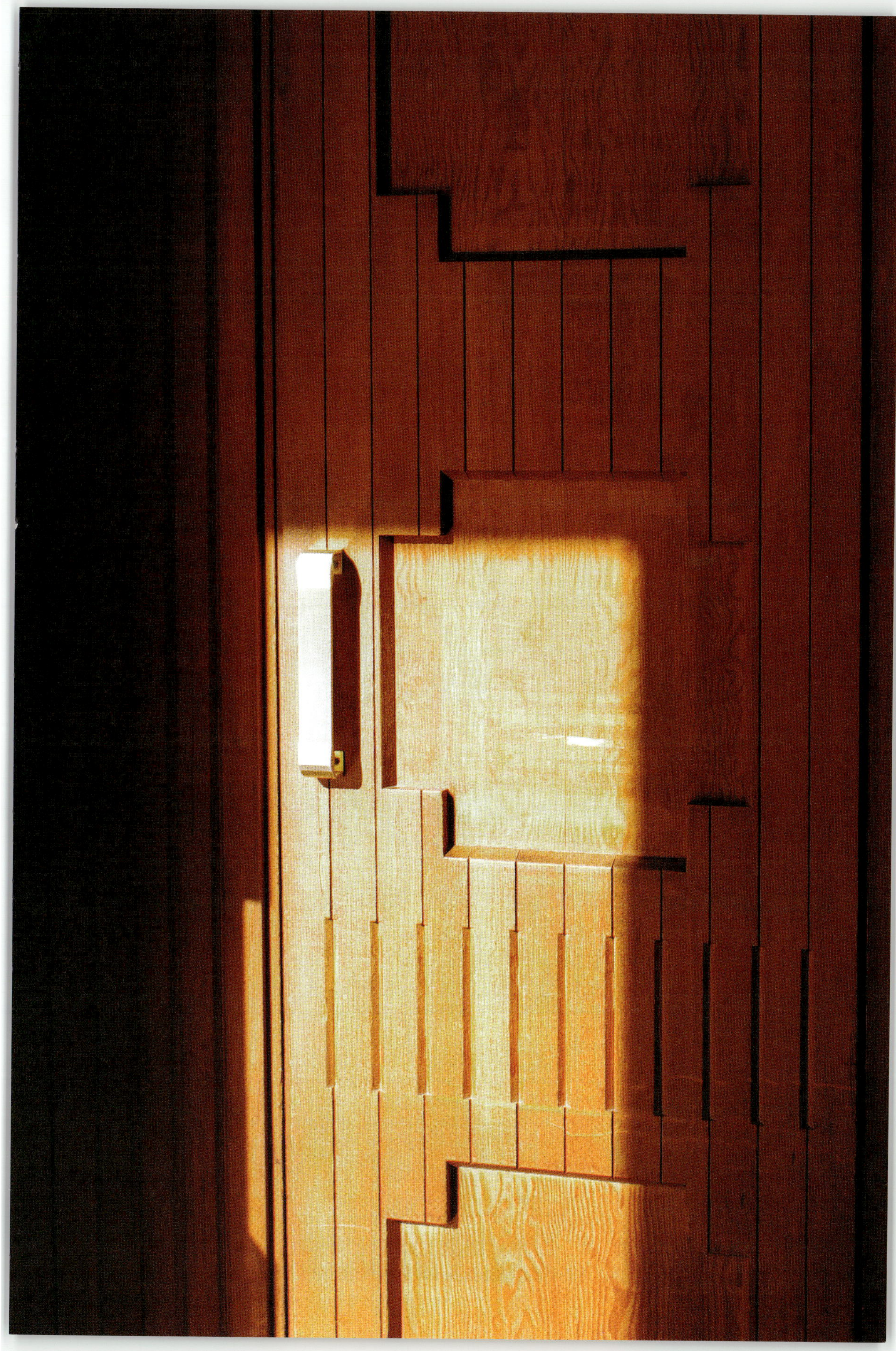

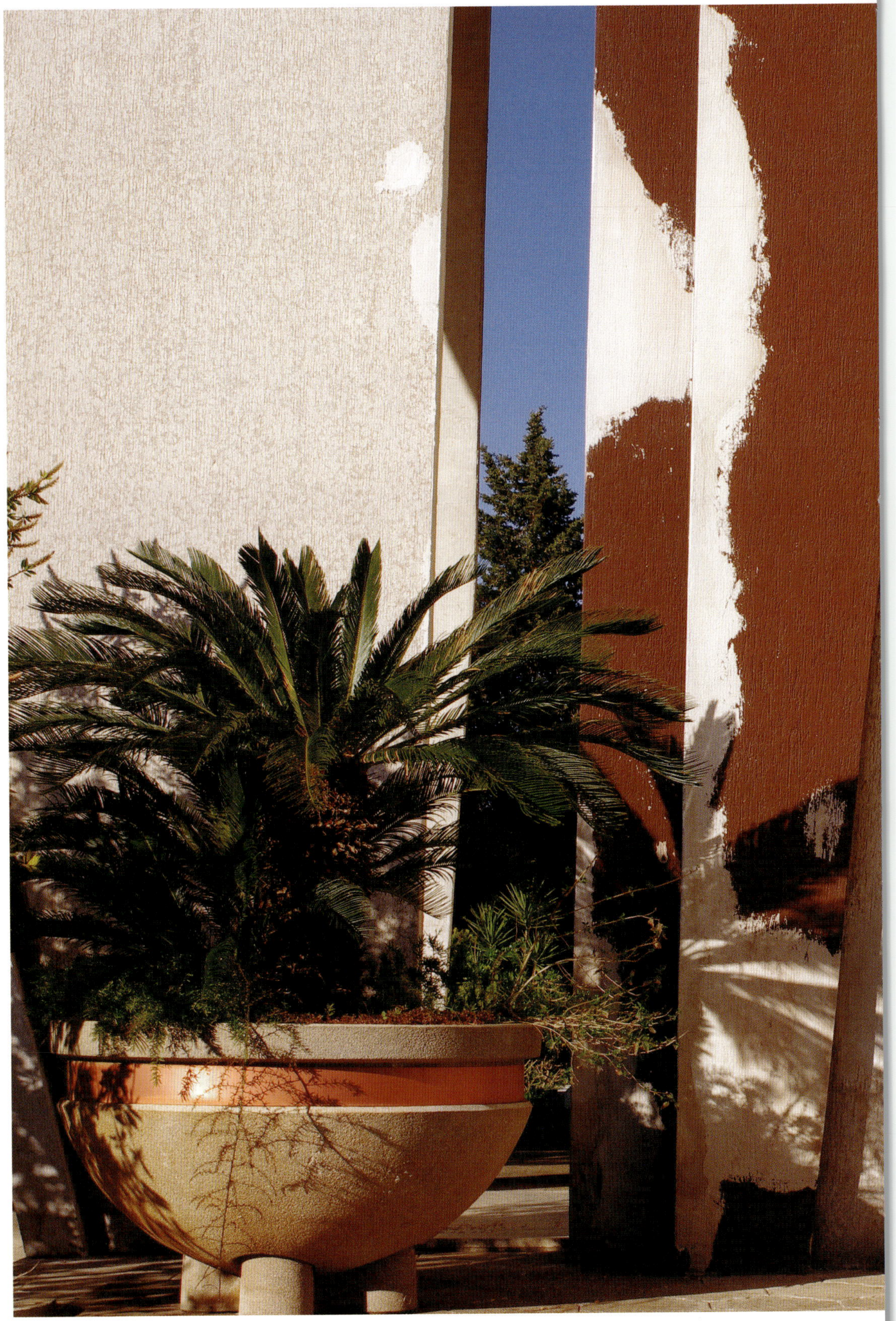

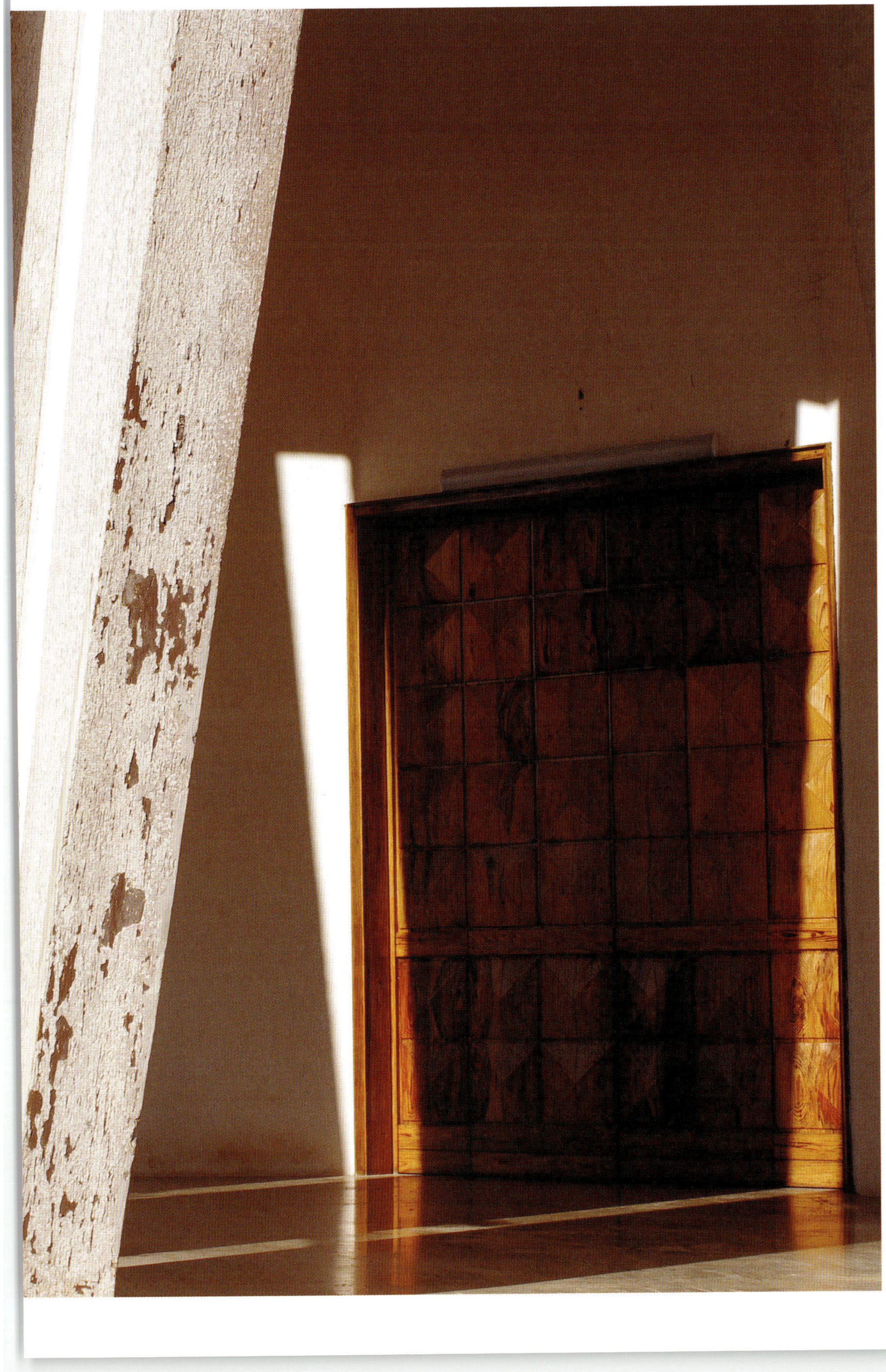

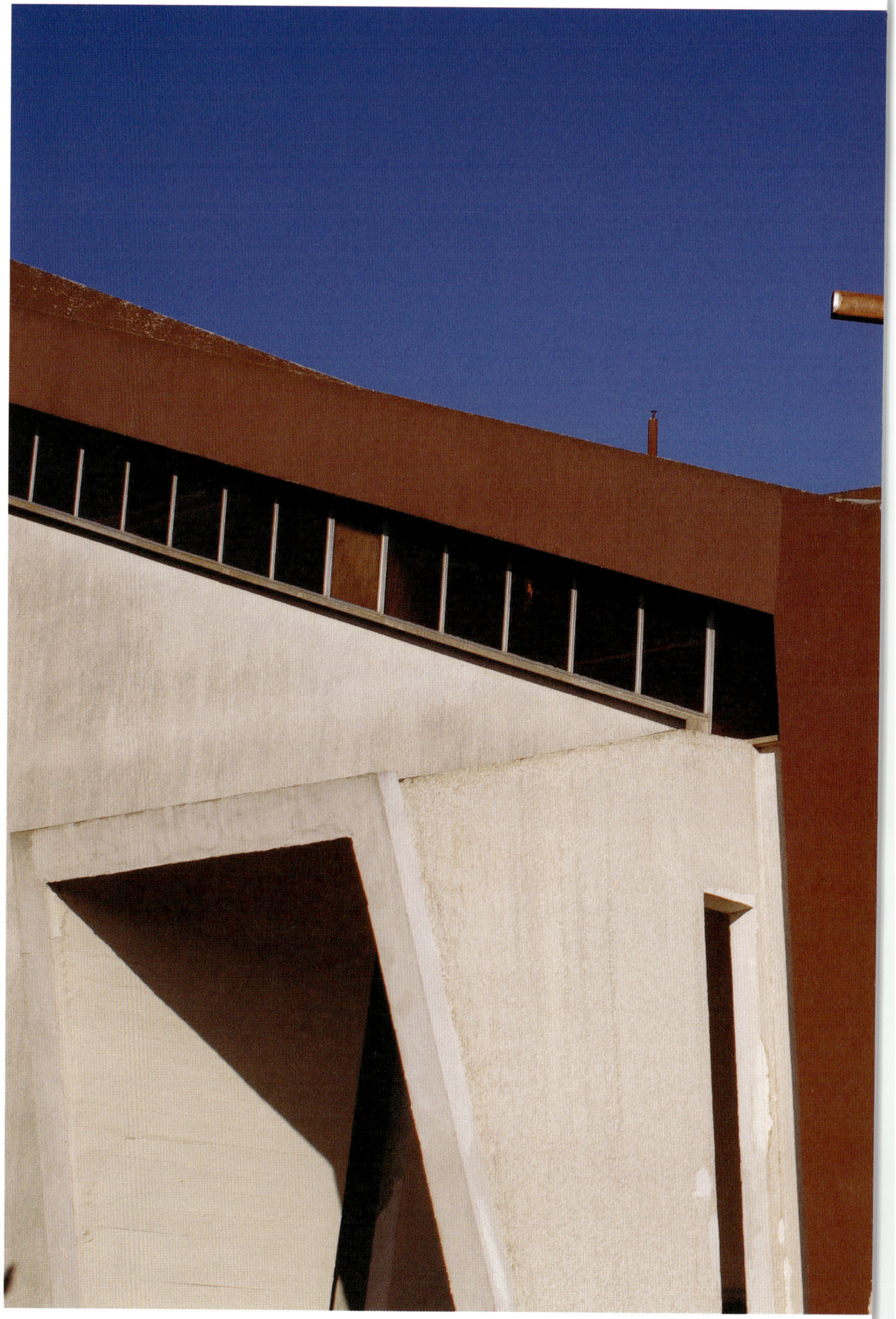

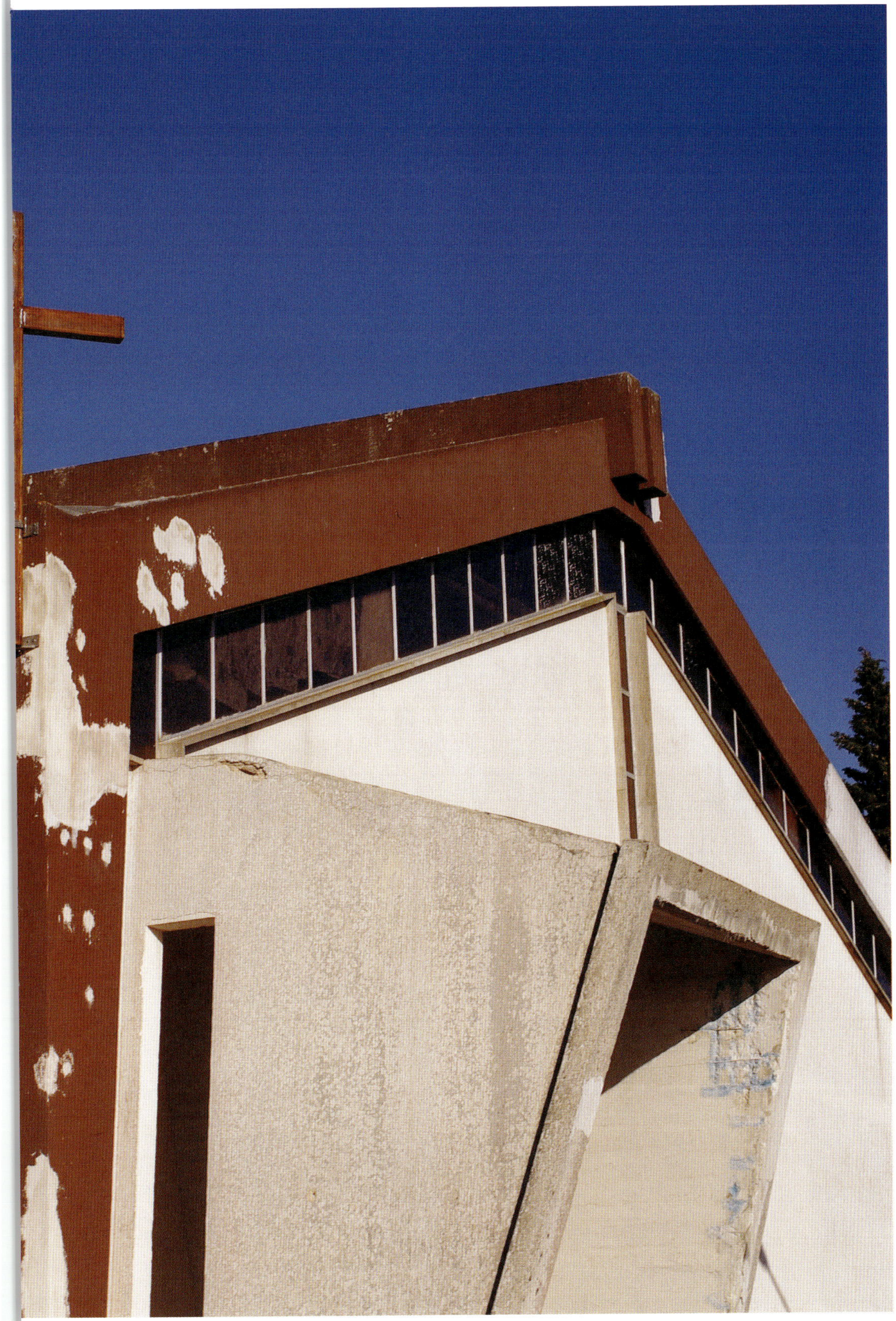

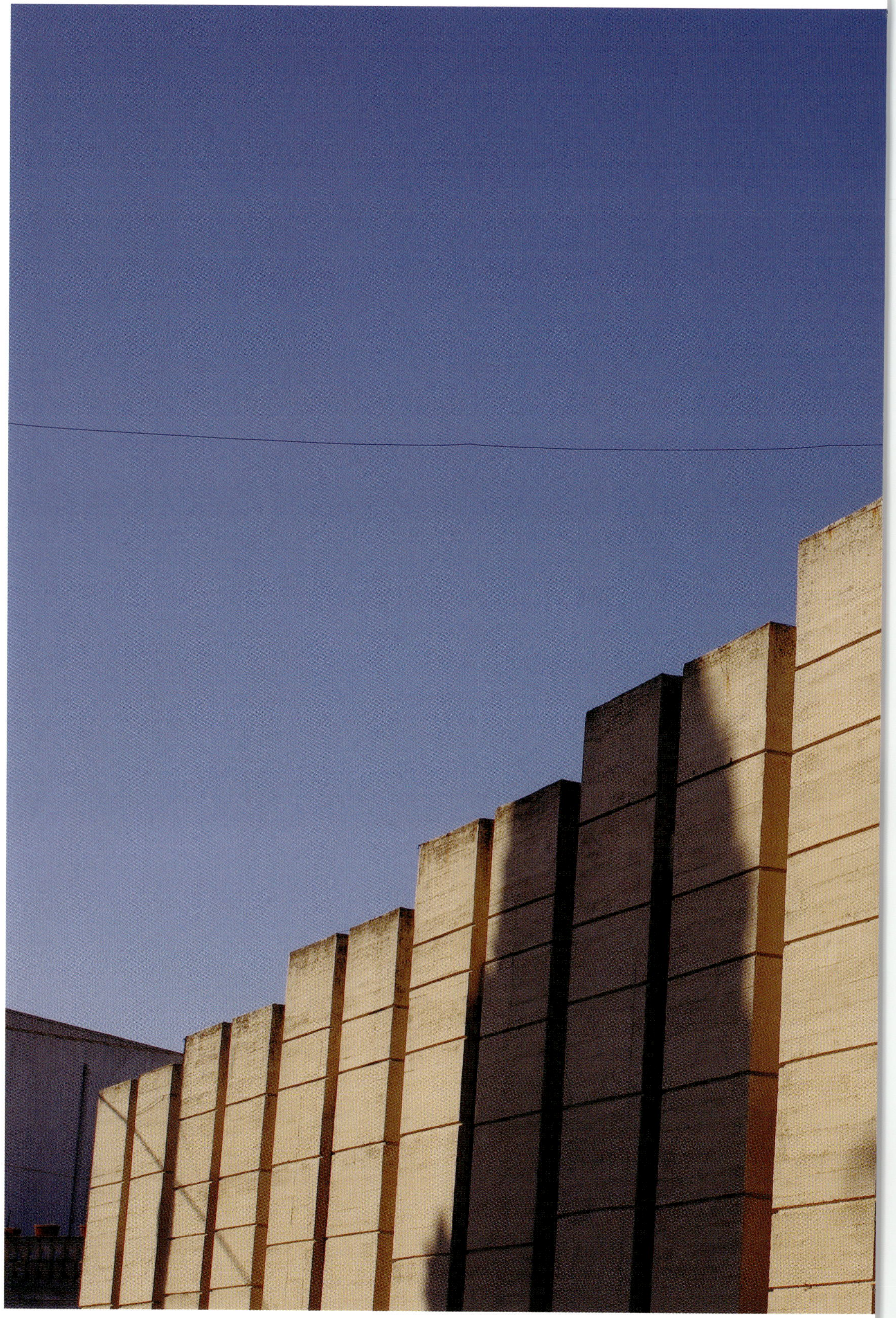

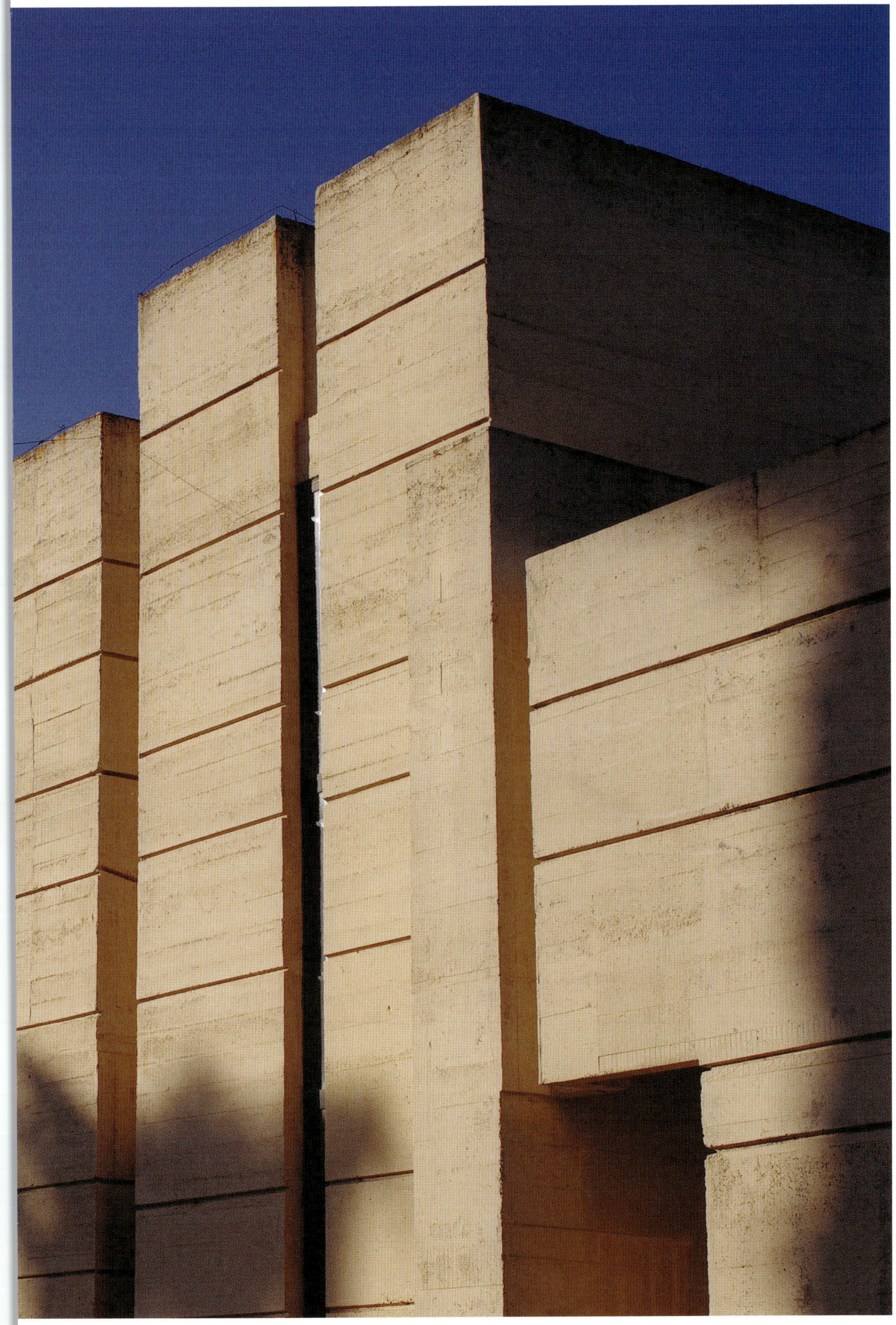

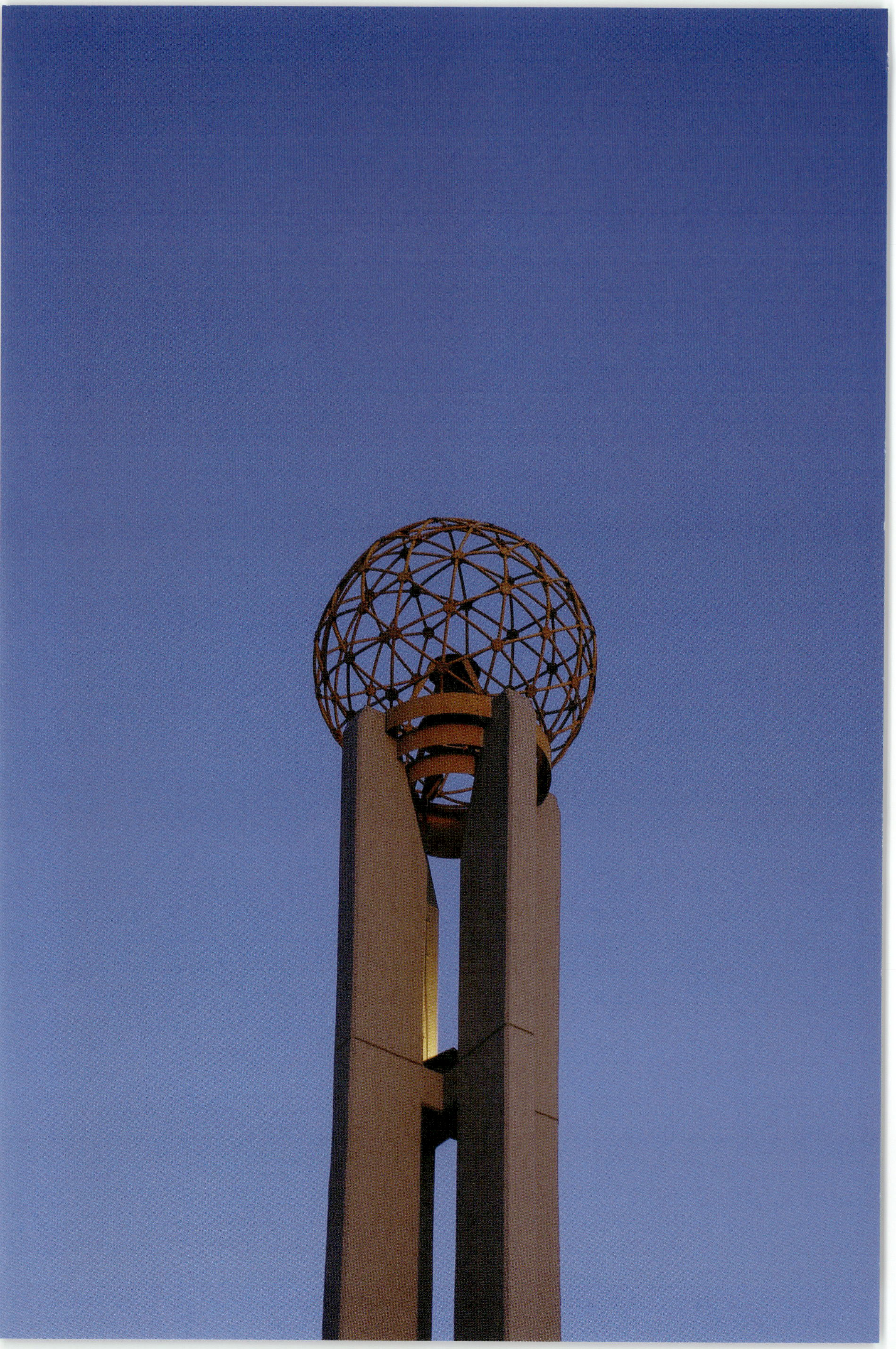

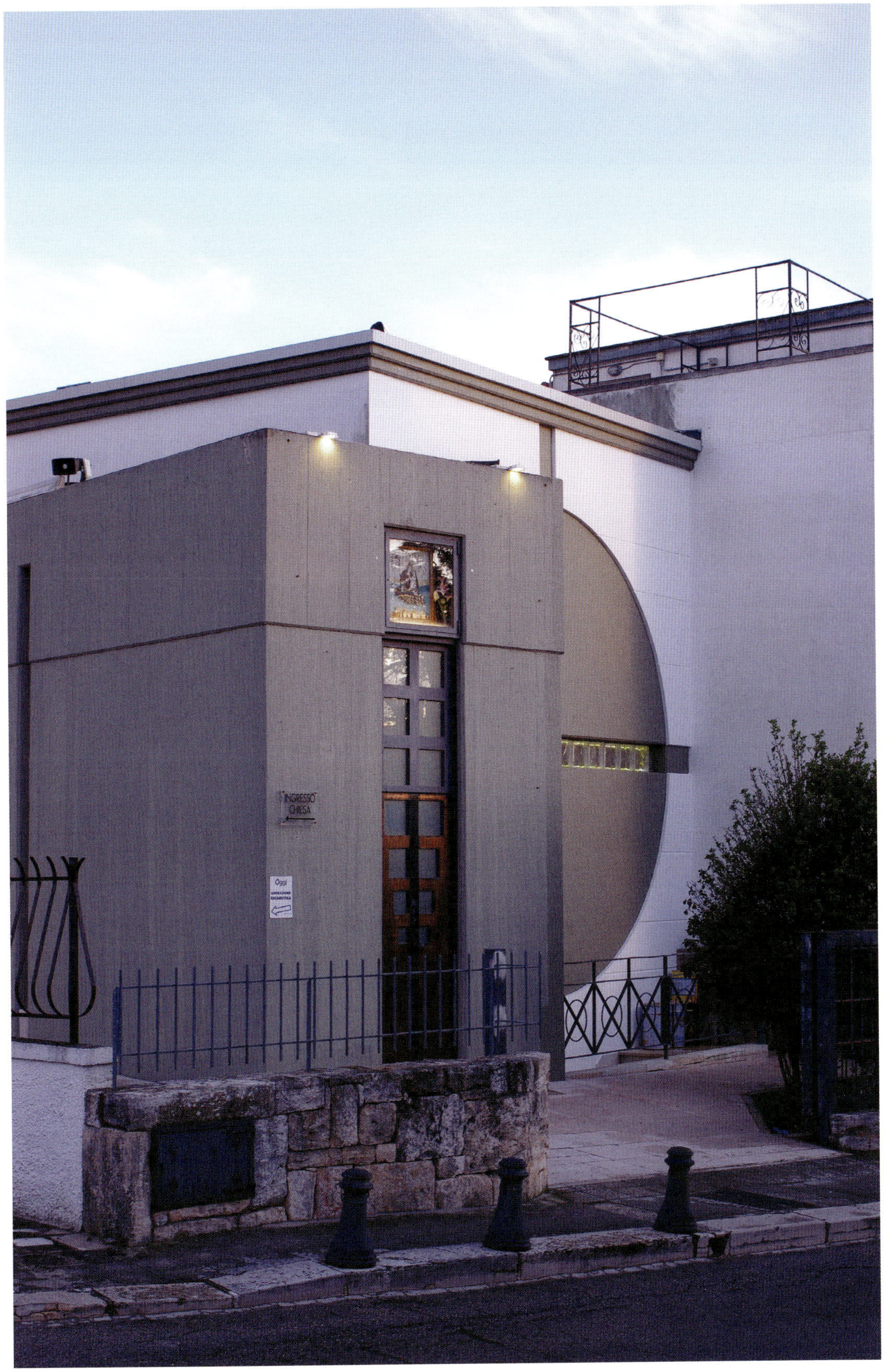
INGRESSO CHIESA
Oggi

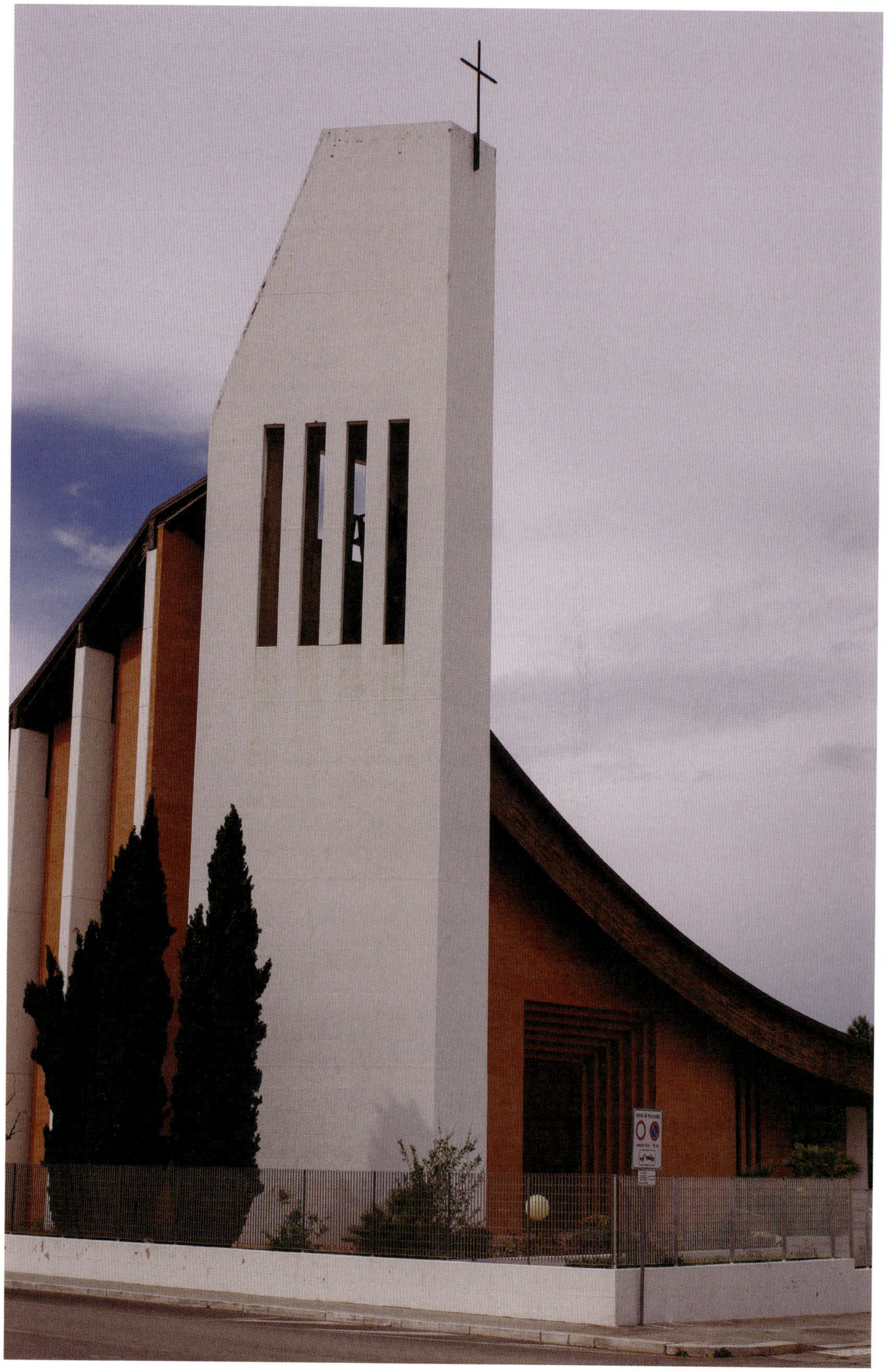

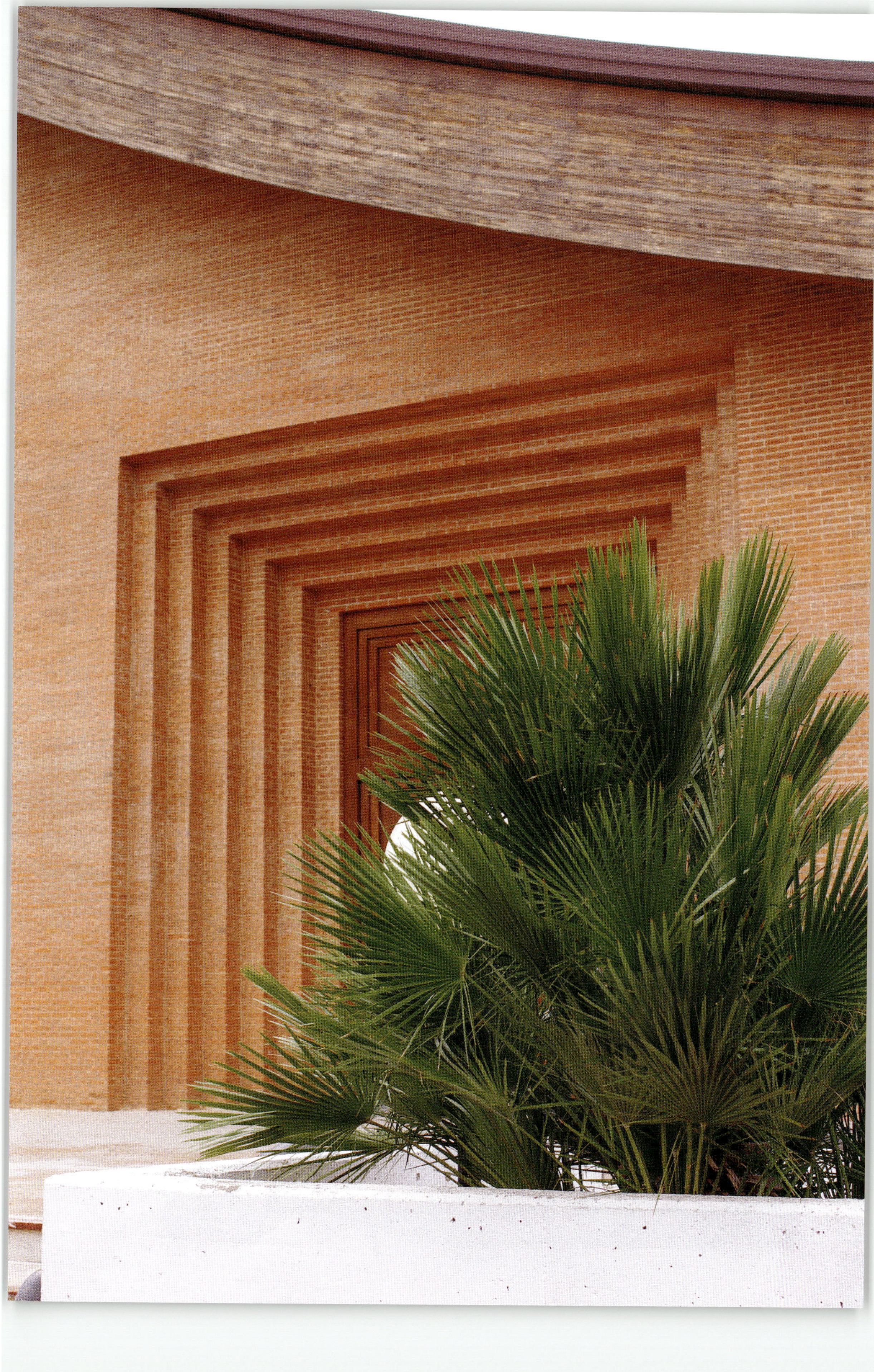

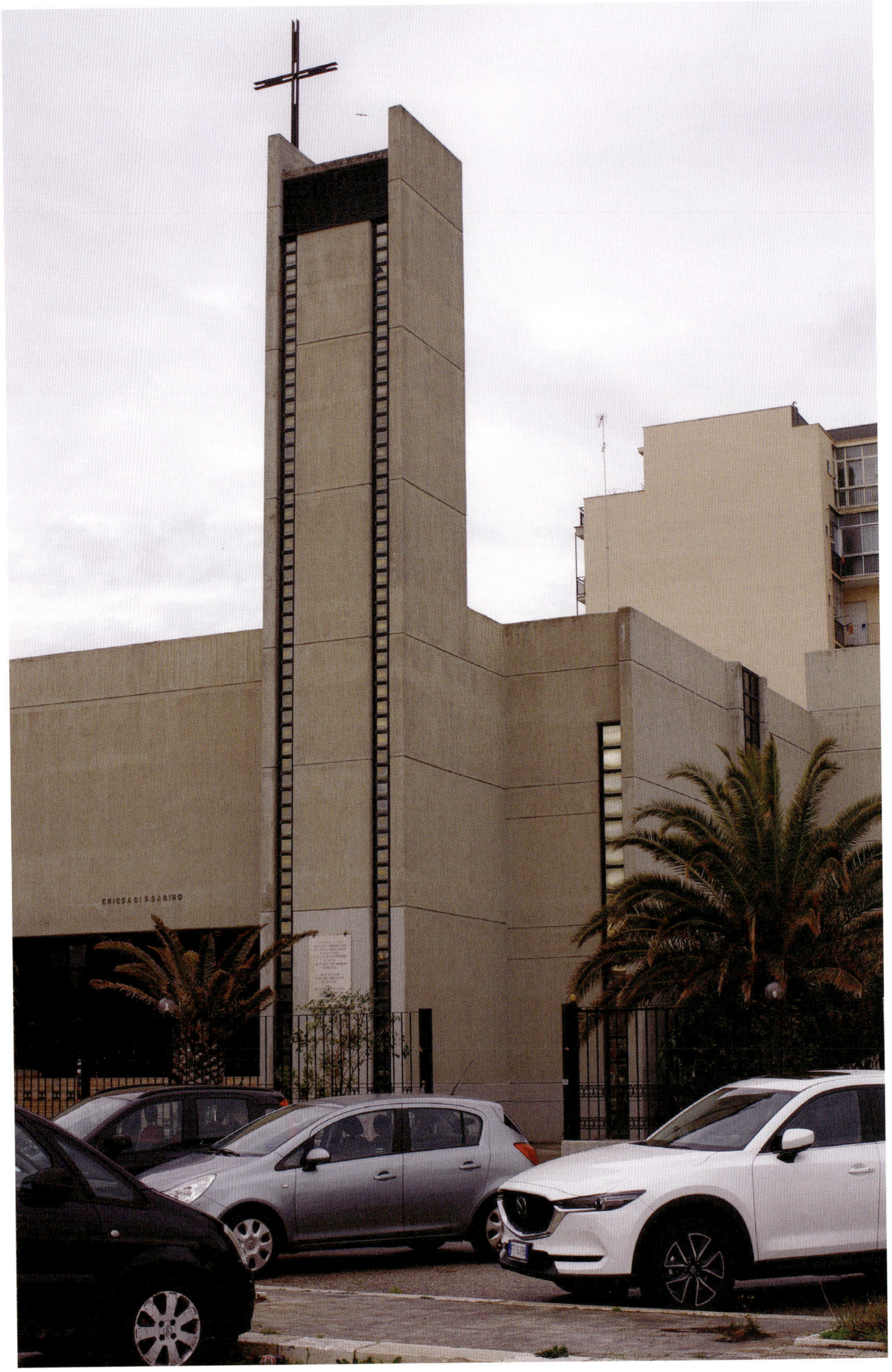

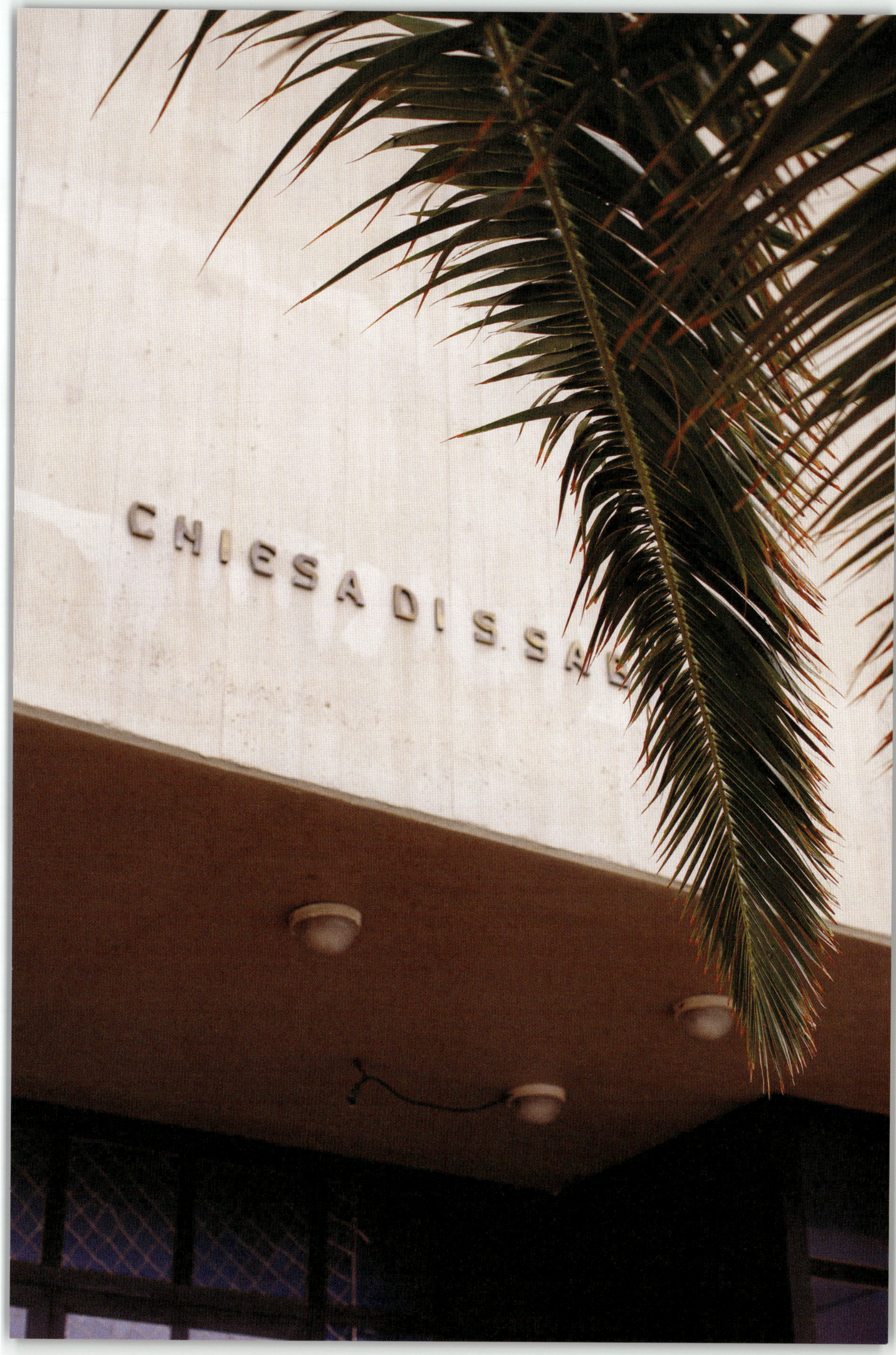
CHIESA DI S.SA

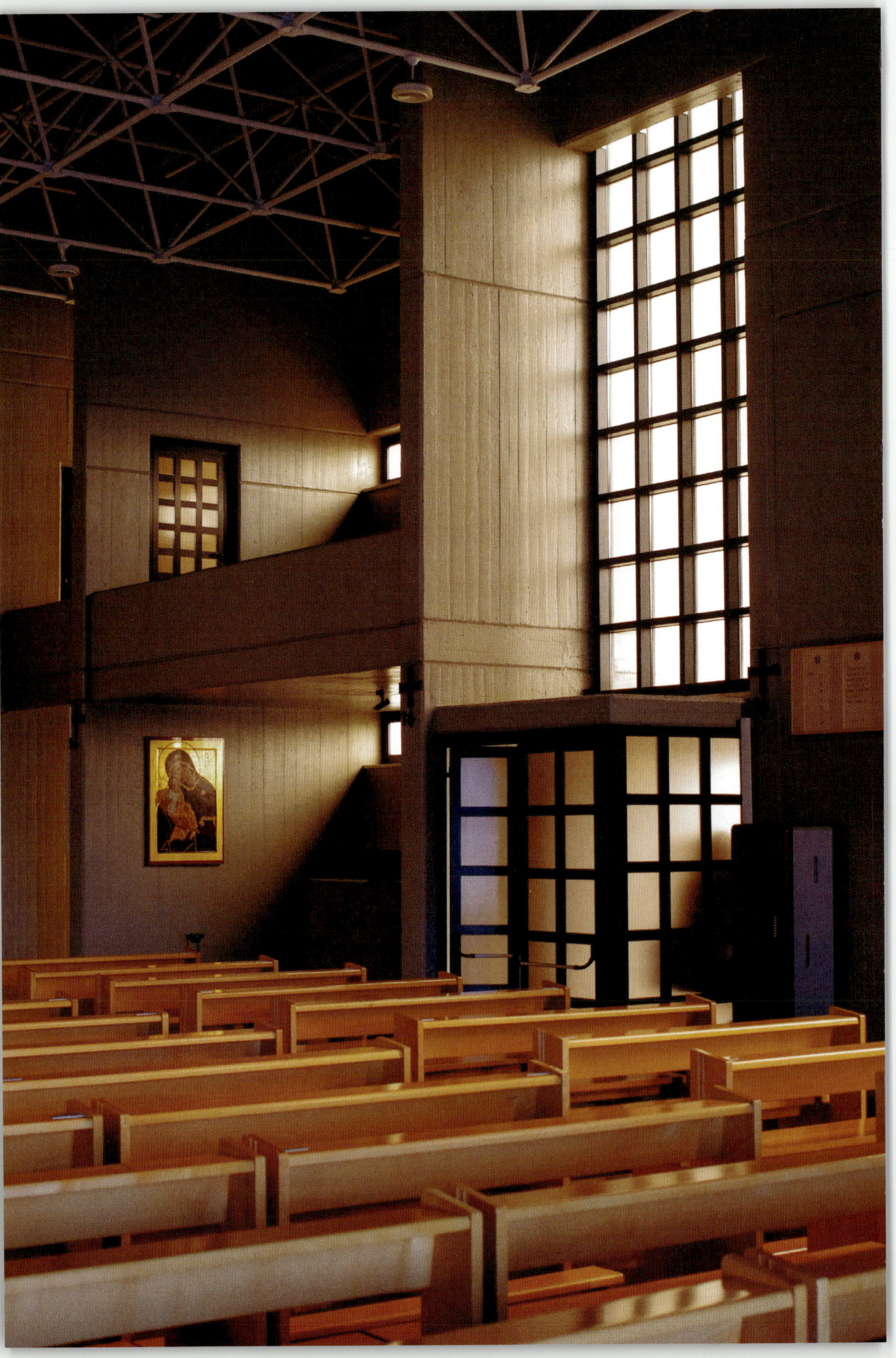

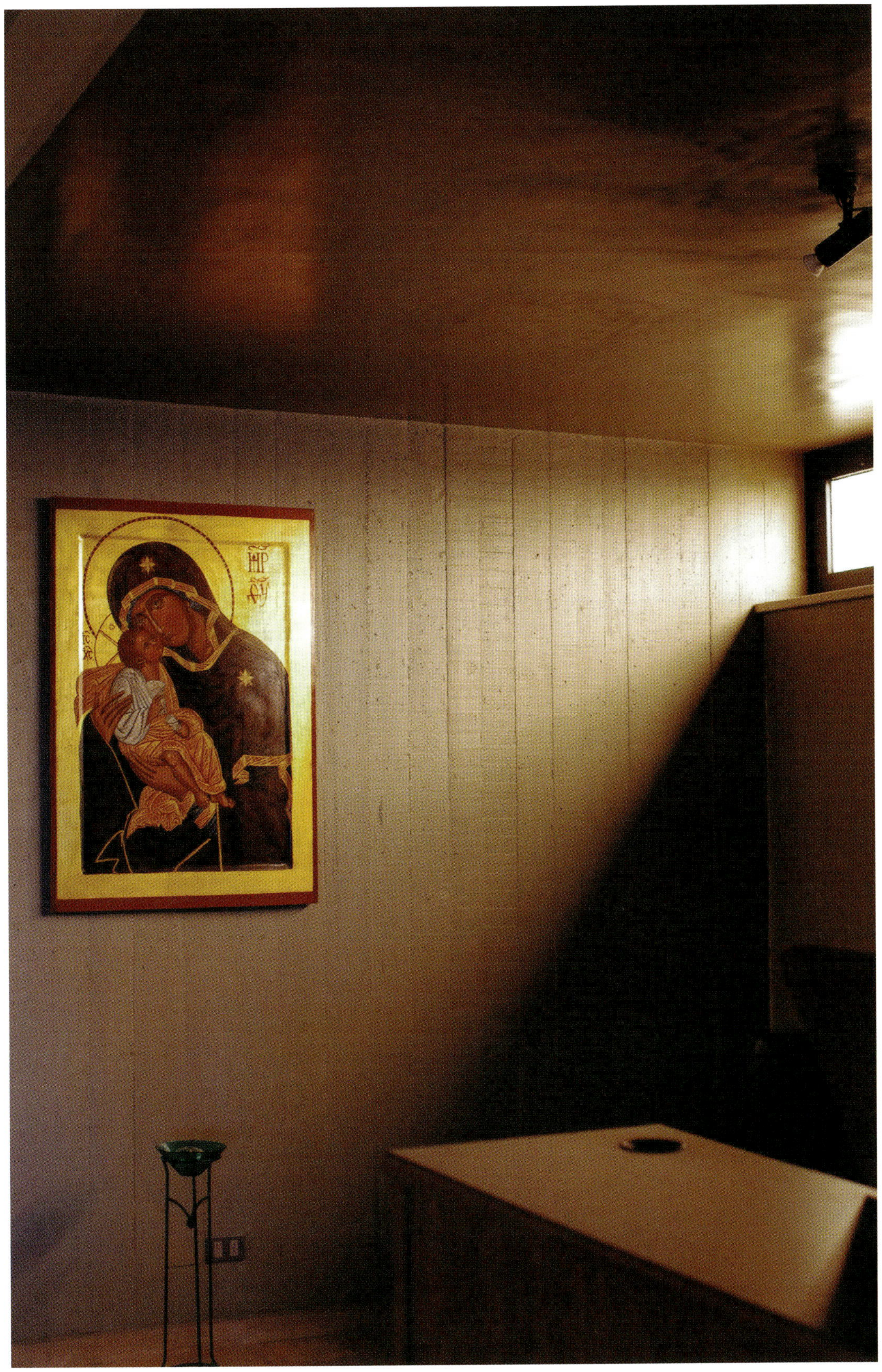

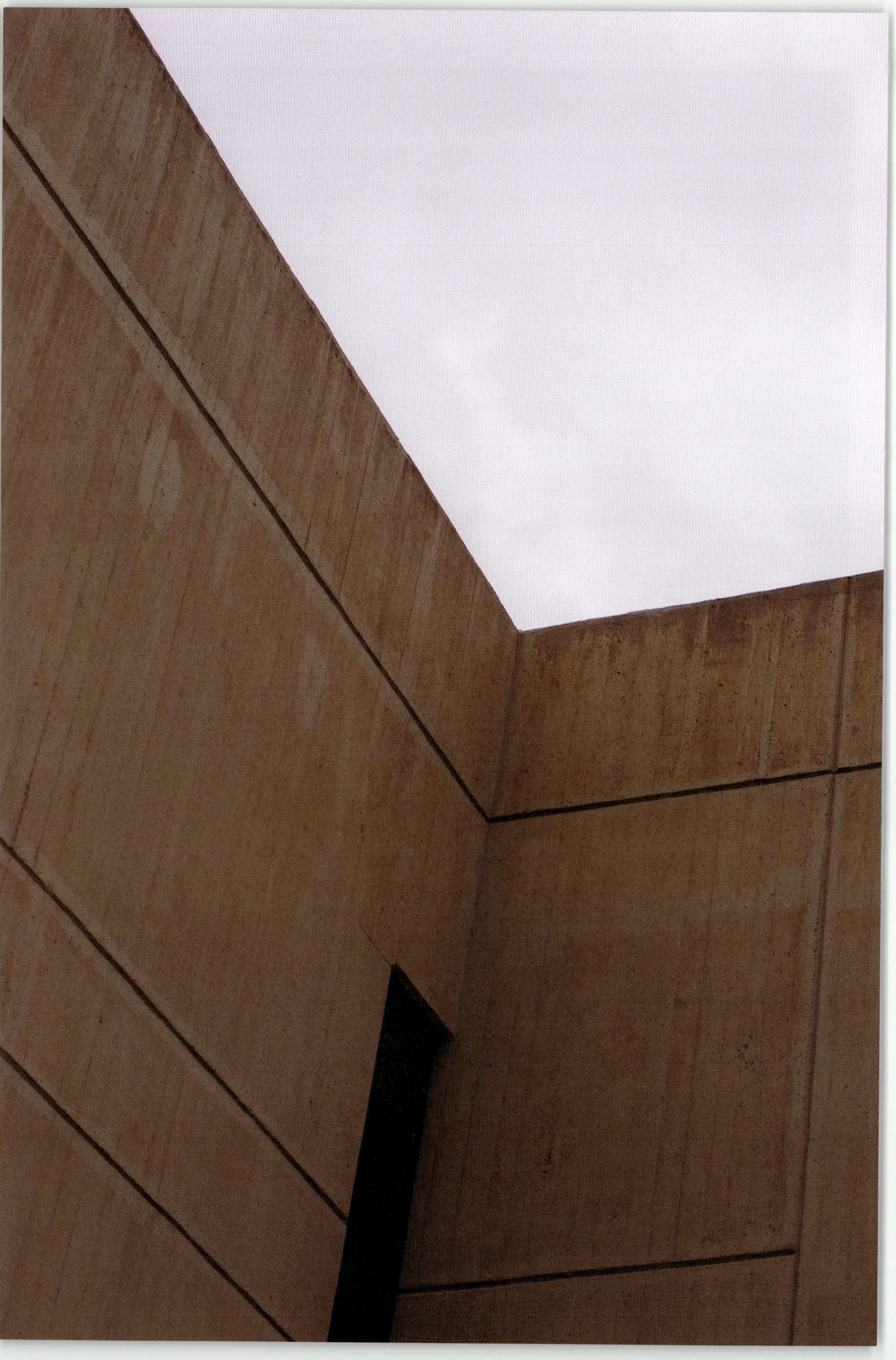

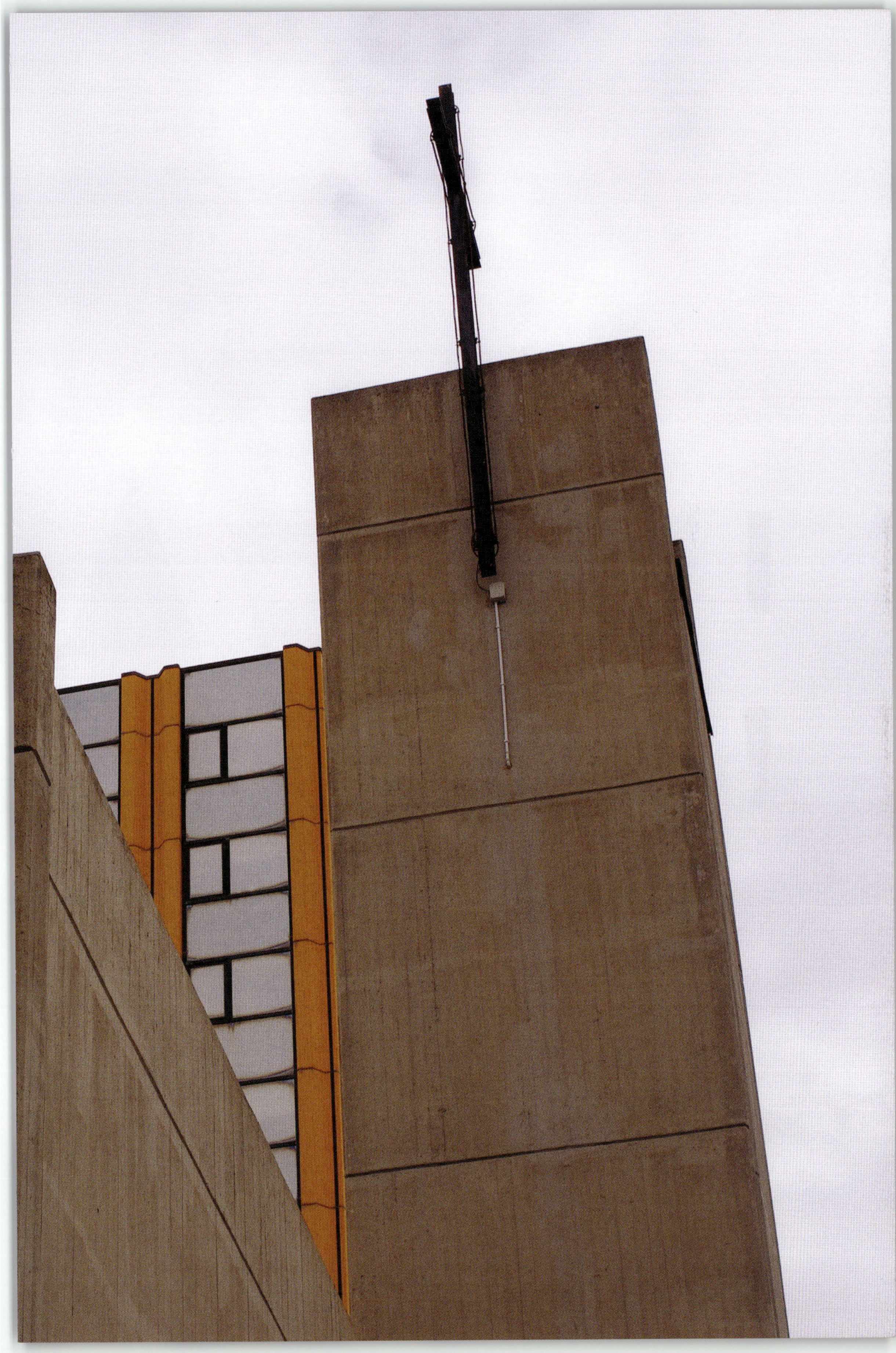

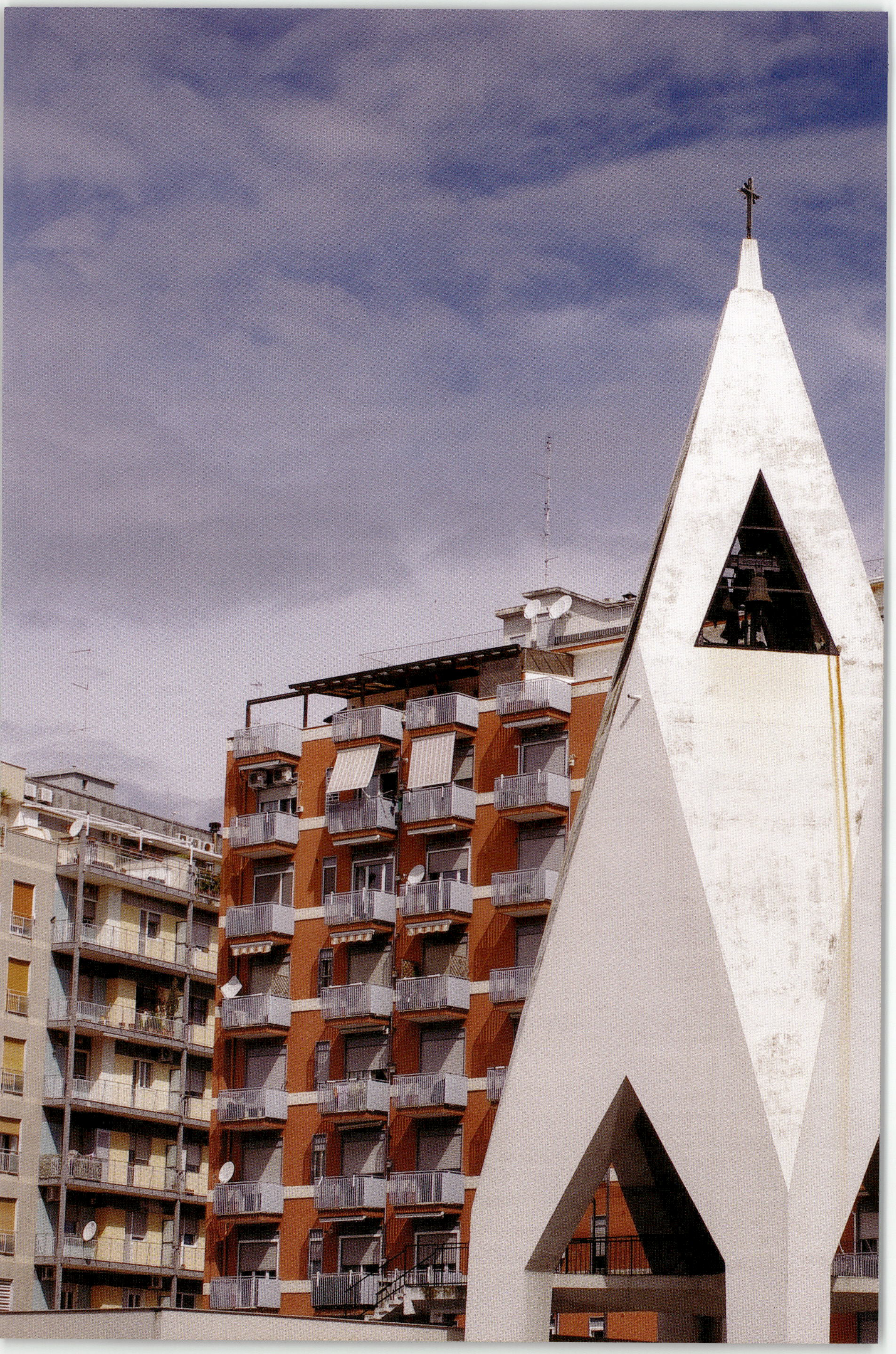

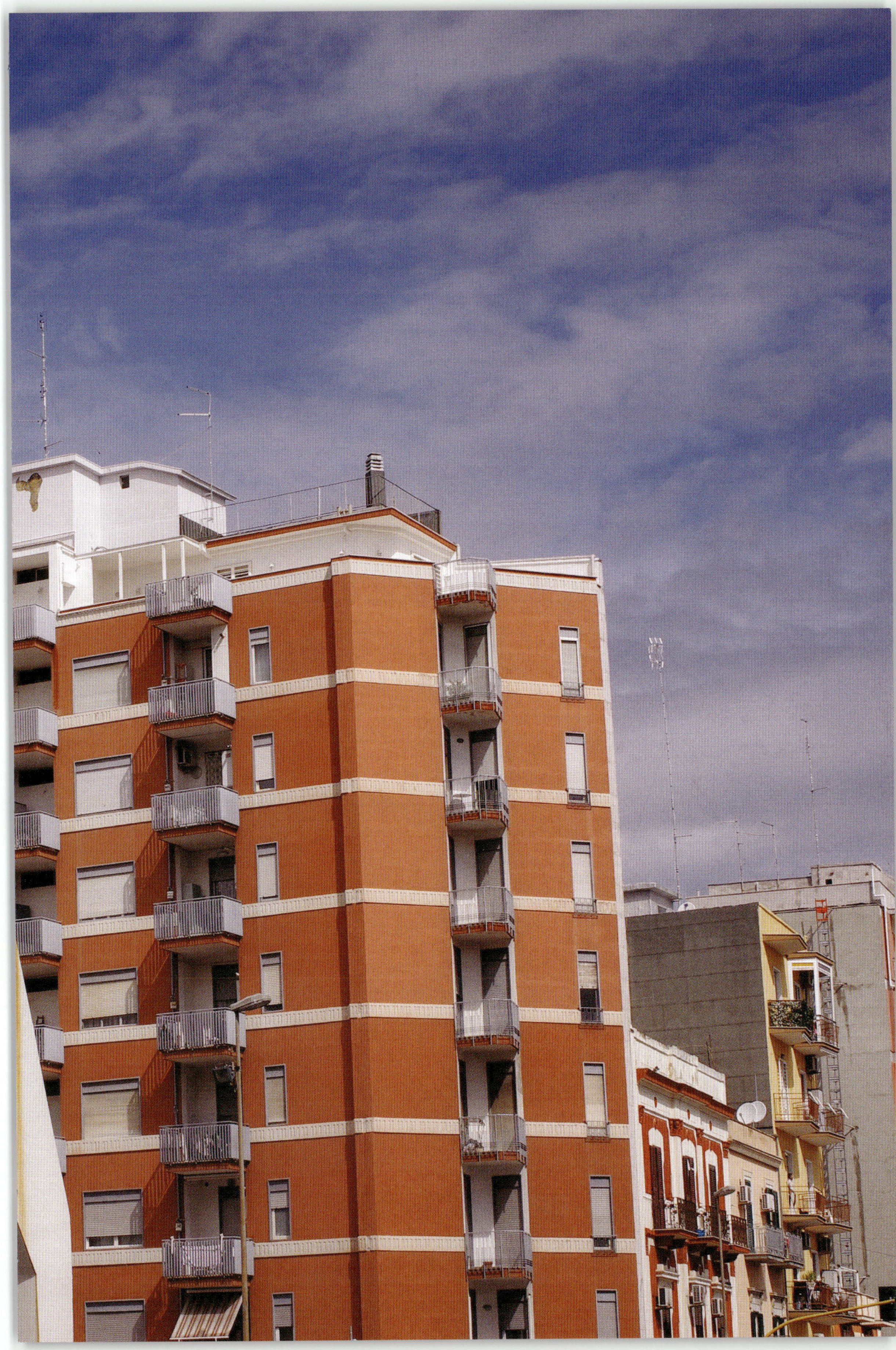

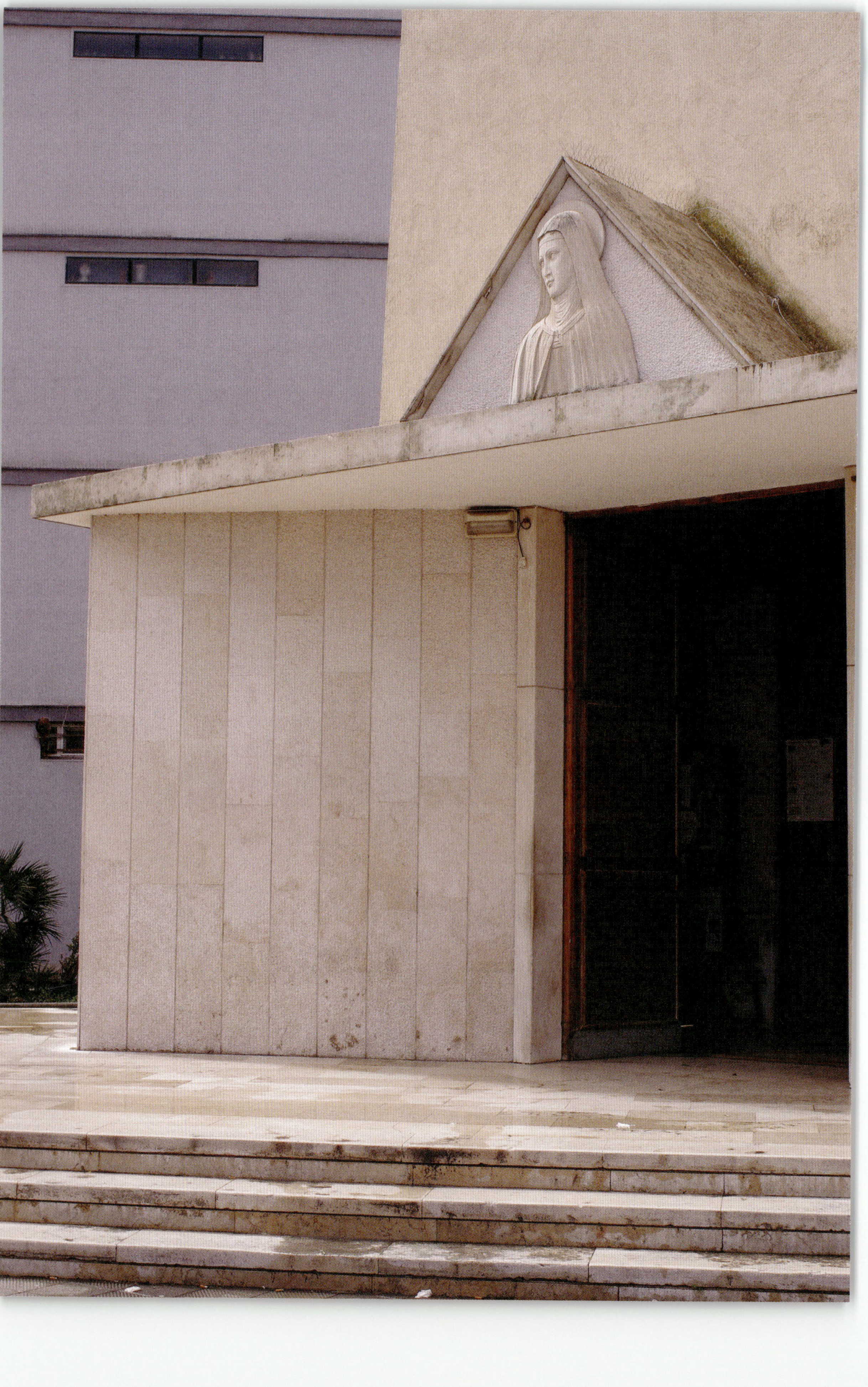

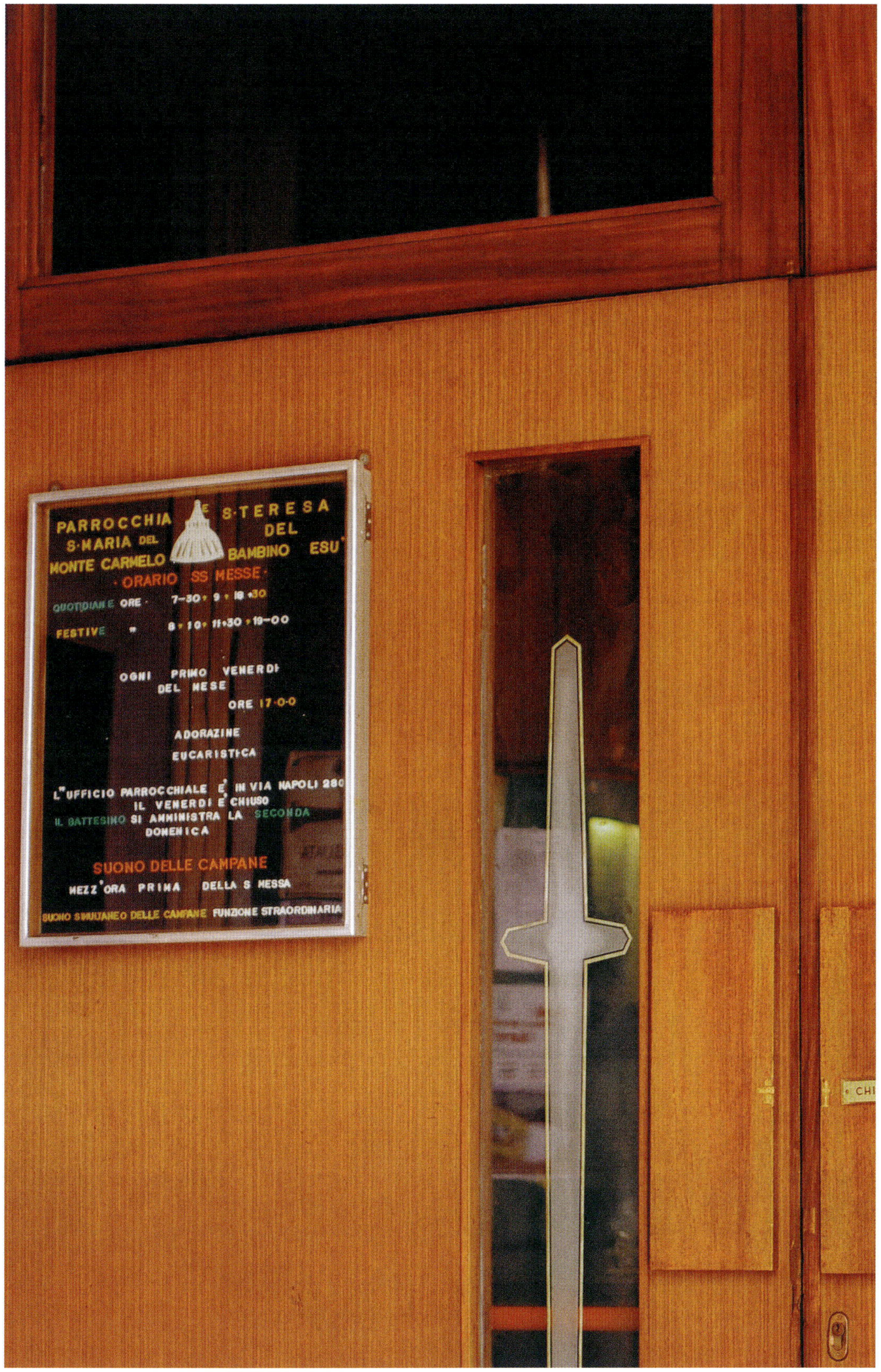
PARROCCHIA S·MARIA DEL MONTE CARMELO
E S·TERESA DEL BAMBINO ESU'
· ORARIO SS MESSE ·
QUOTIDIANE ORE · 7-30 · 9 · 18 ·30
FESTIVE " 8 · 10 · 11·30 · 19-00
OGNI PRIMO VENERDI DEL MESE
ORE 17·0·0
ADORAZINE
EUCARISTICA
L'UFFICIO PARROCCHIALE E' IN VIA NAPOLI 280
IL VENERDI E' CHIUSO
IL BATTESIMO SI AMMINISTRA LA SECONDA DOMENICA
SUONO DELLE CAMPANE
MEZZ'ORA PRIMA DELLA S MESSA
SUONO SIMULTANEO DELLE CAMPANE FUNZIONE STRAORDINARIA

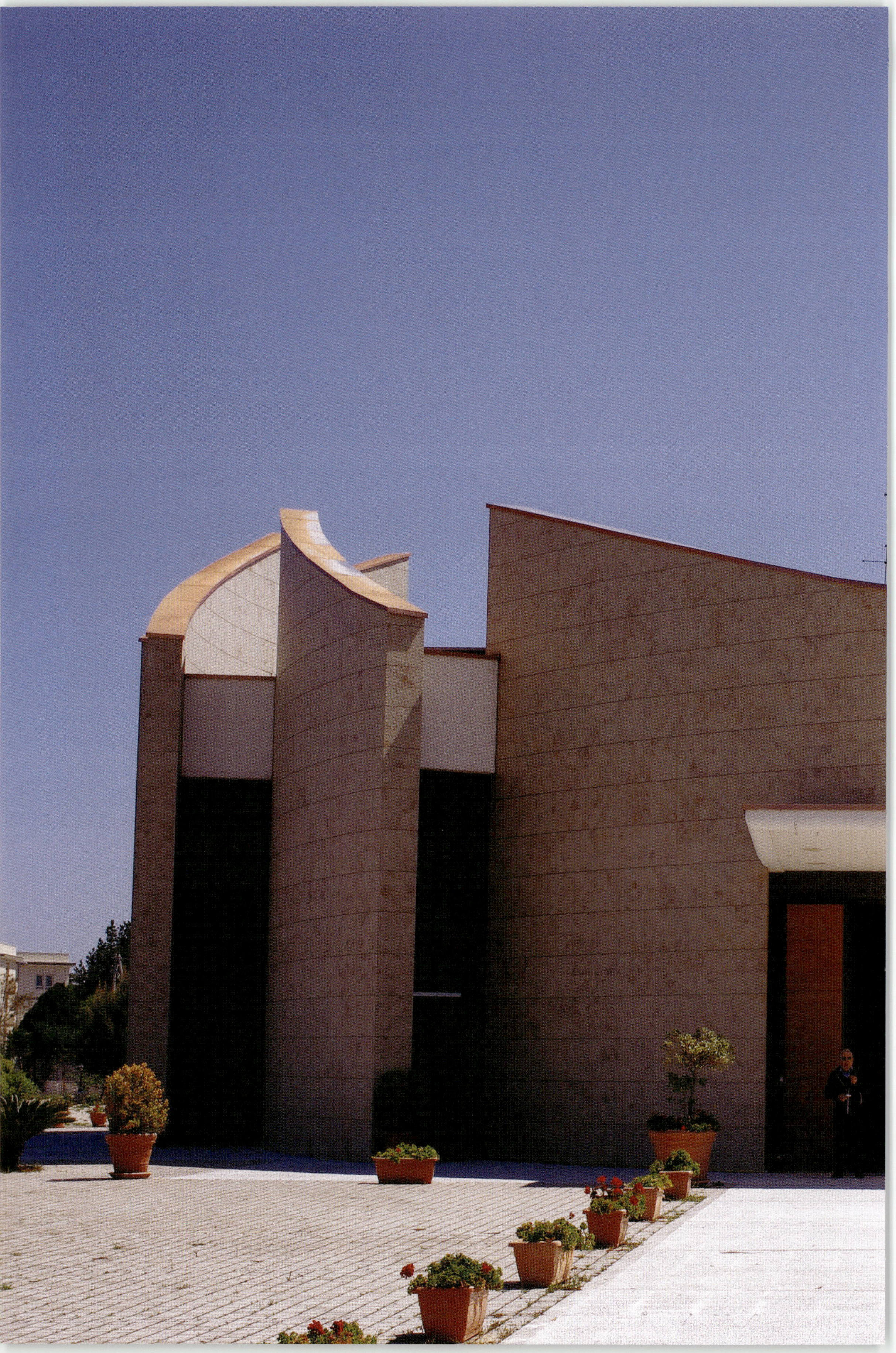

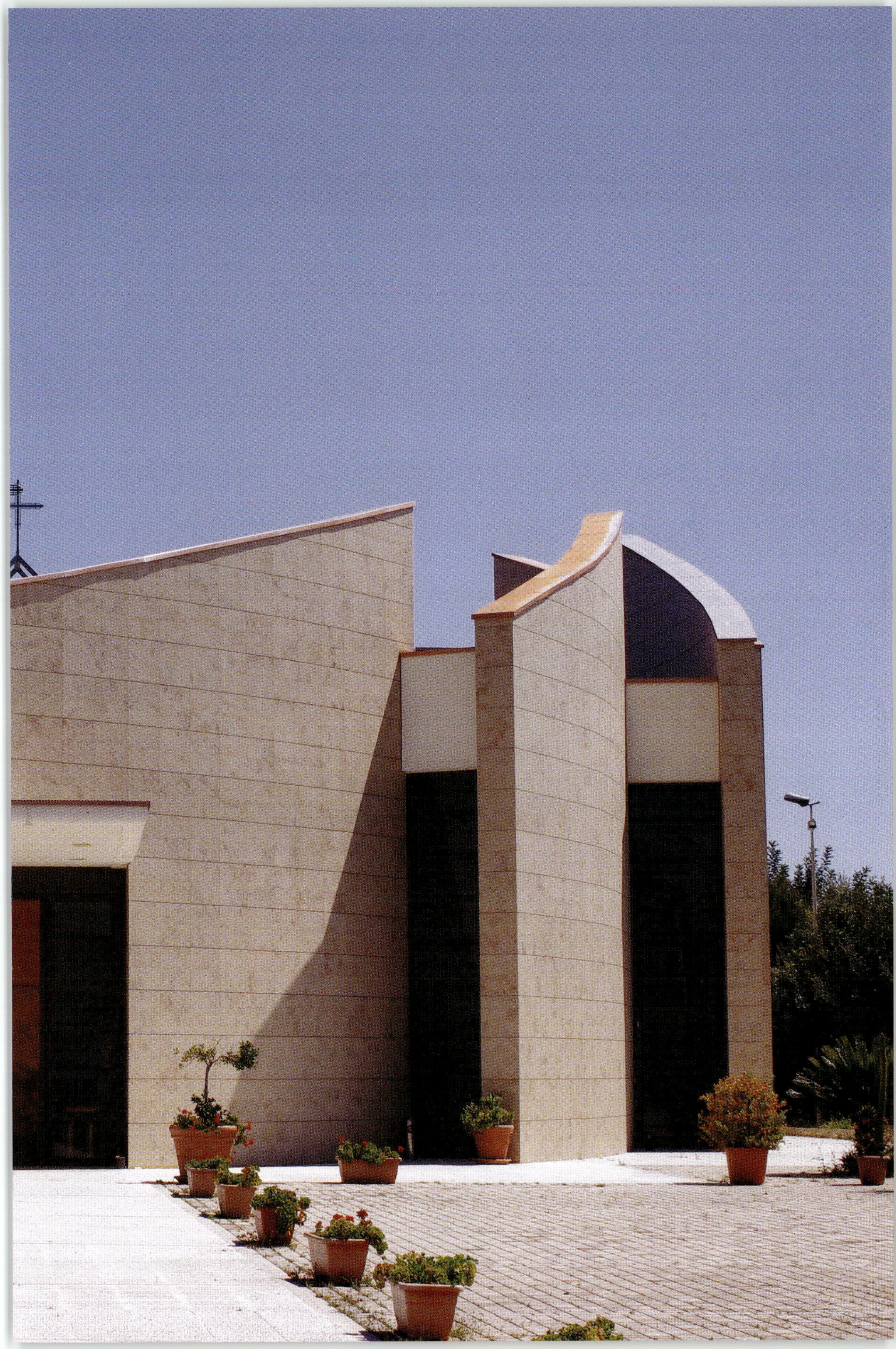

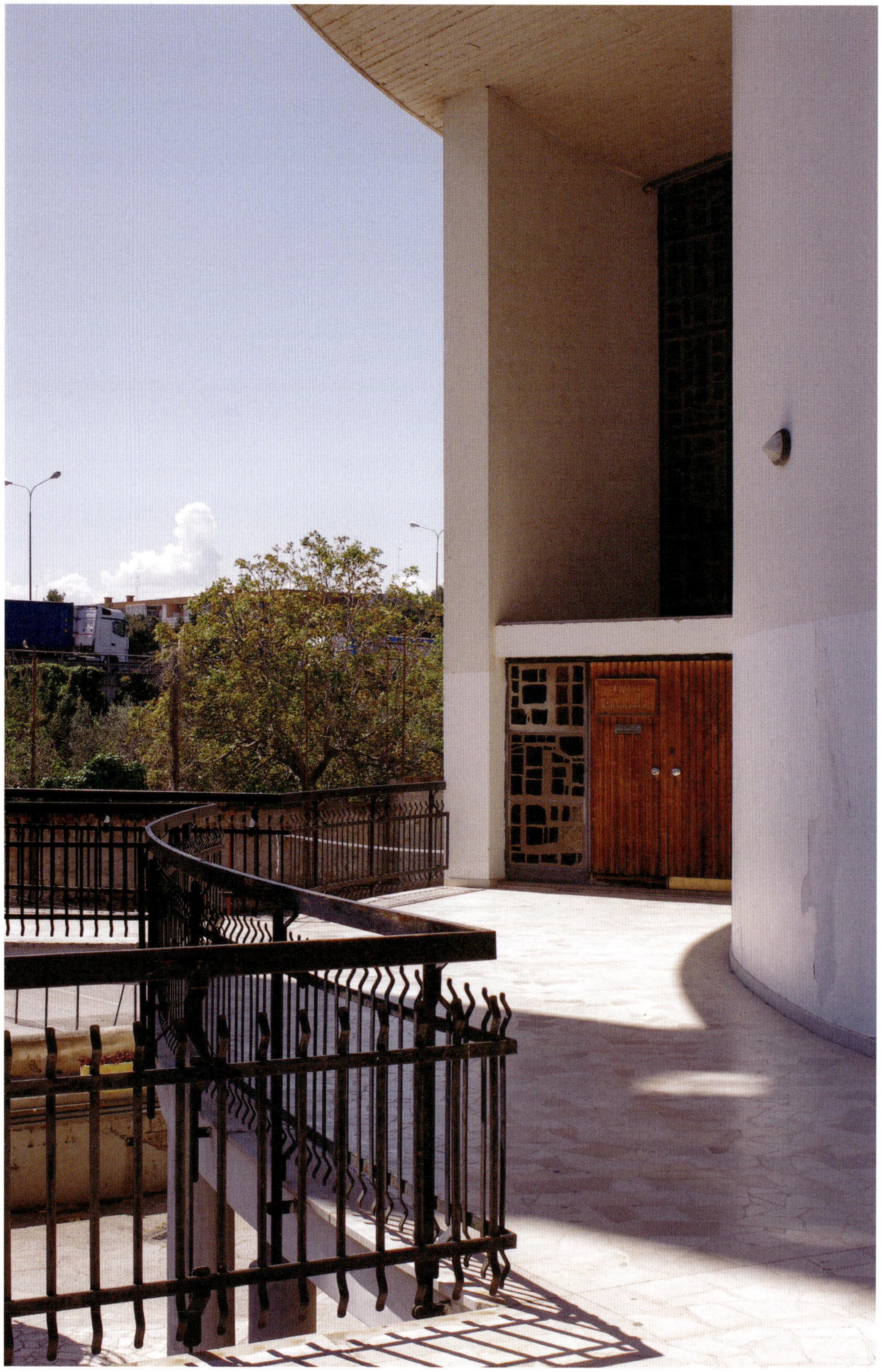

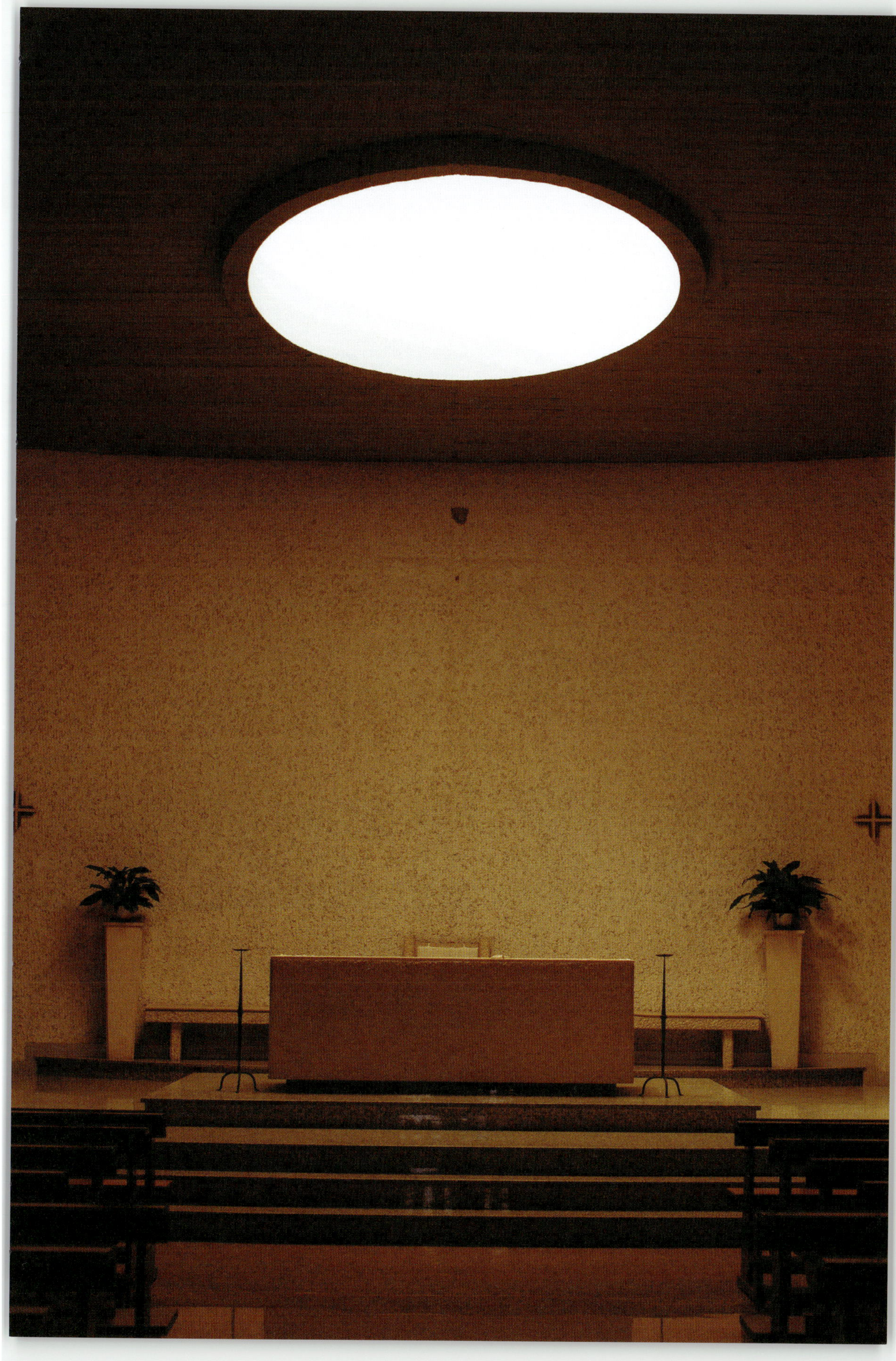

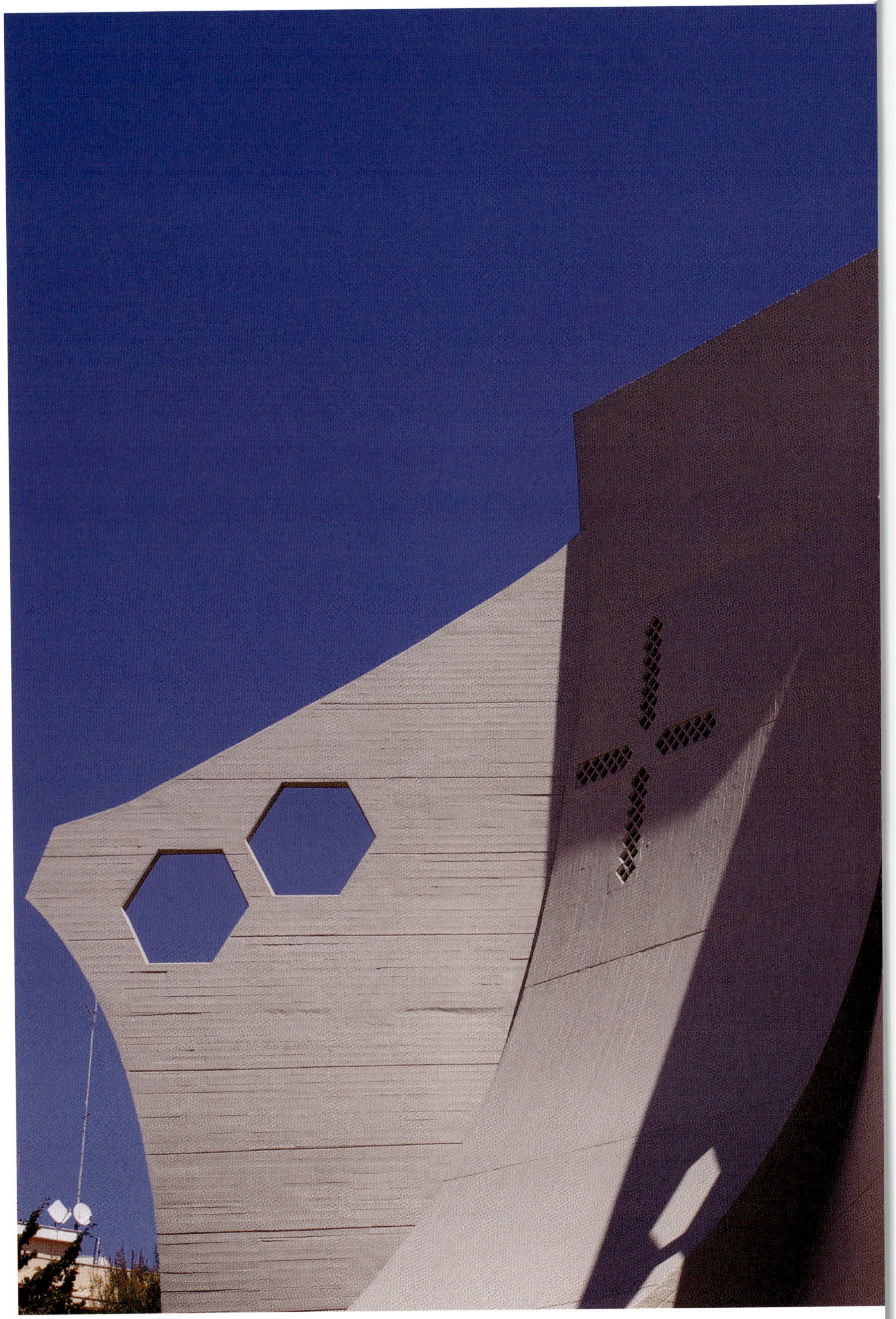

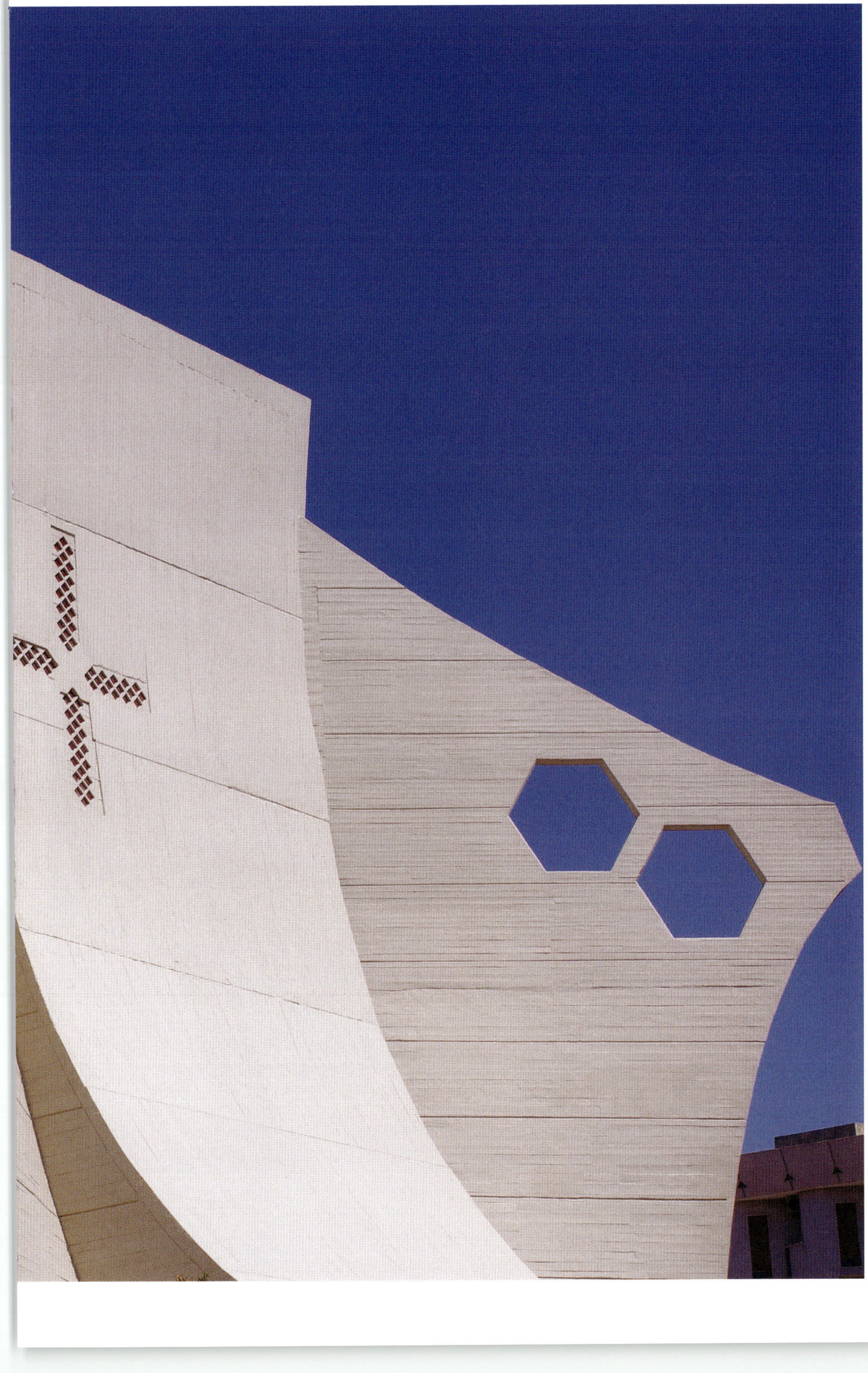

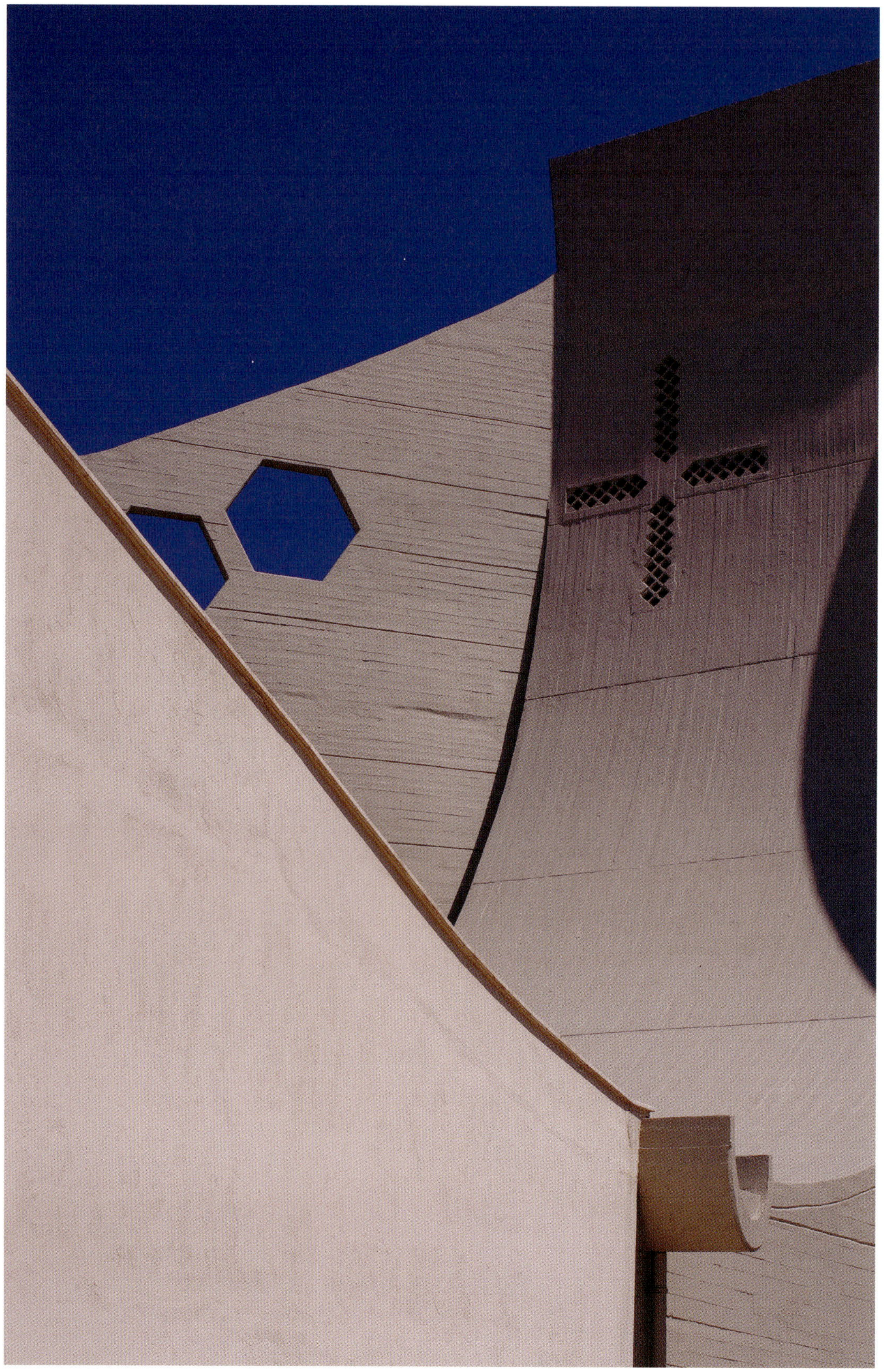

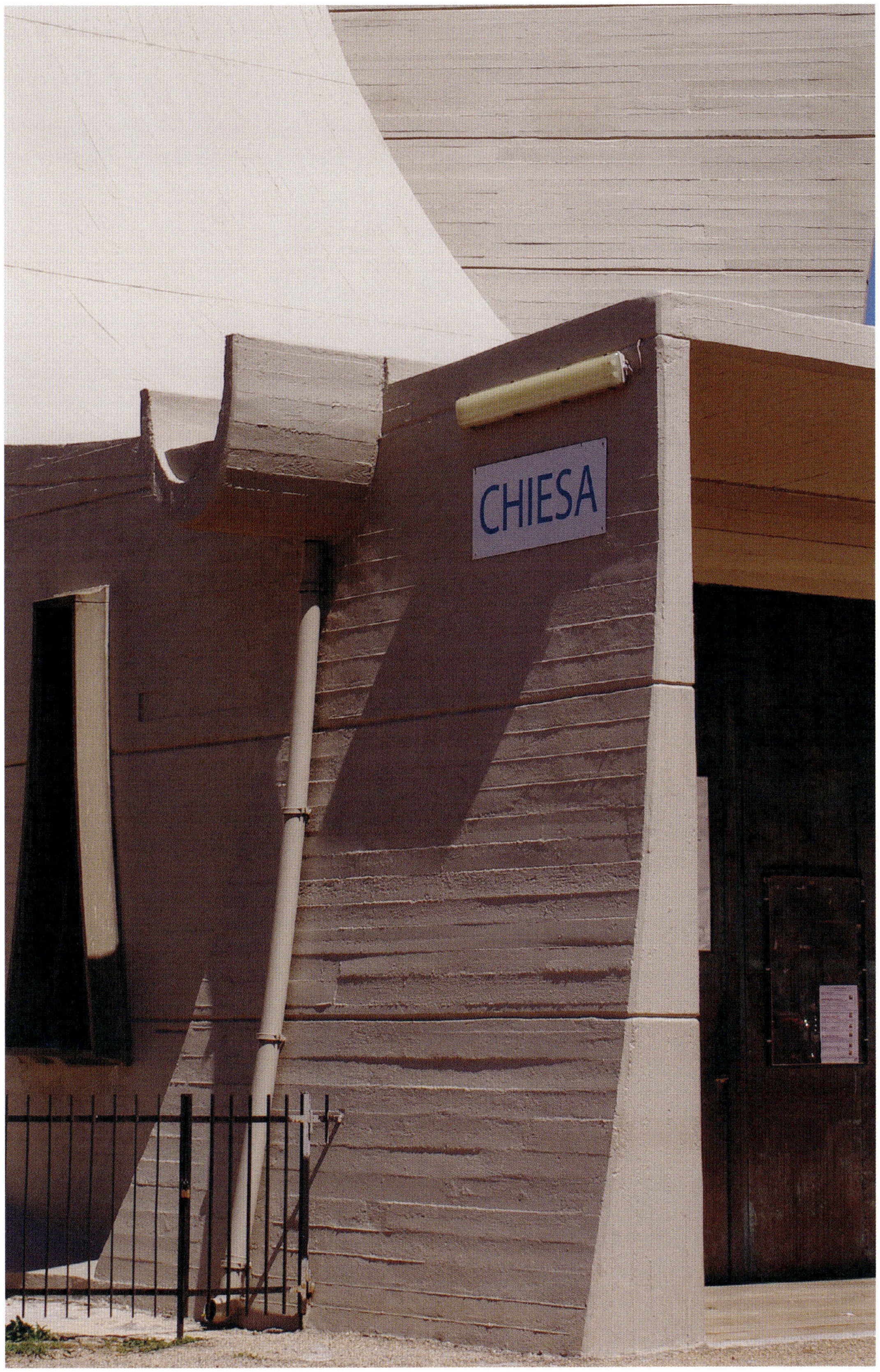
CHIESA

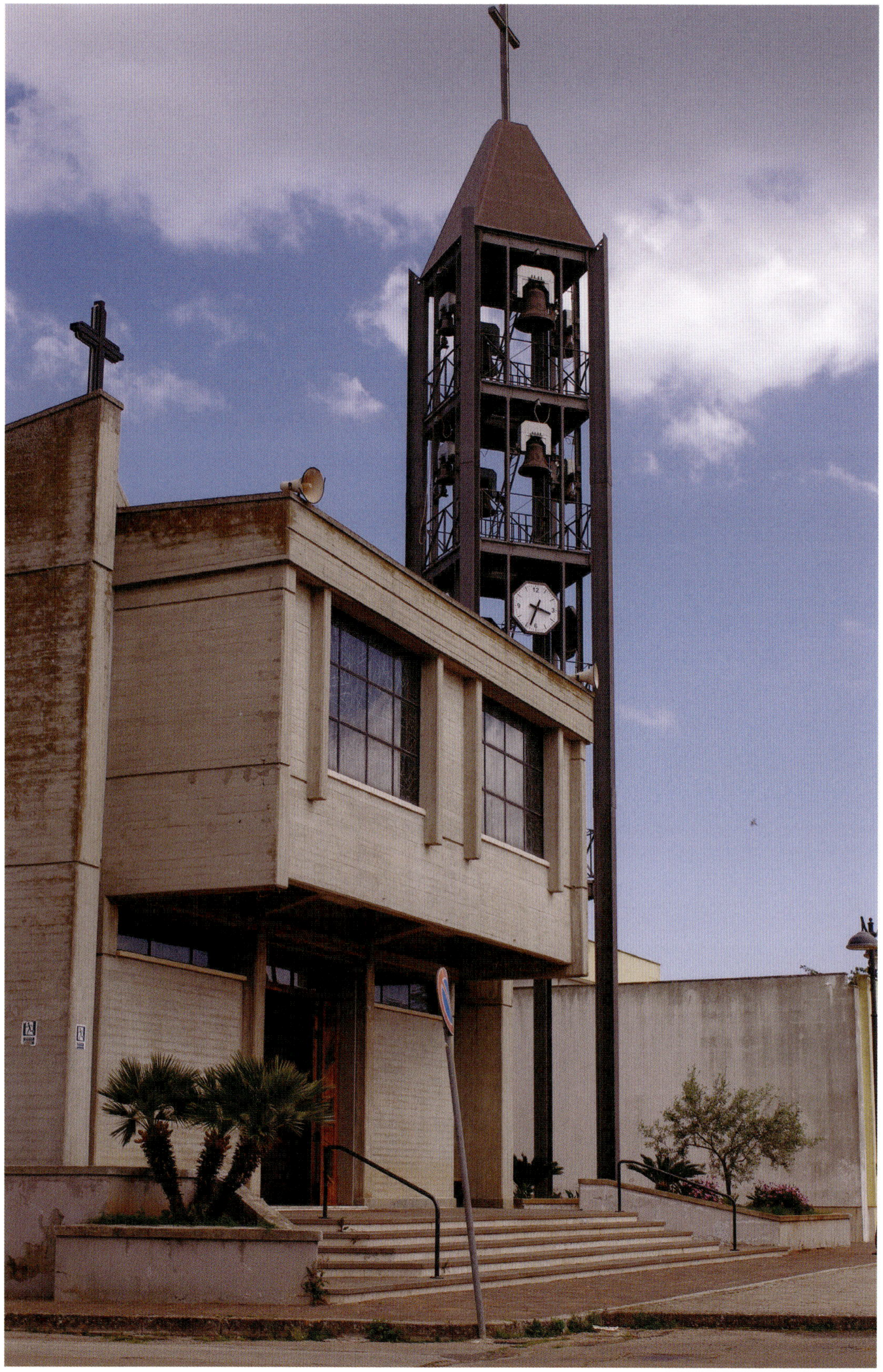

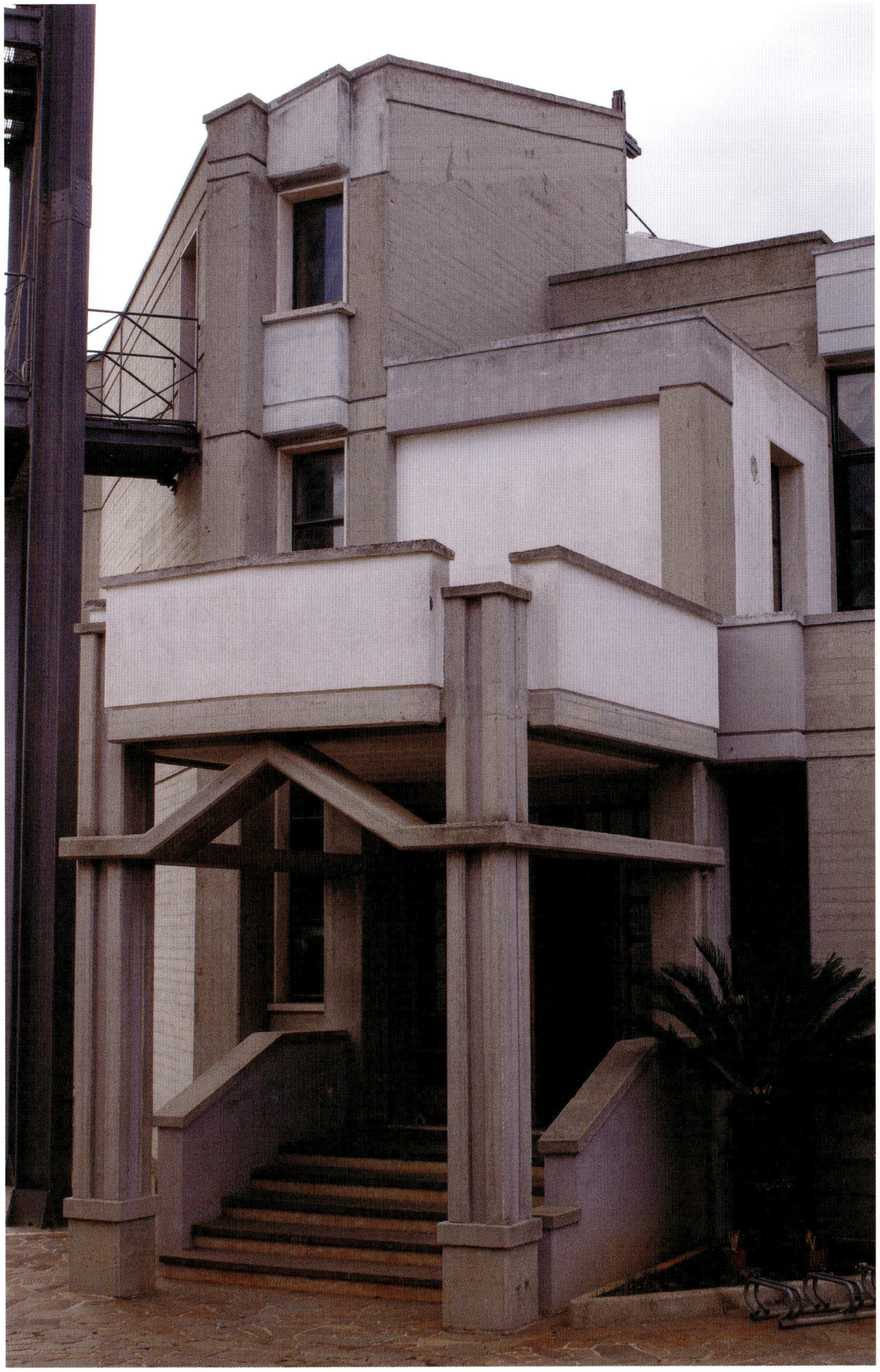

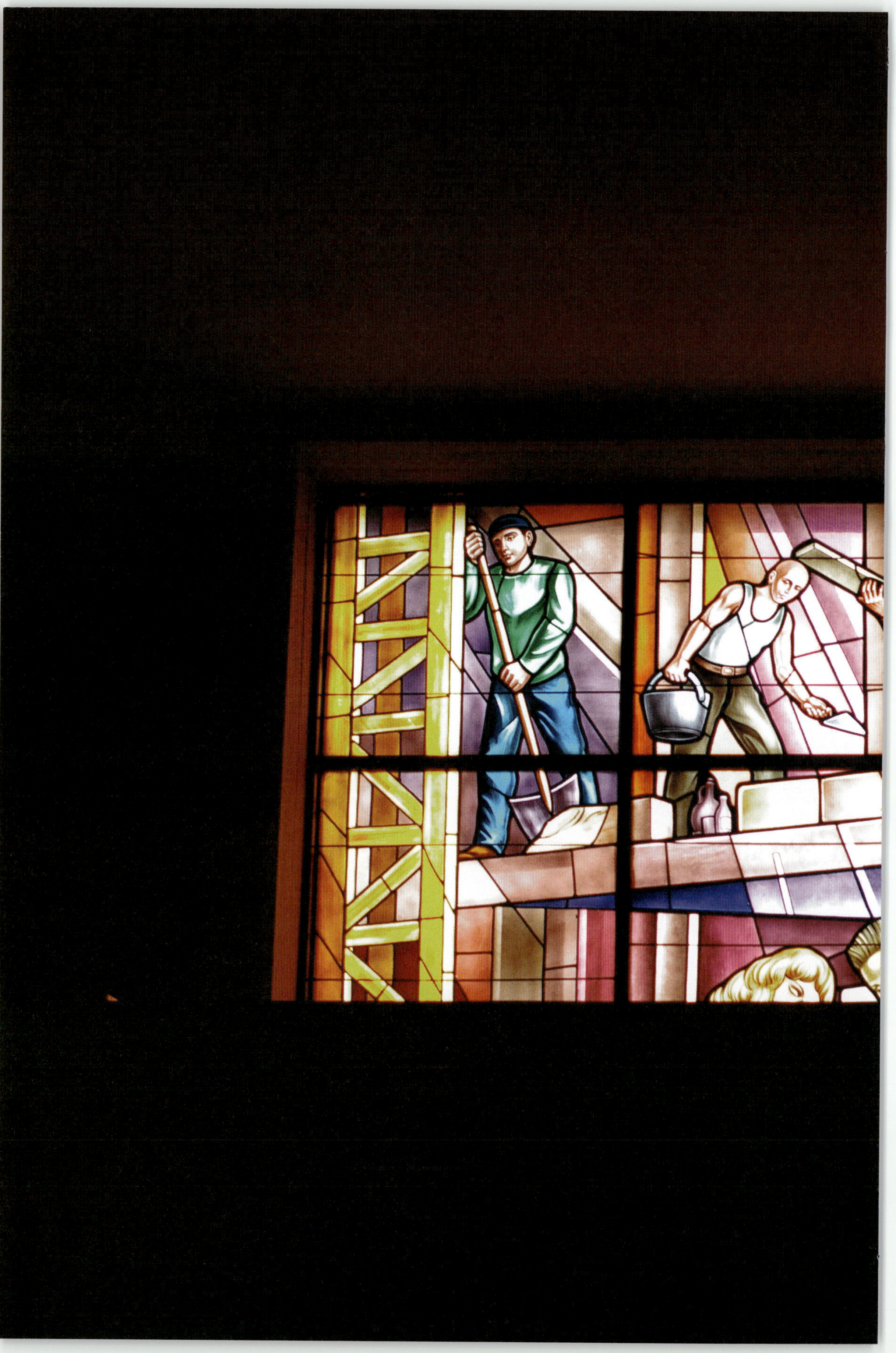

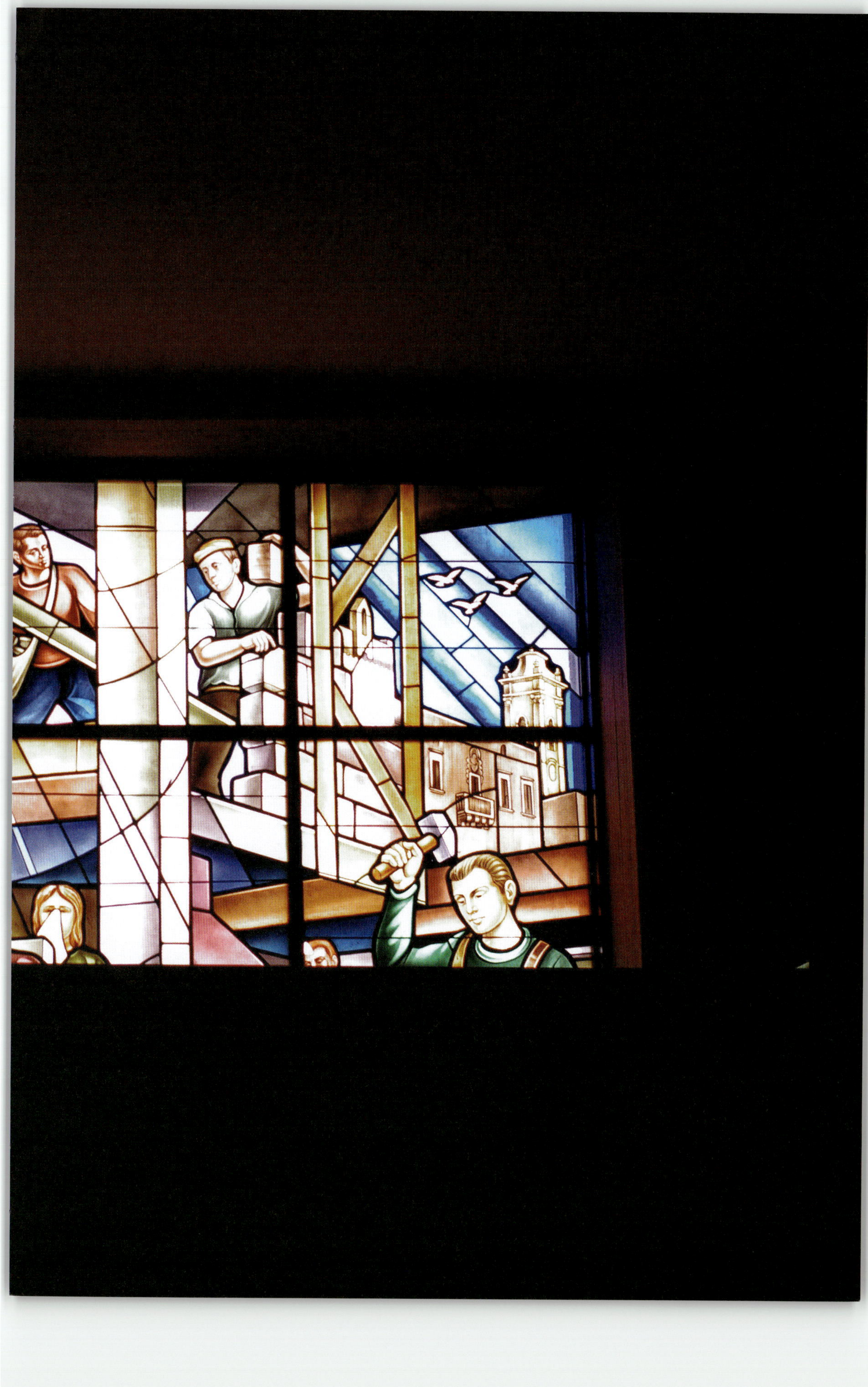

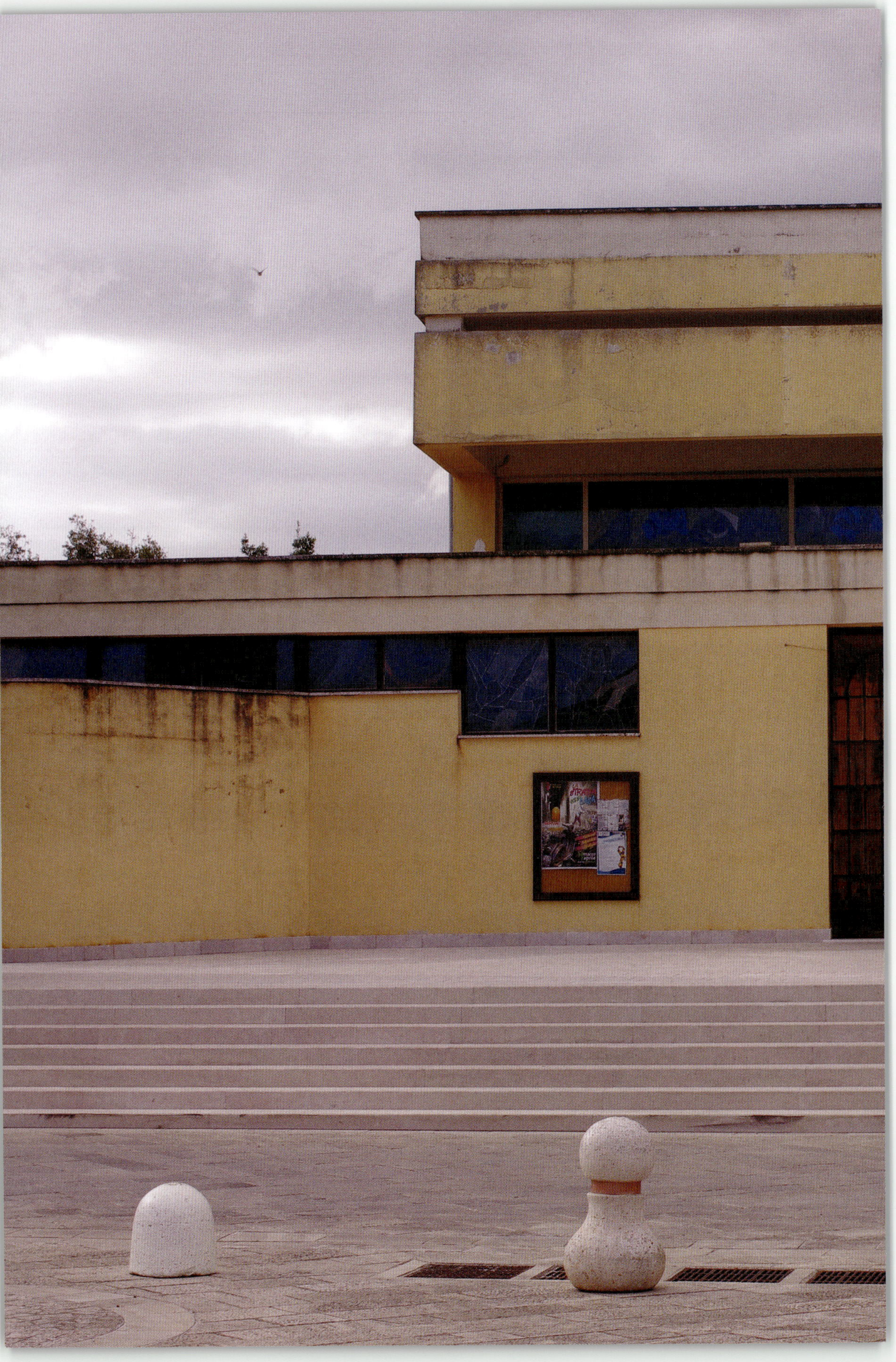

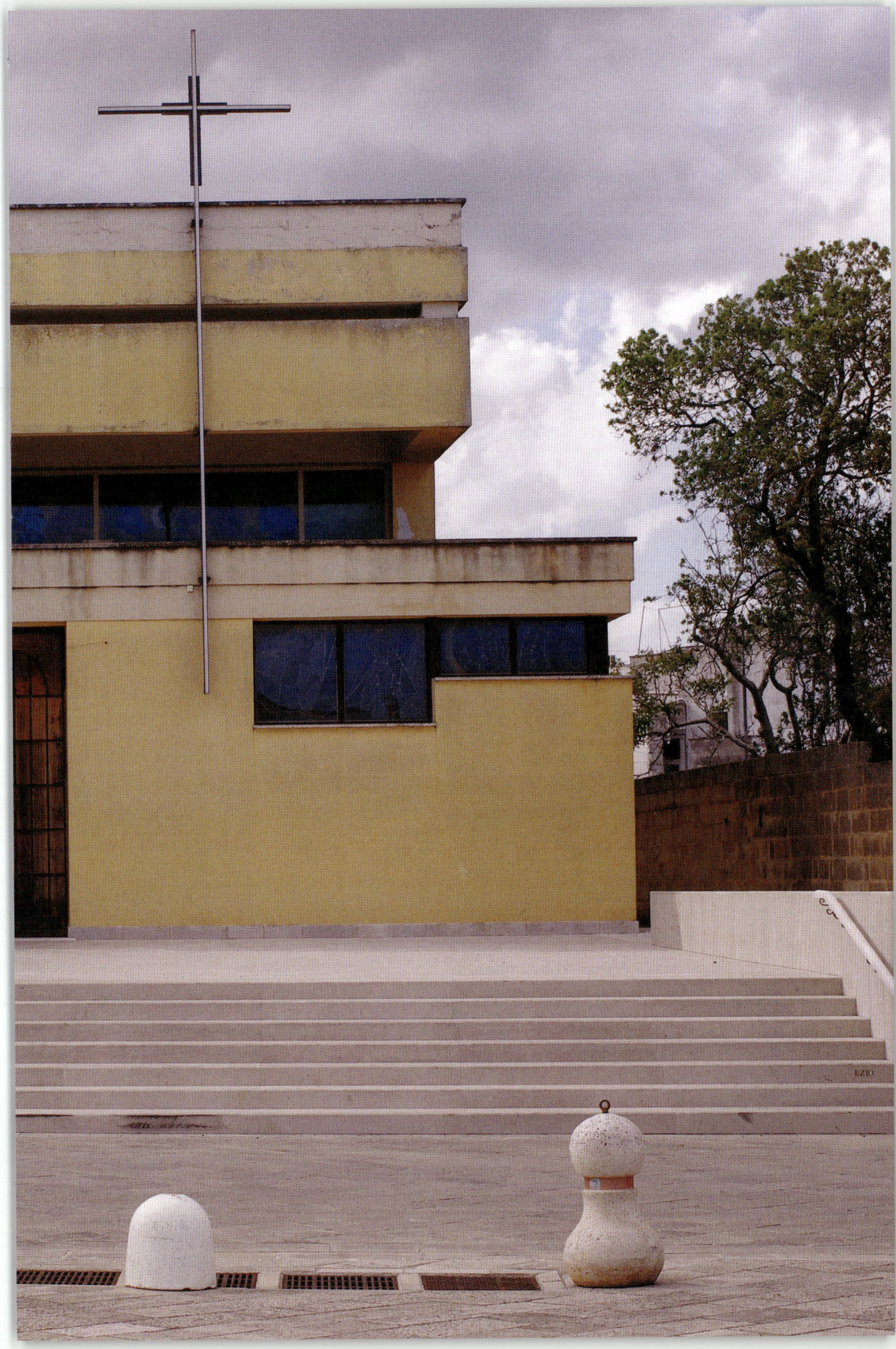
EZIO

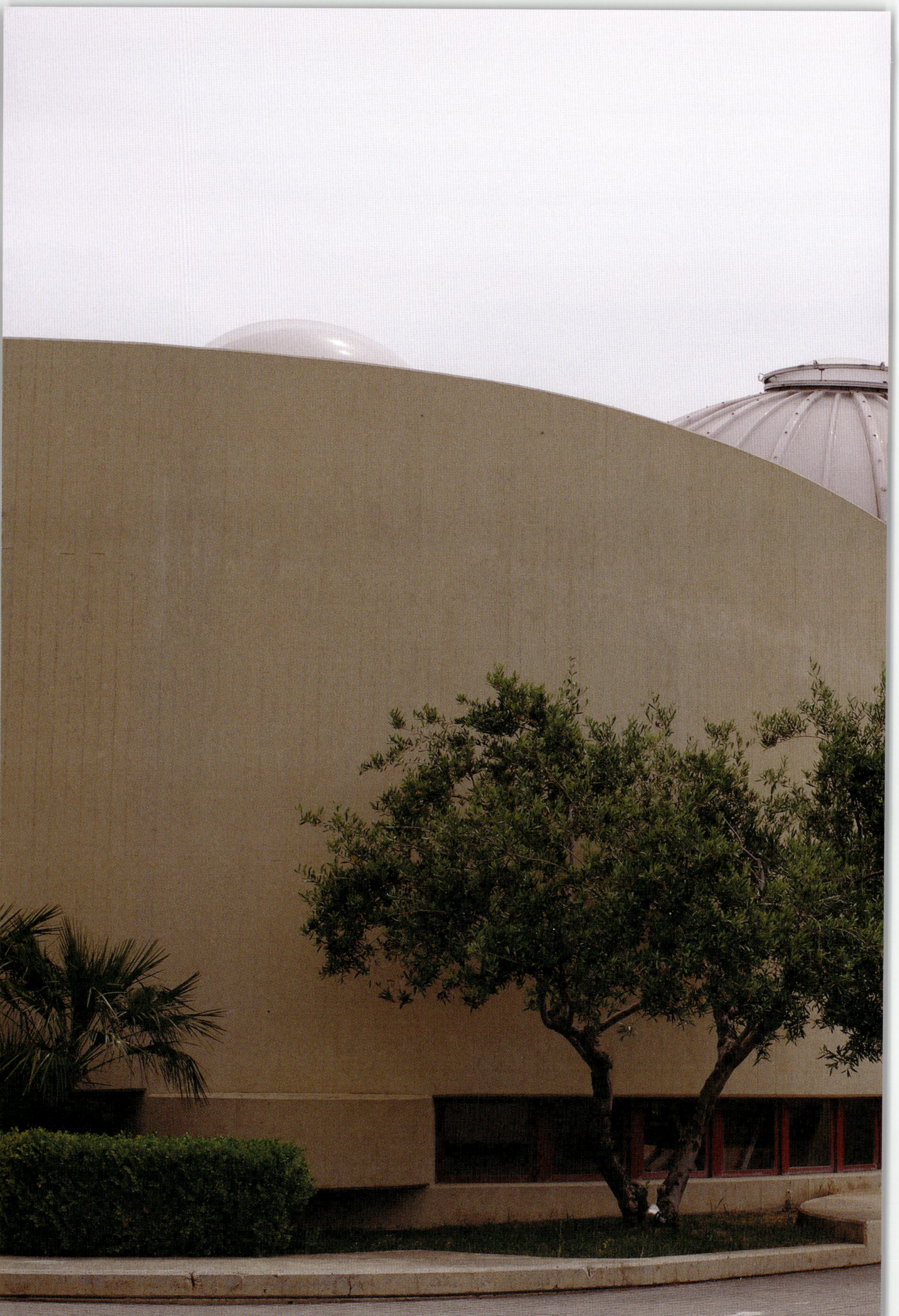

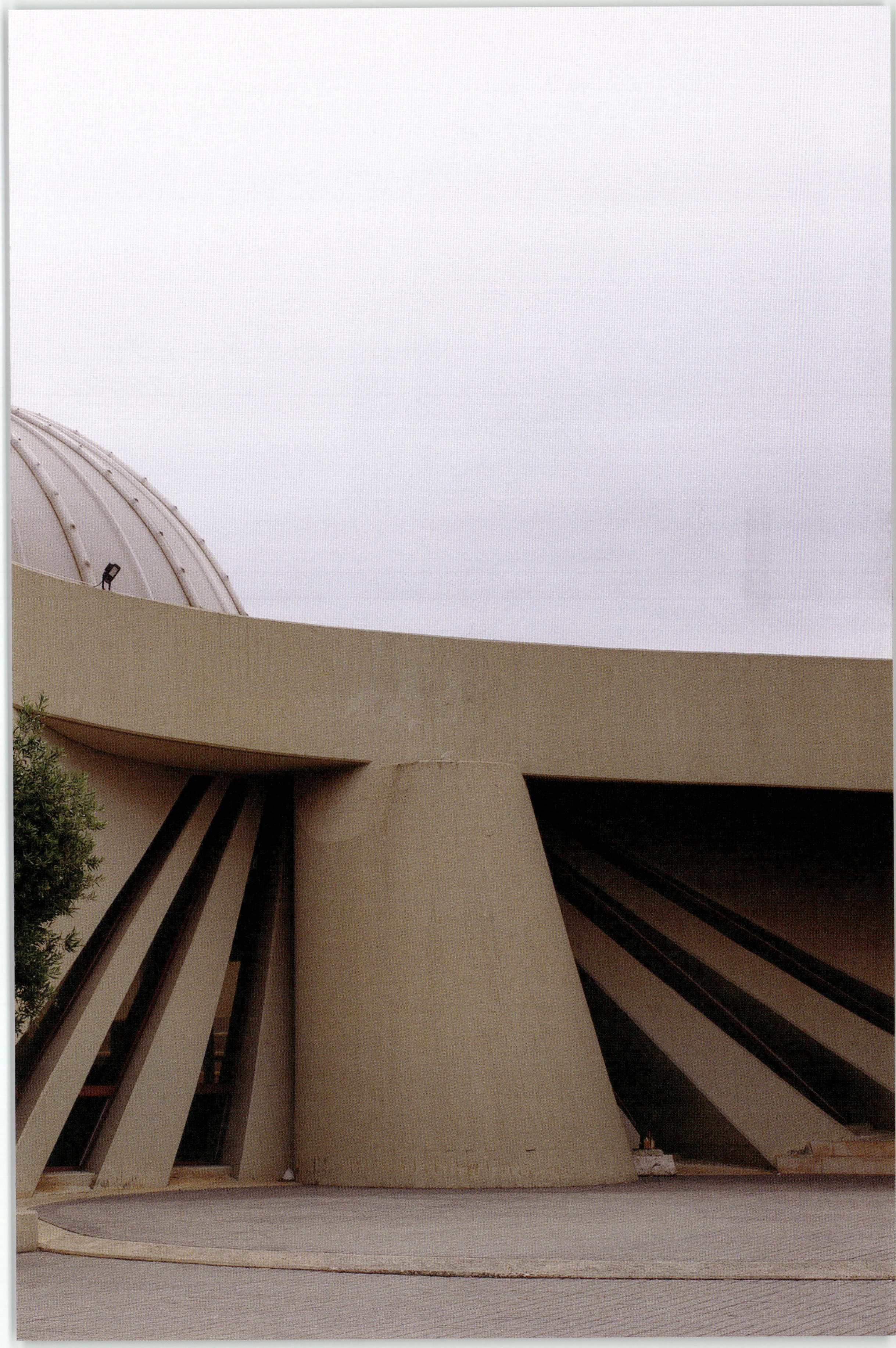

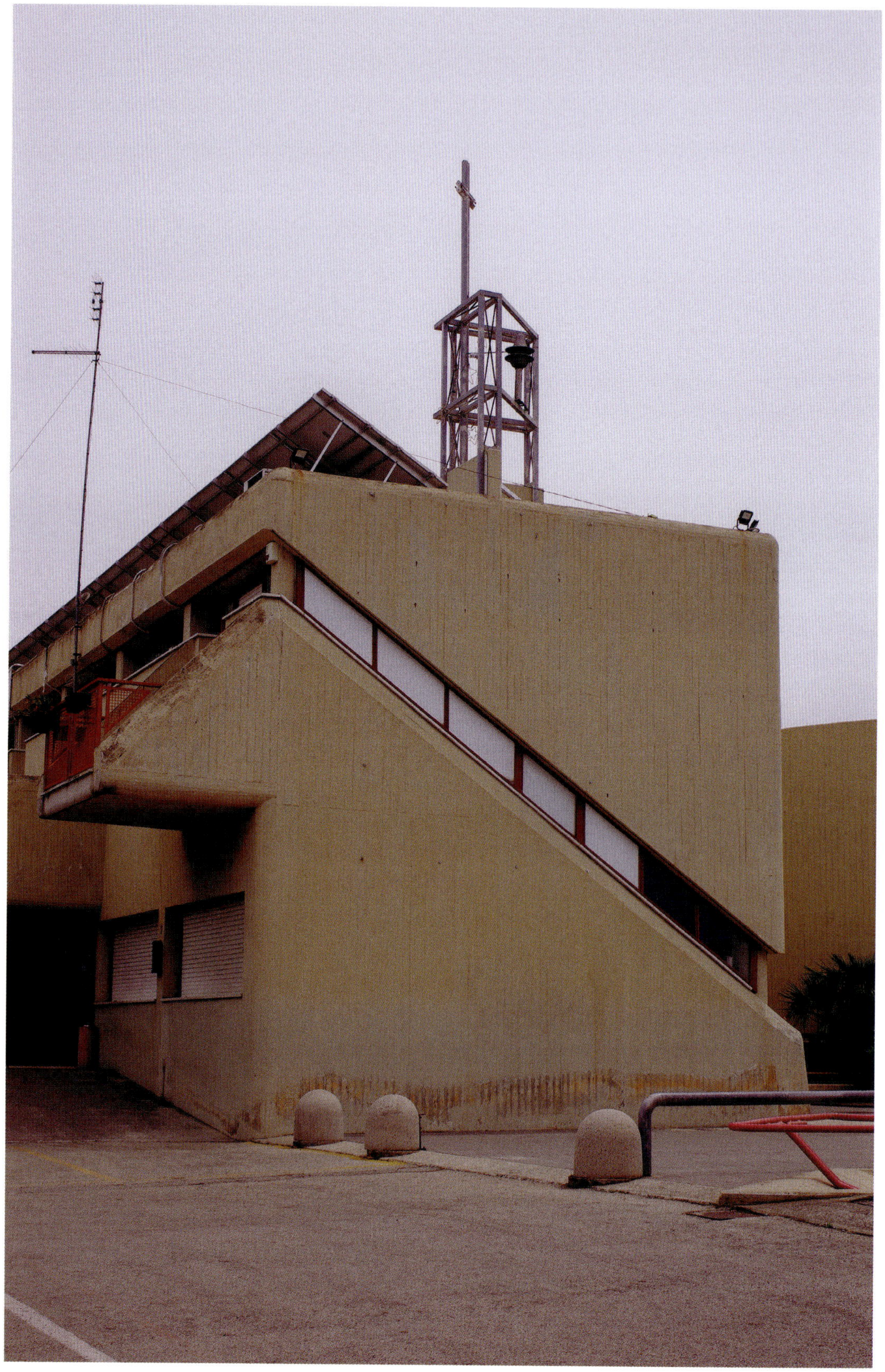

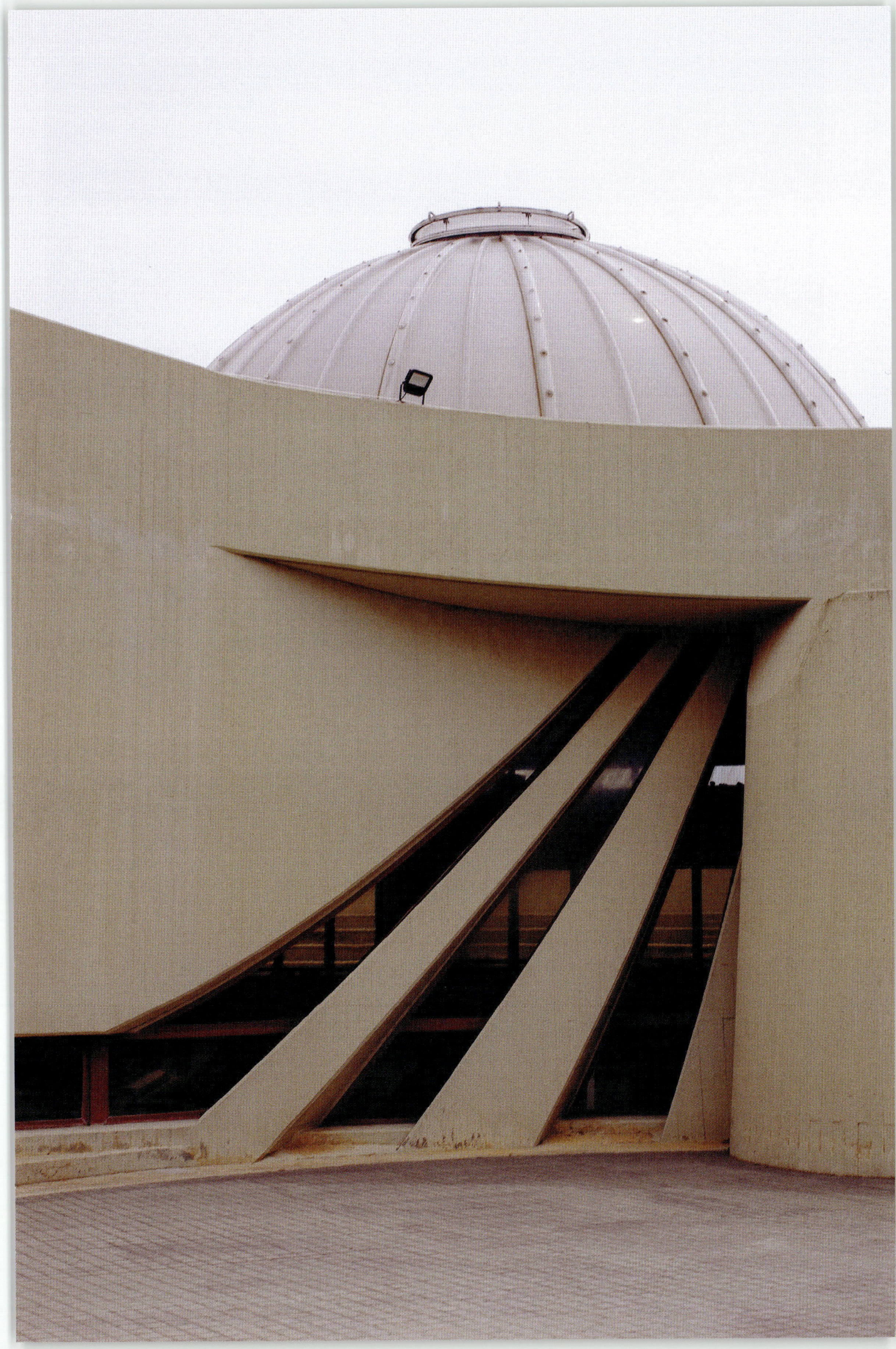

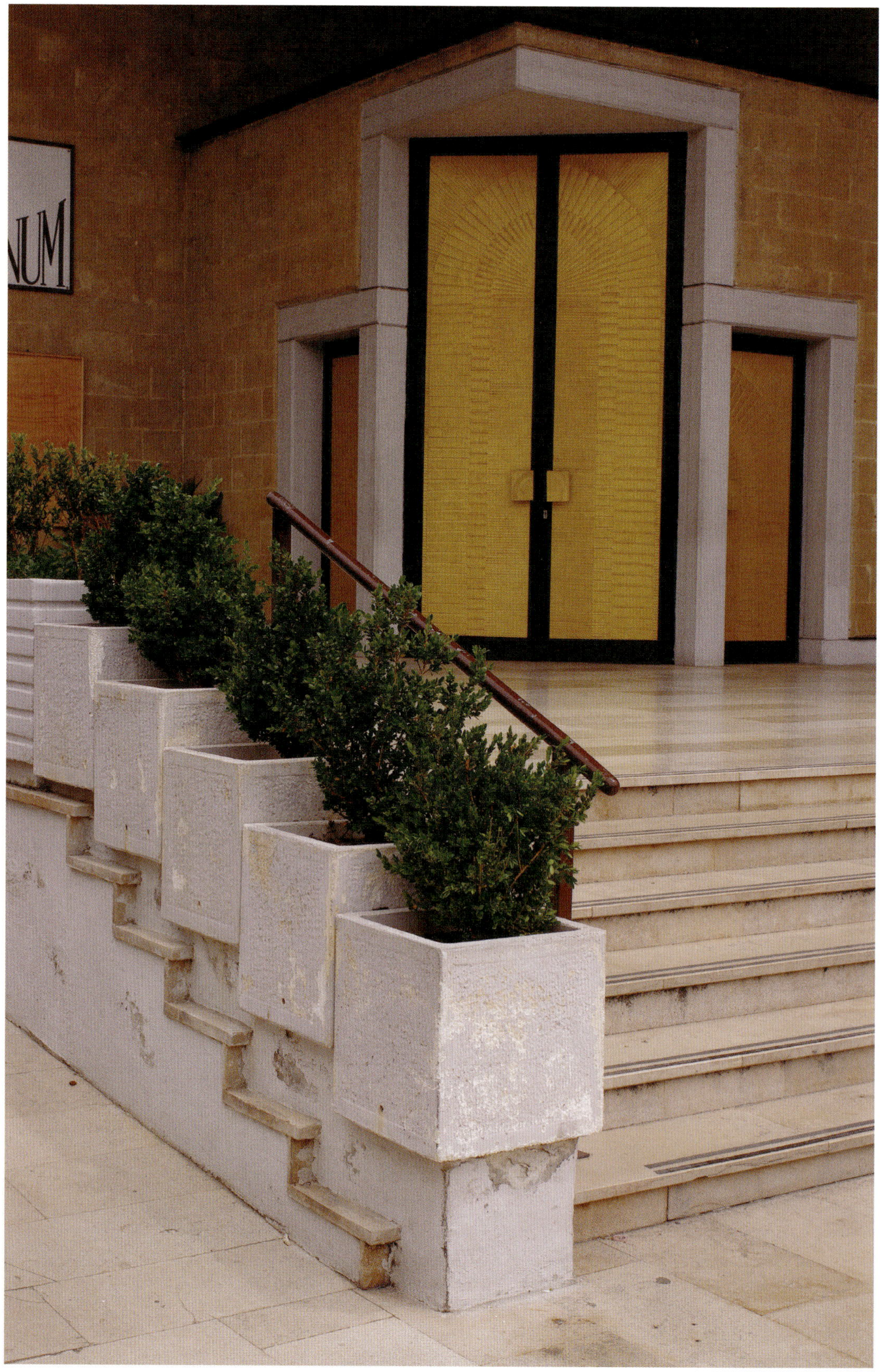
NUM

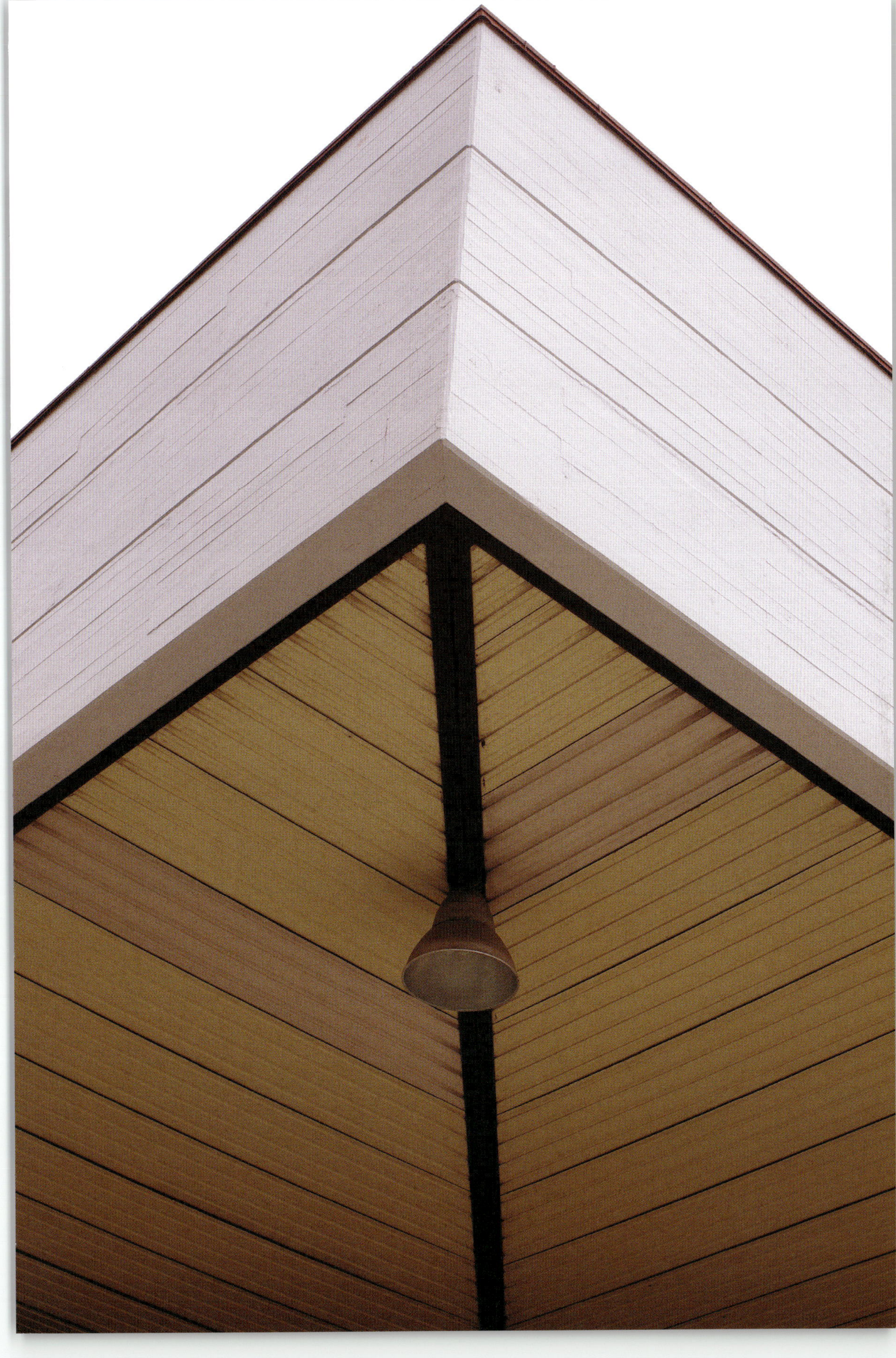

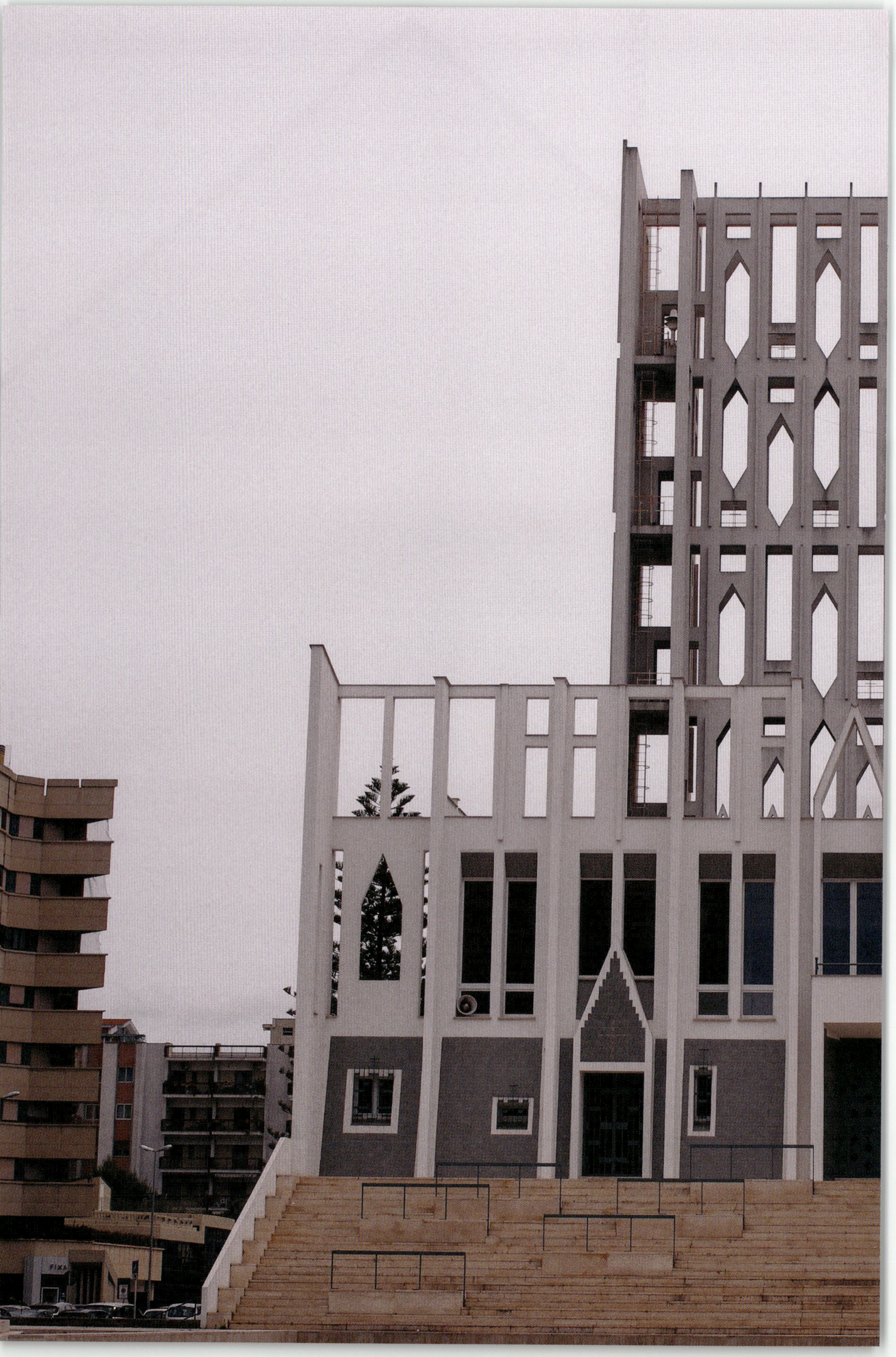

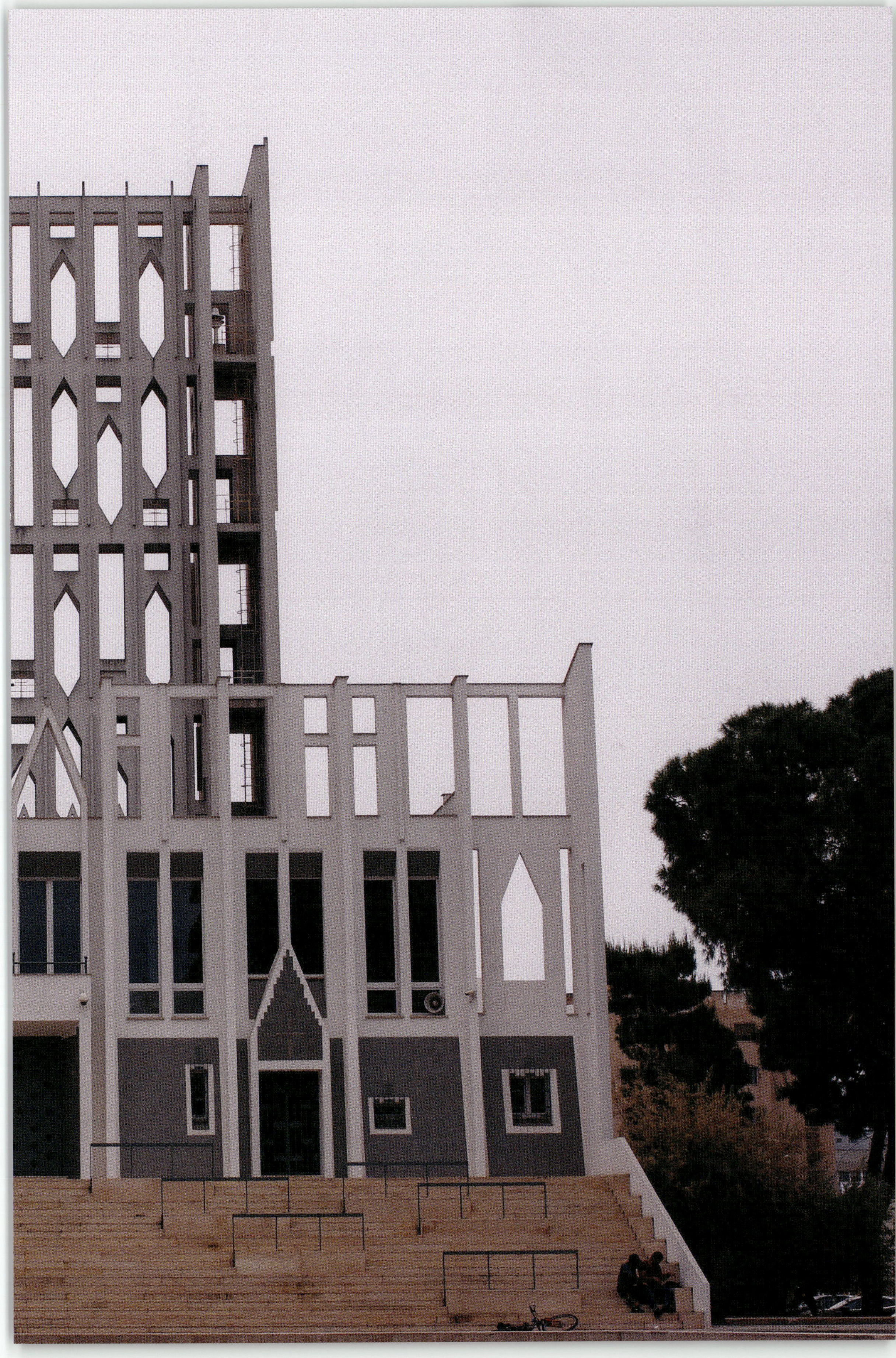

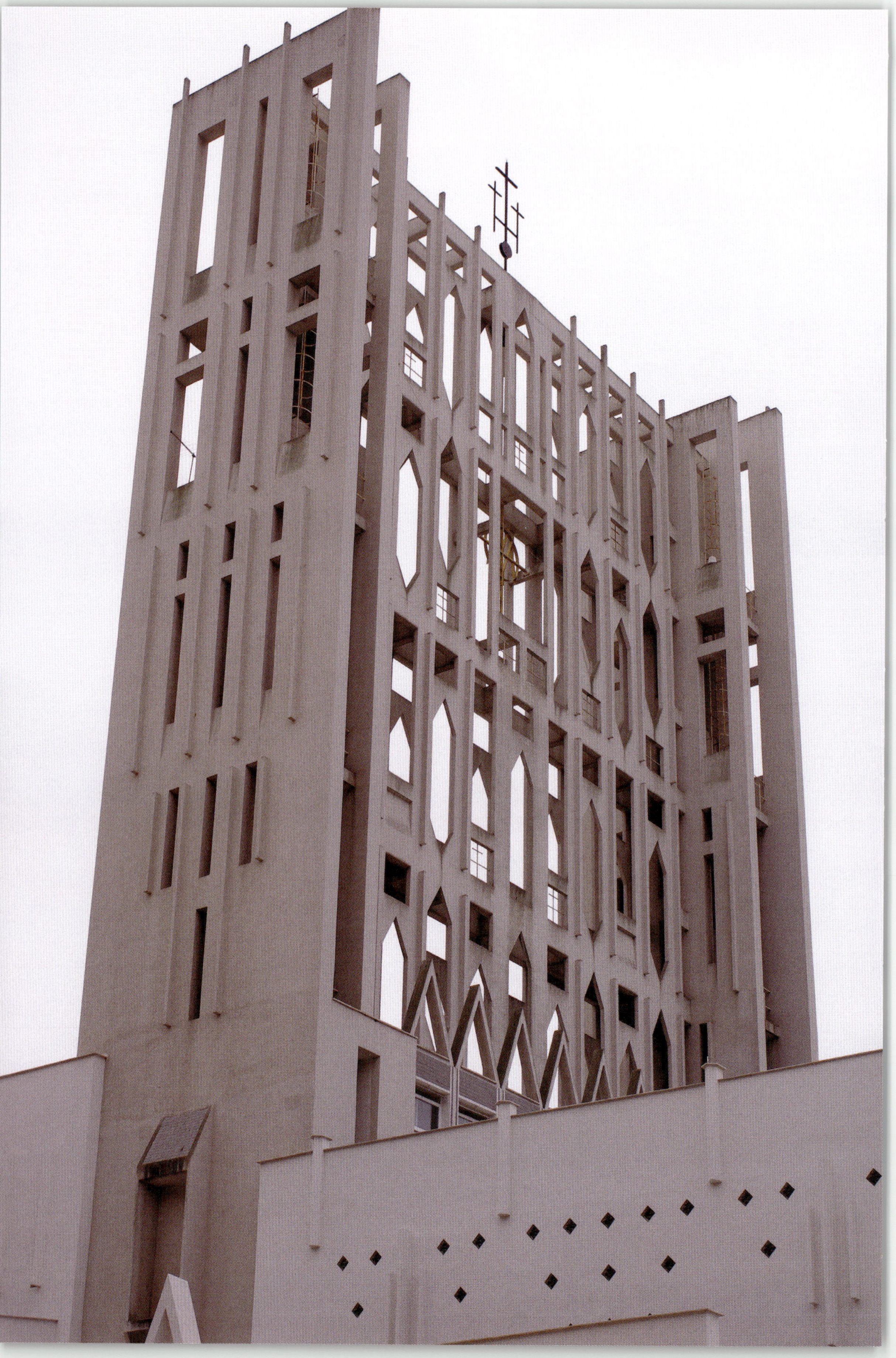

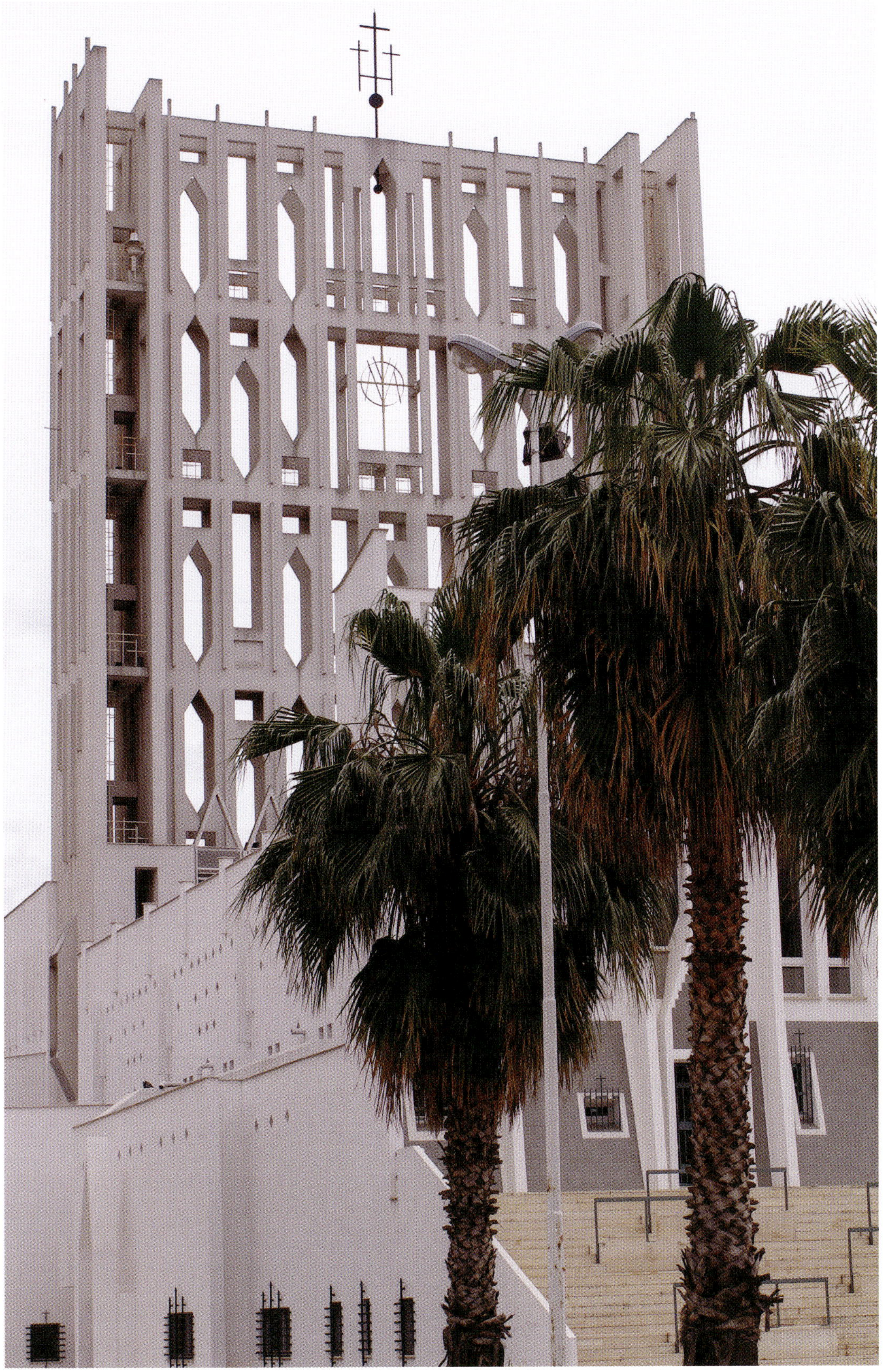

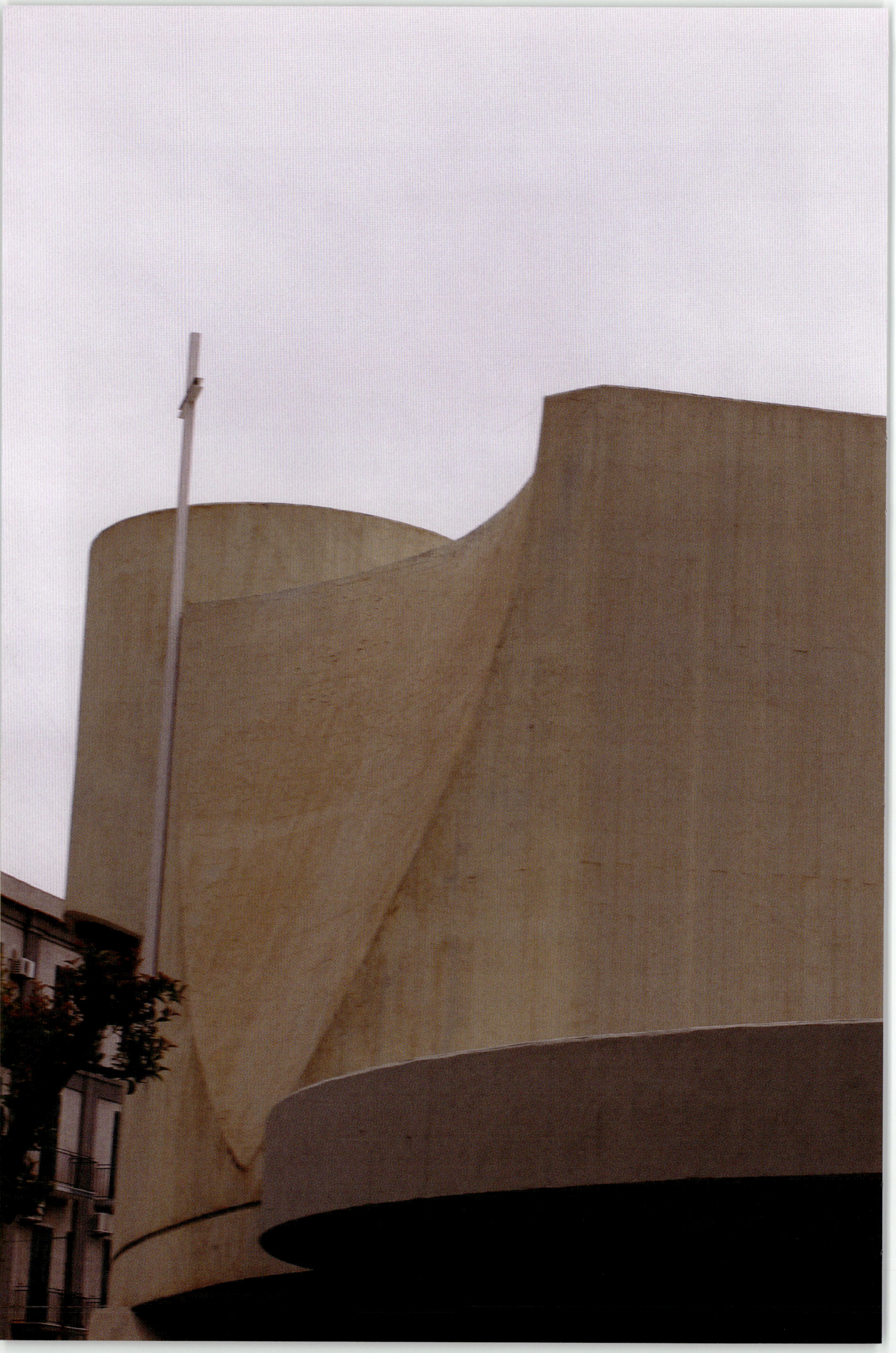

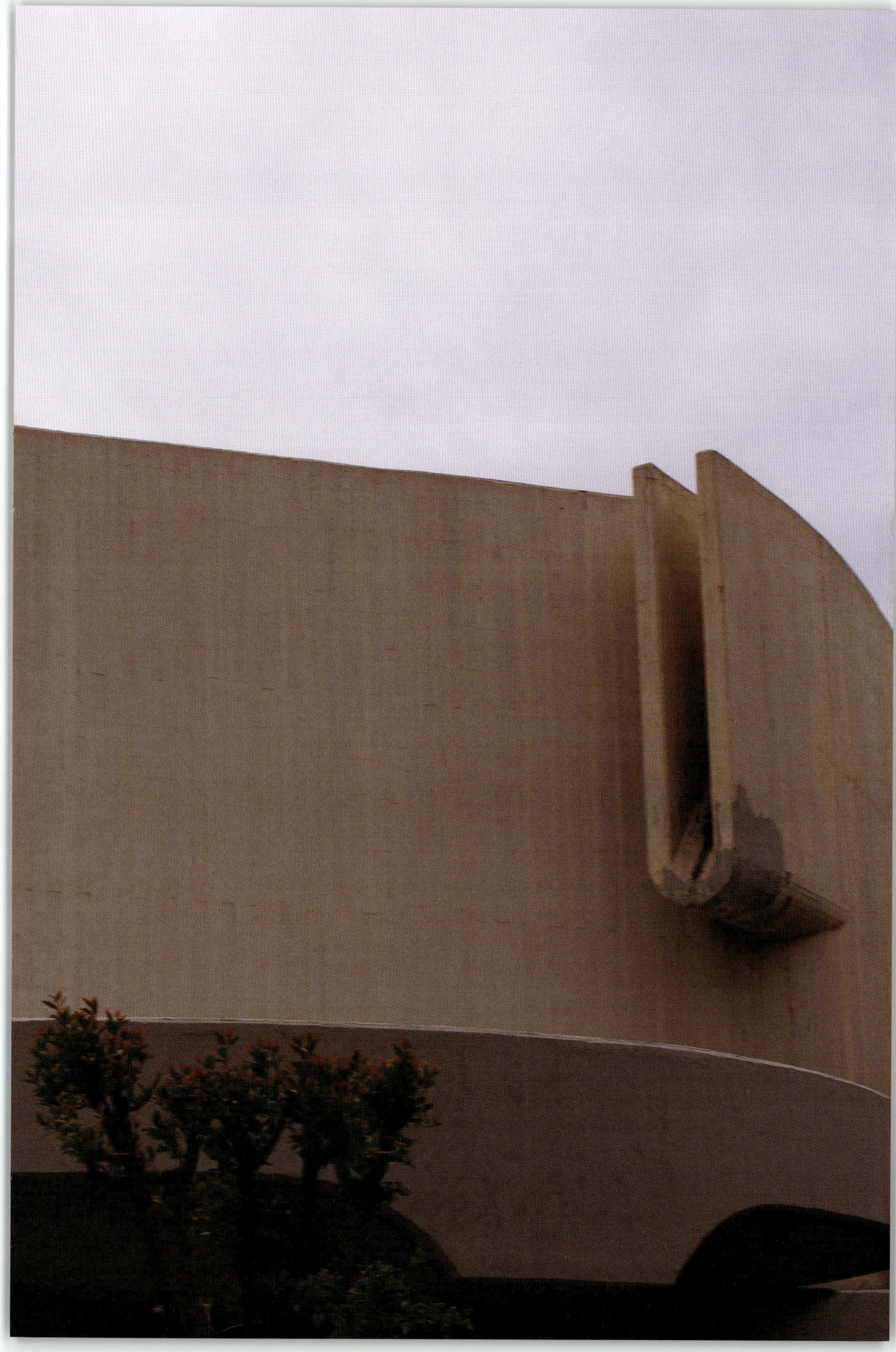

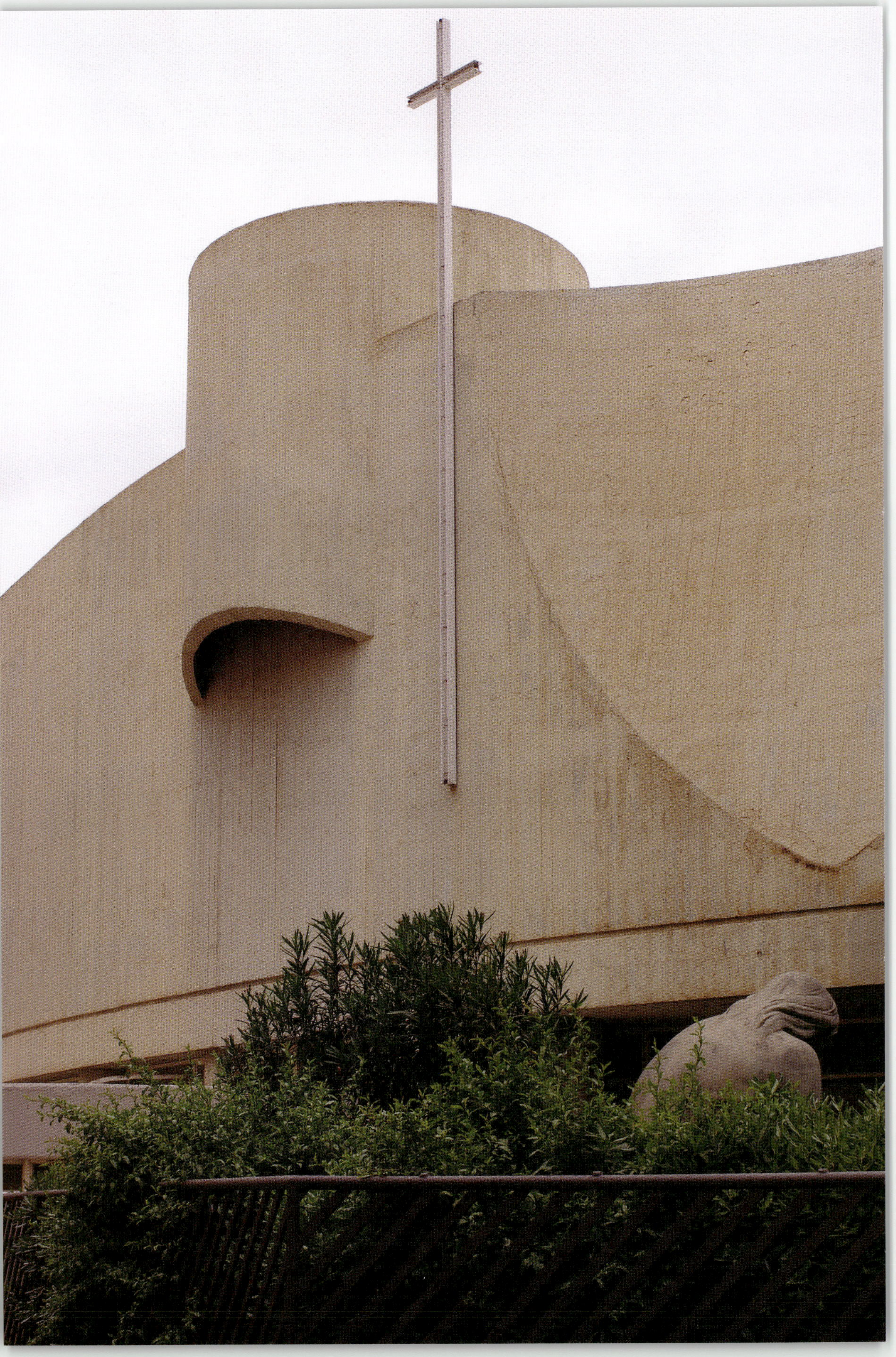

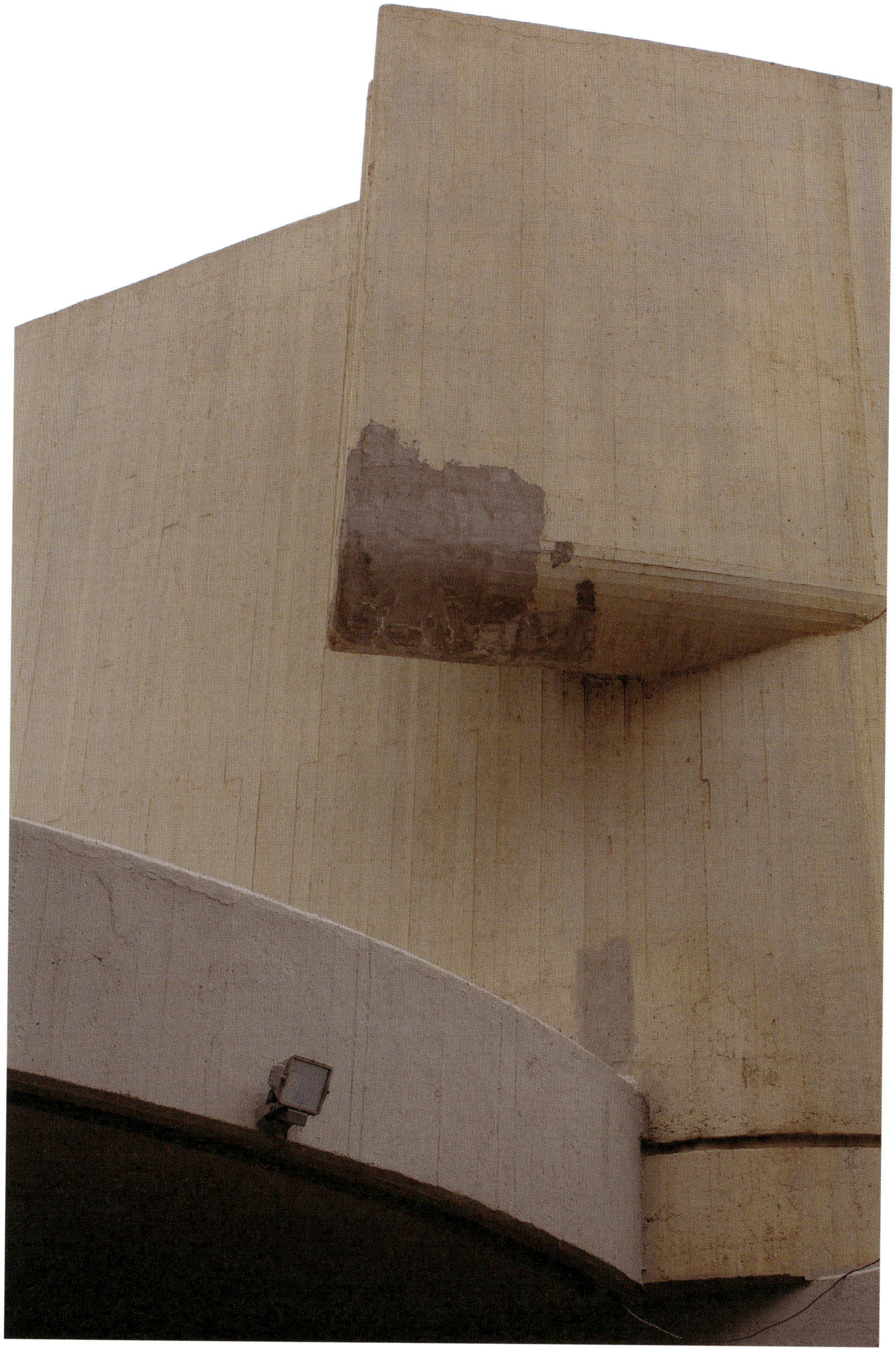

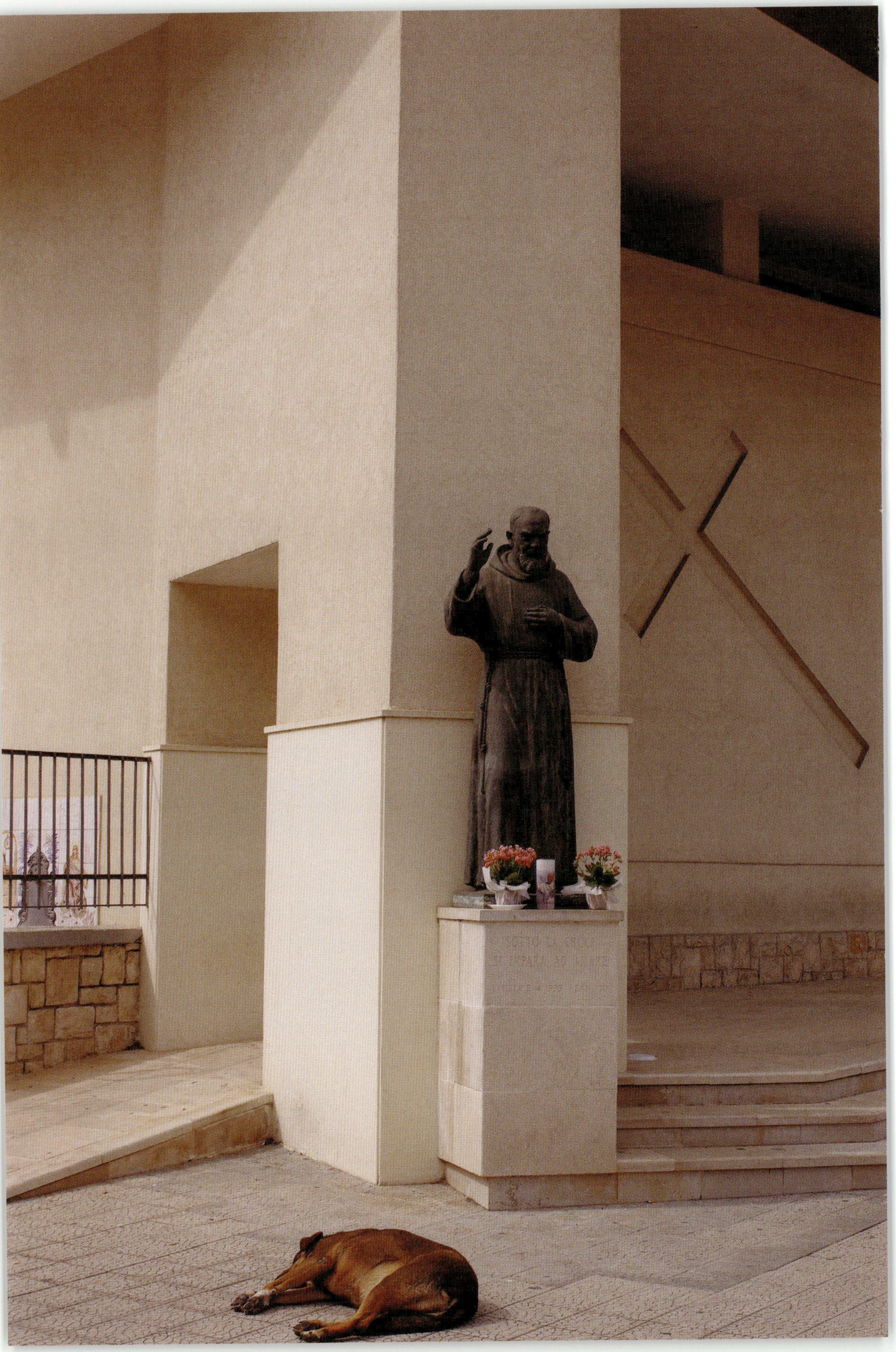

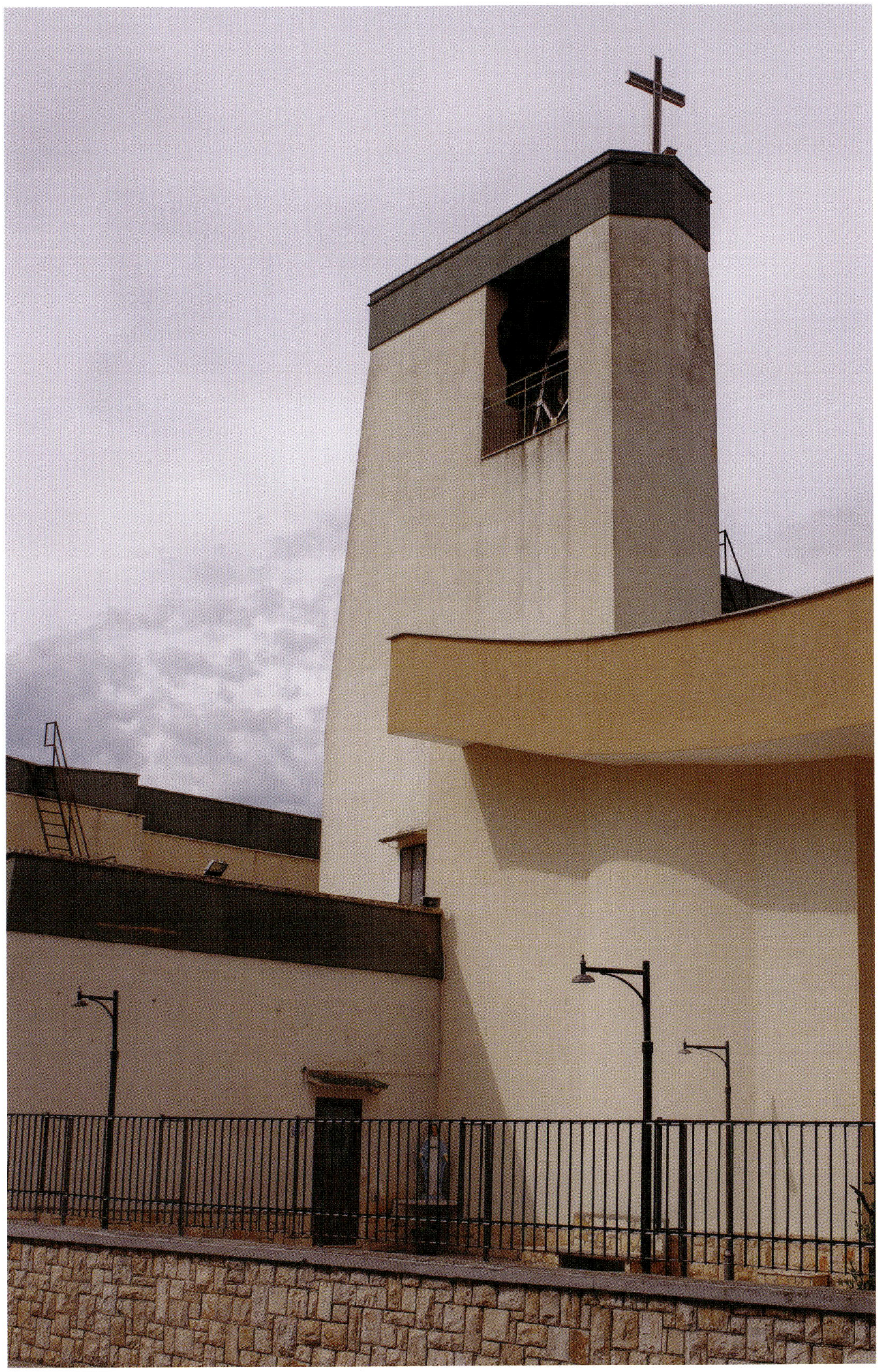

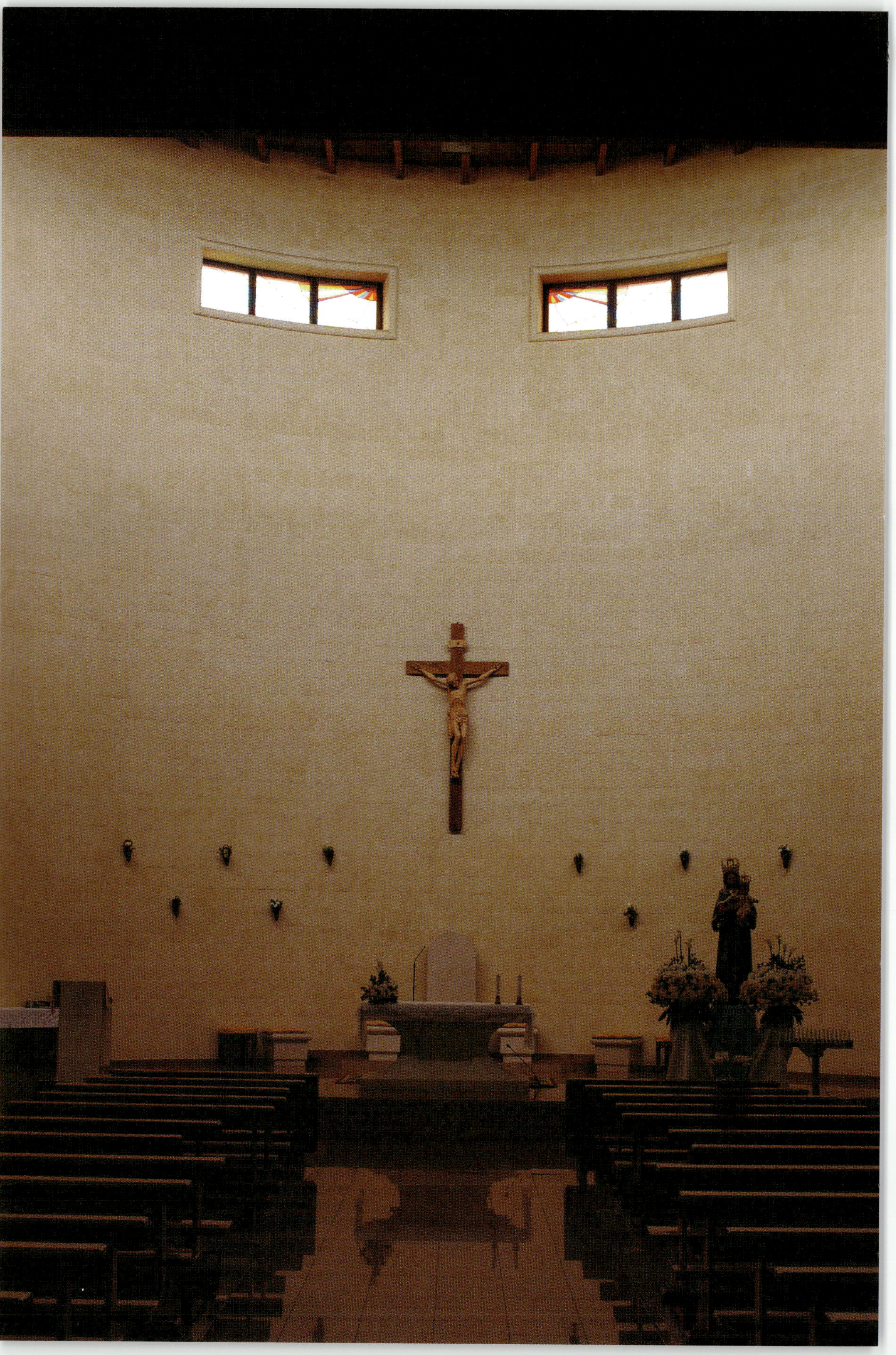

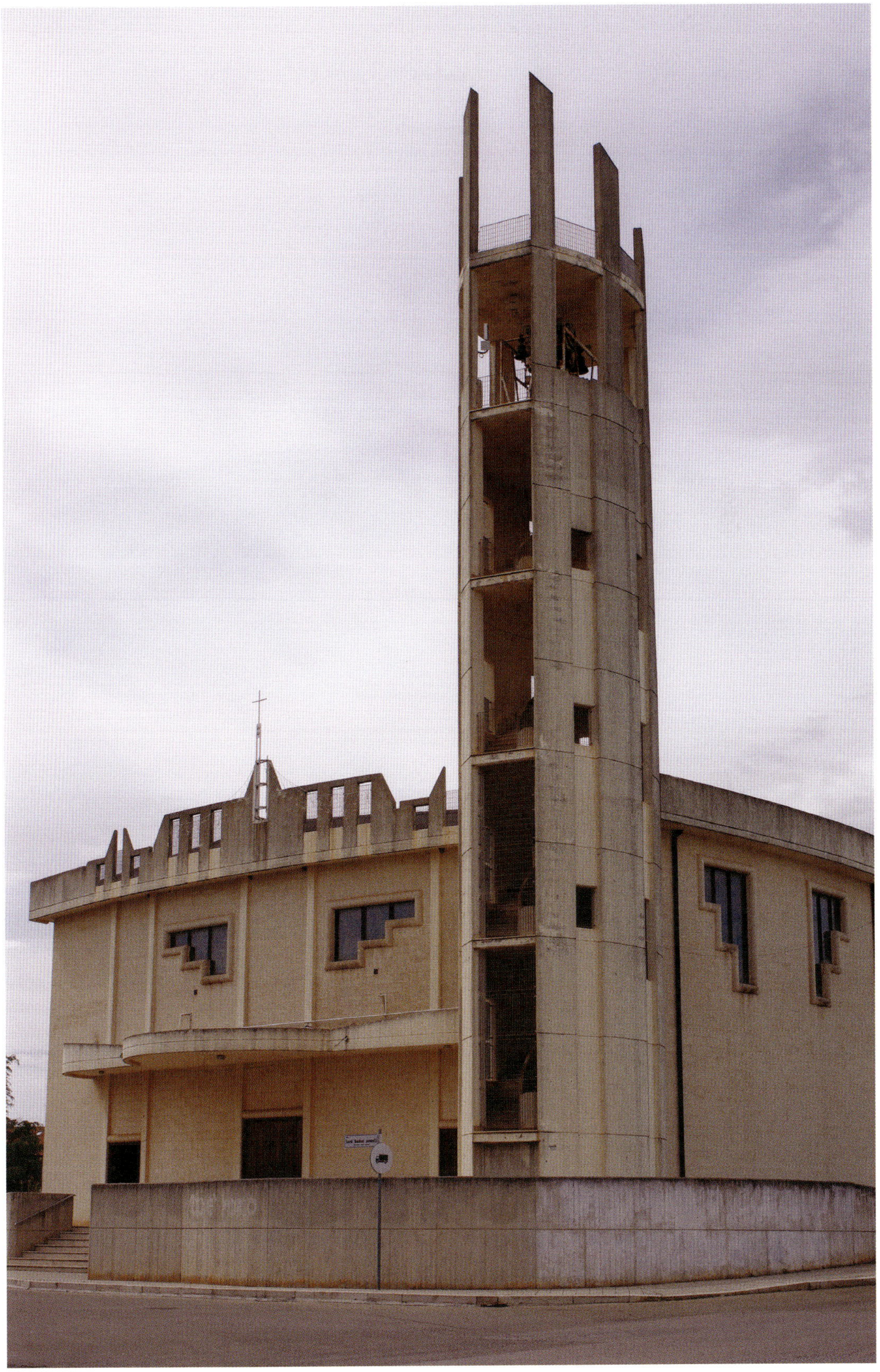

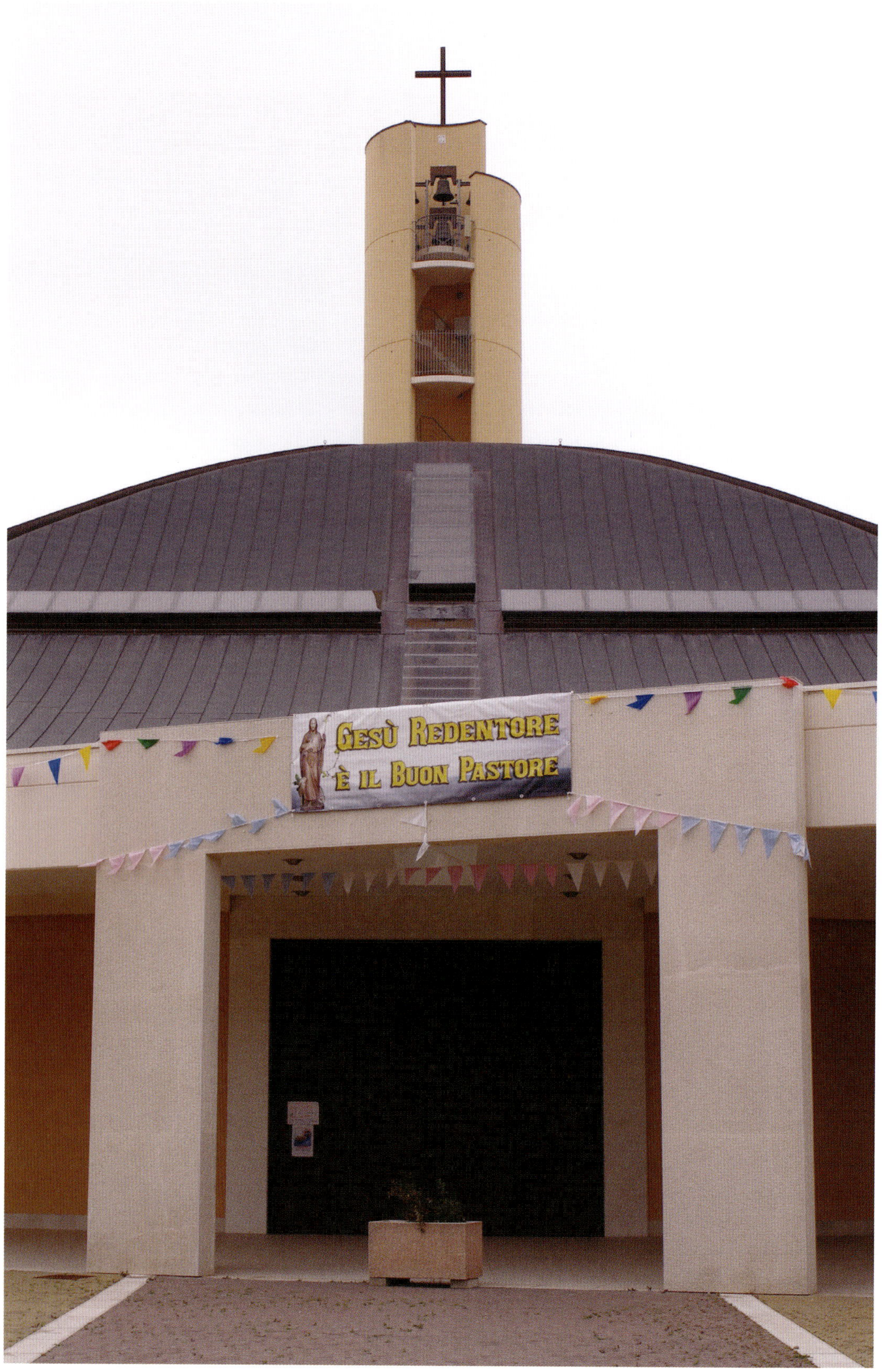
GESÙ REDENTORE
È IL BUON PASTORE

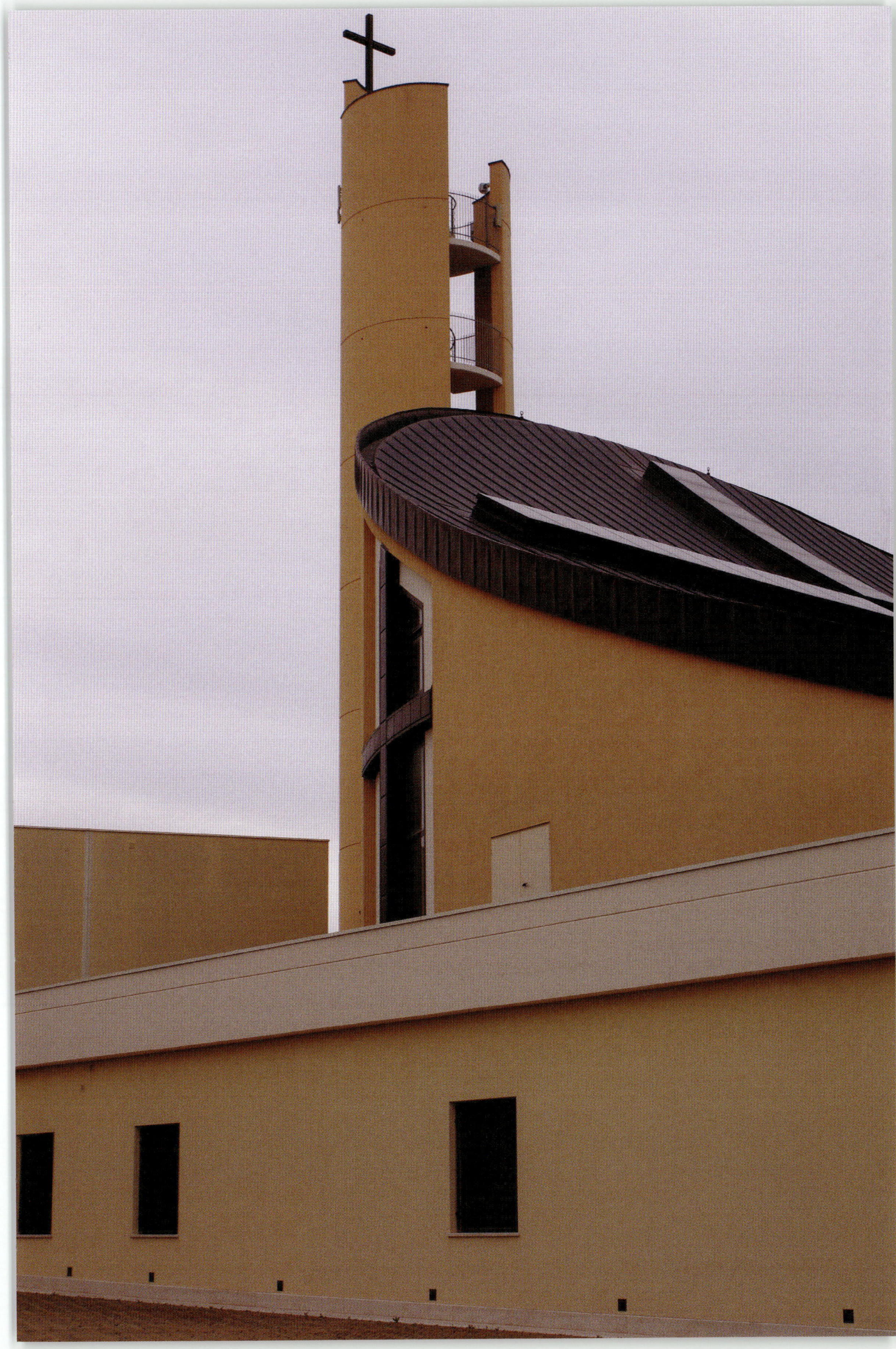

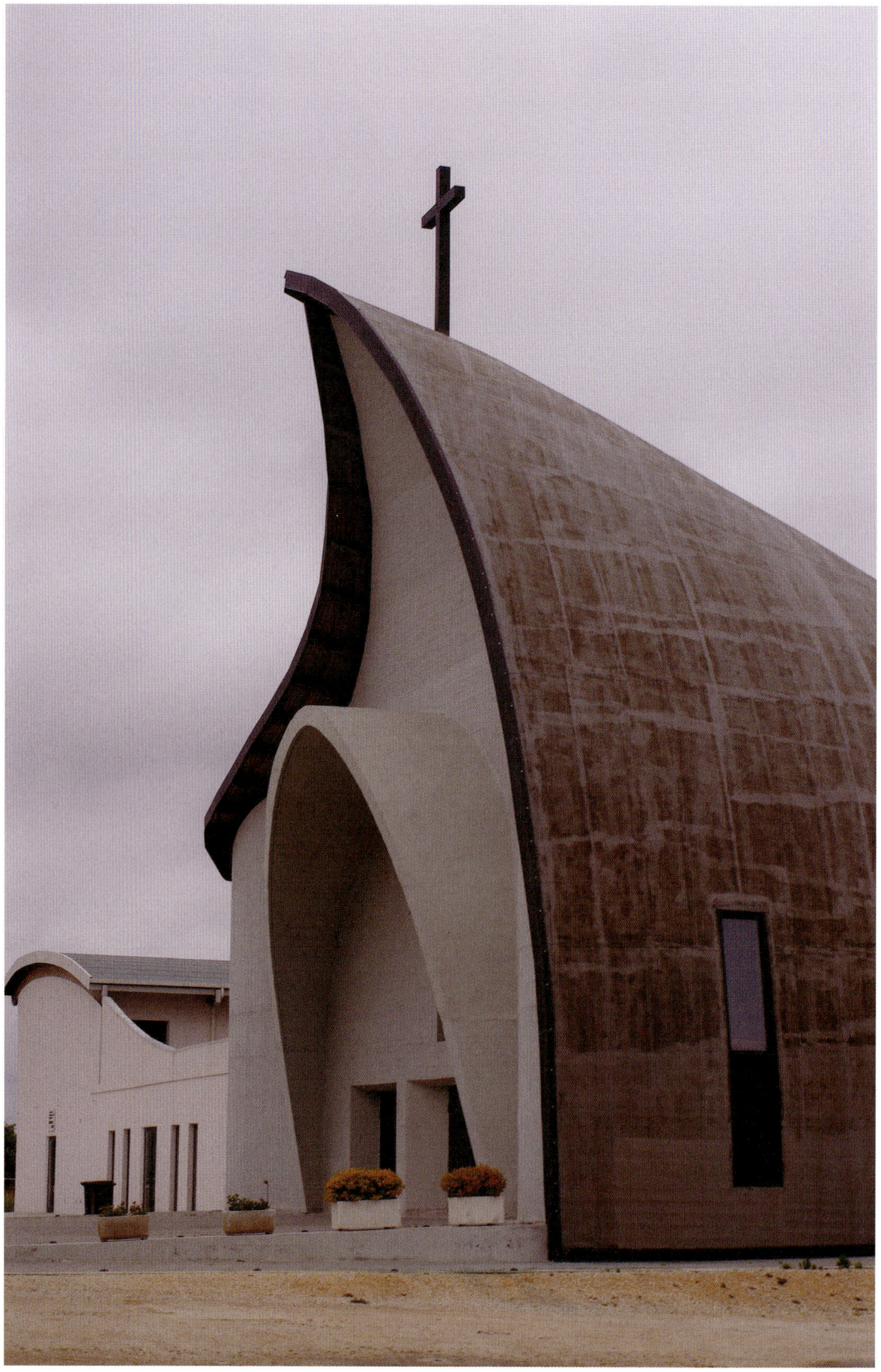

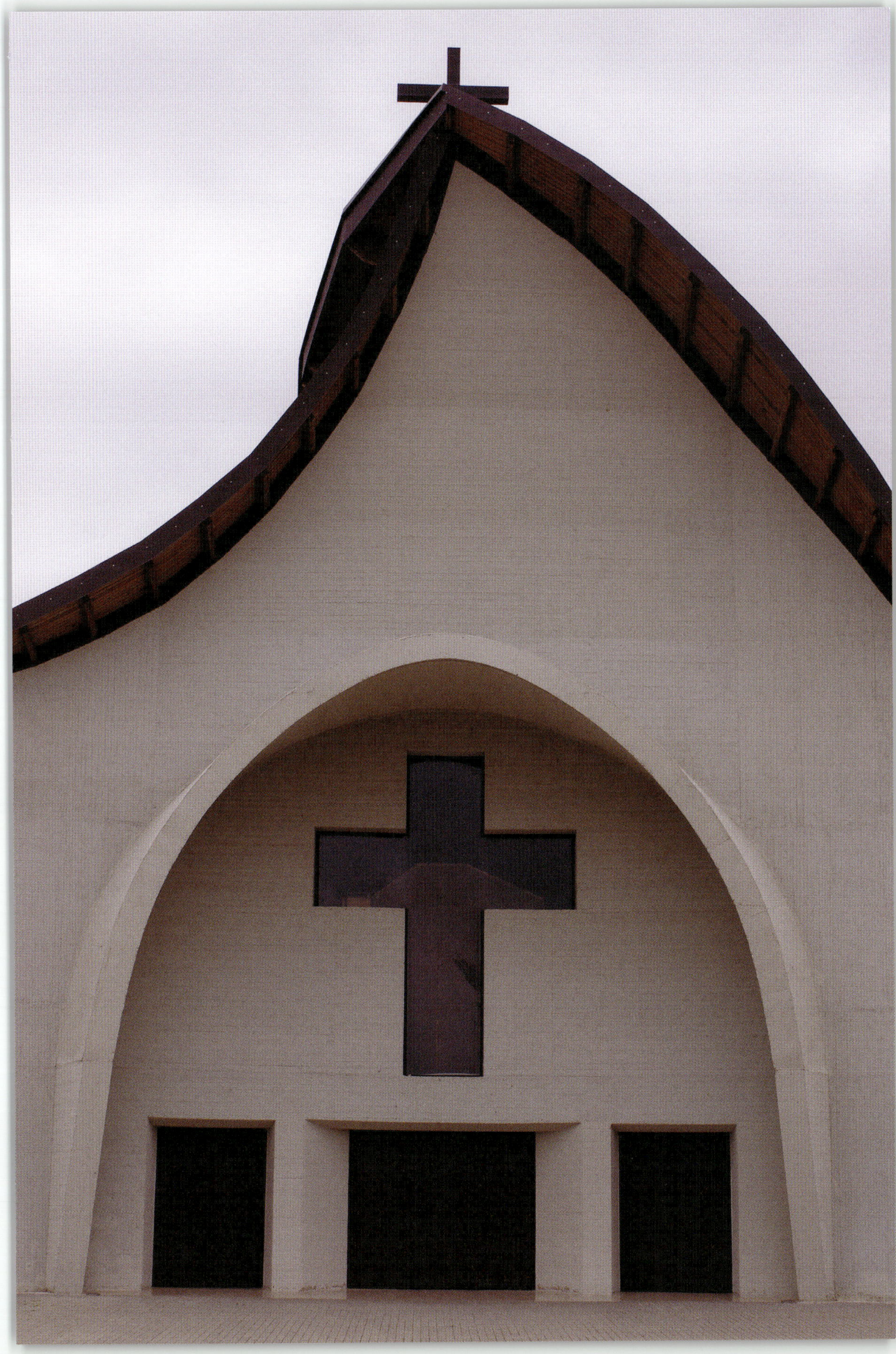

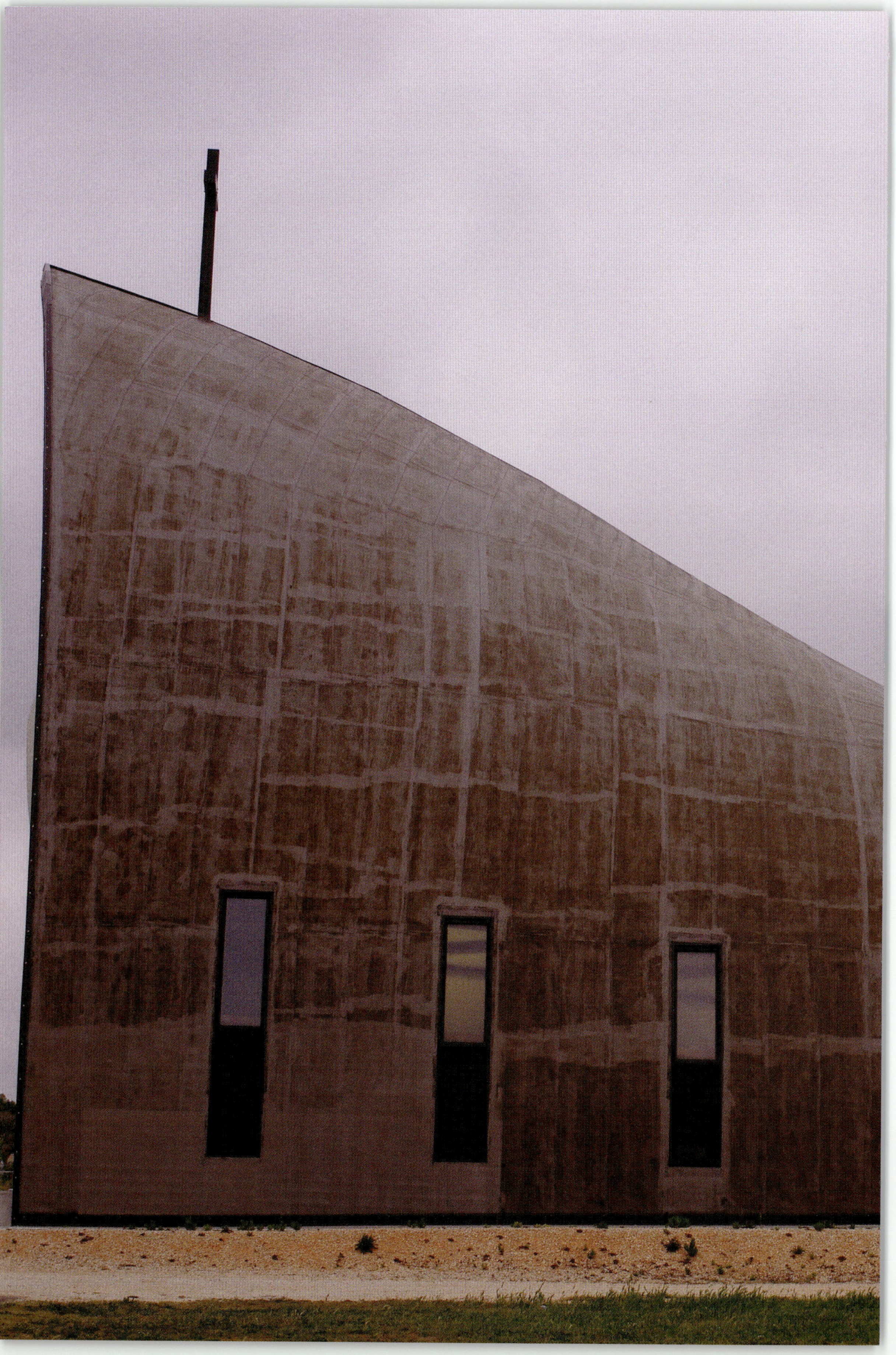

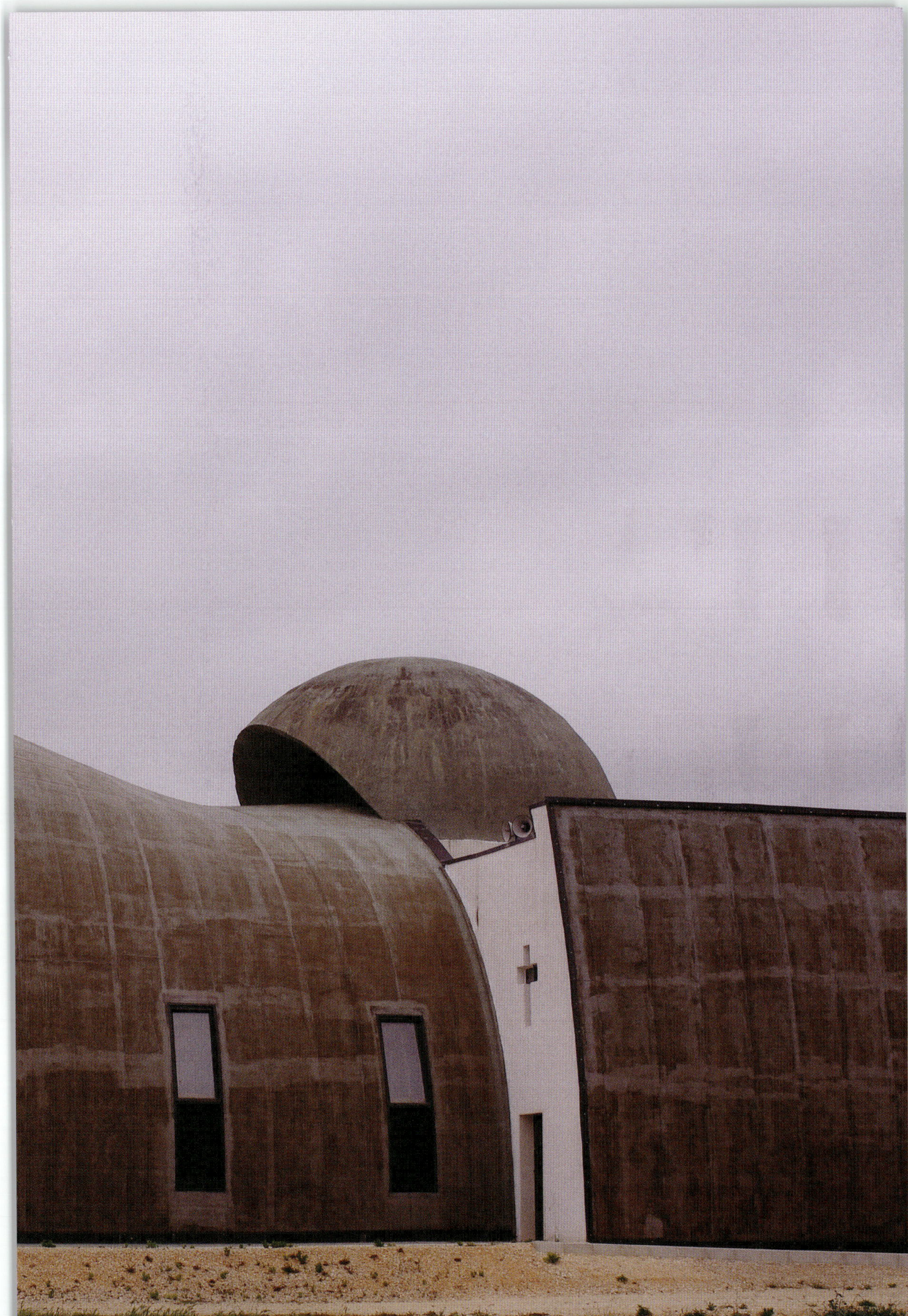

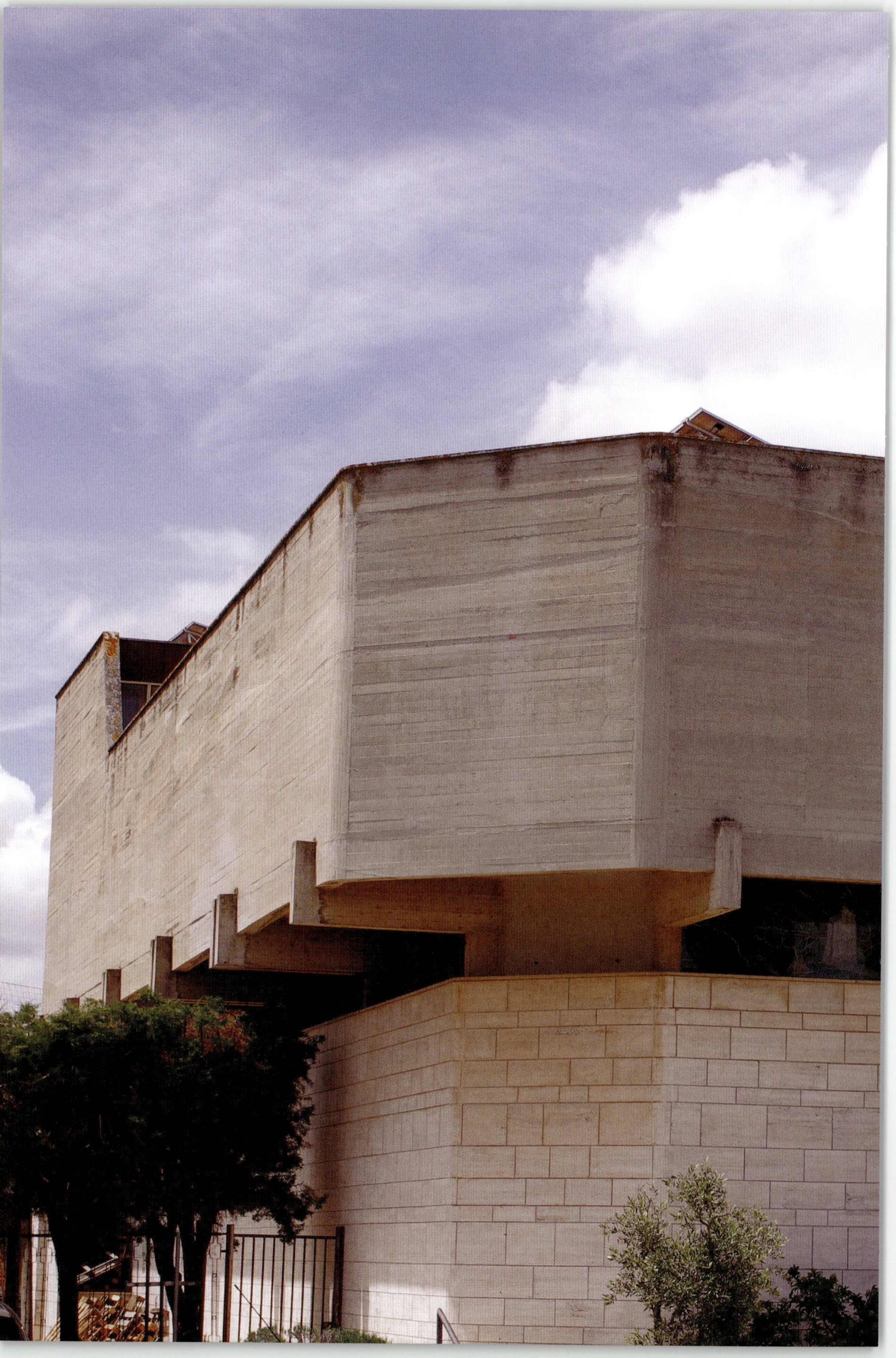

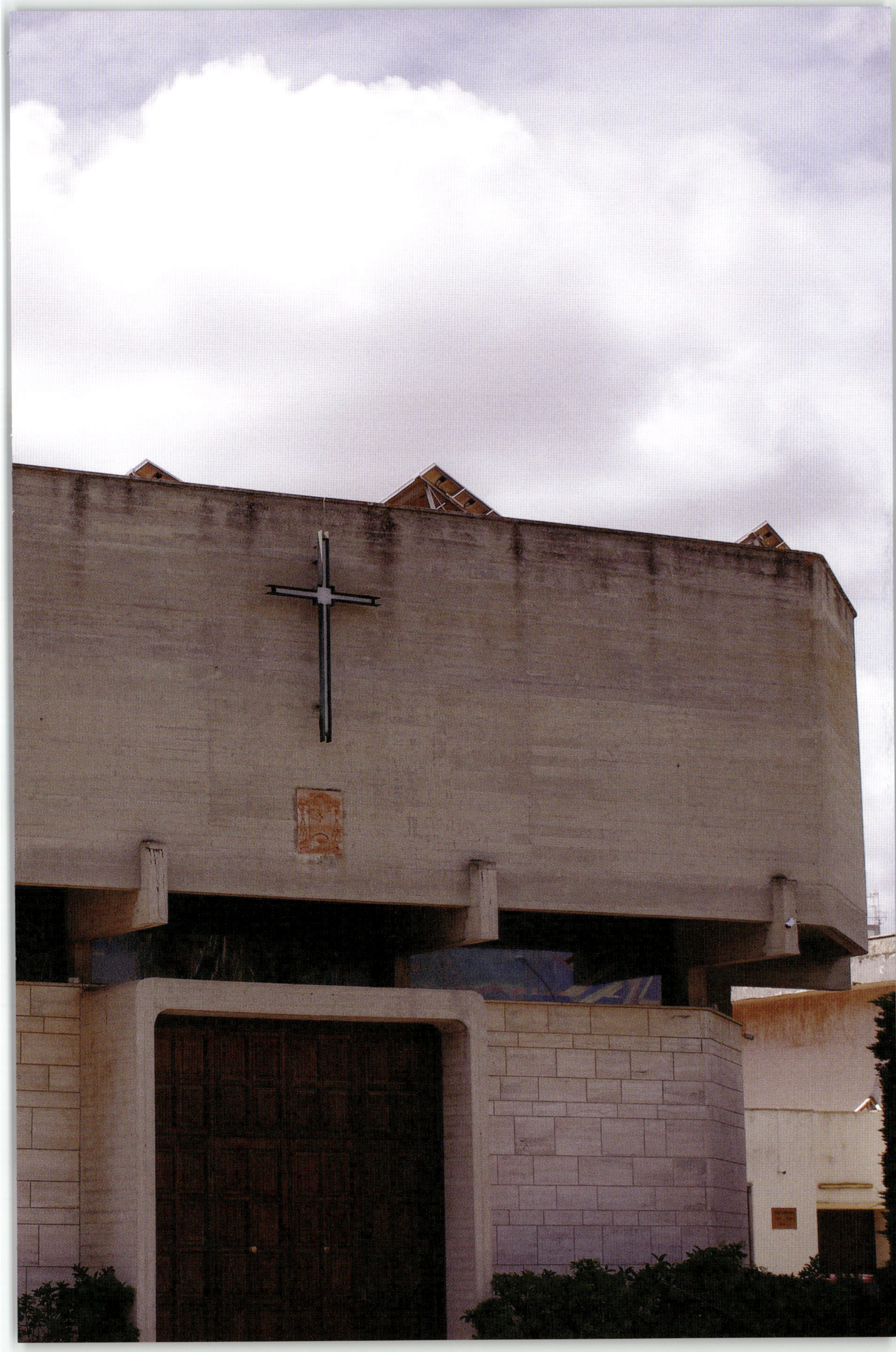

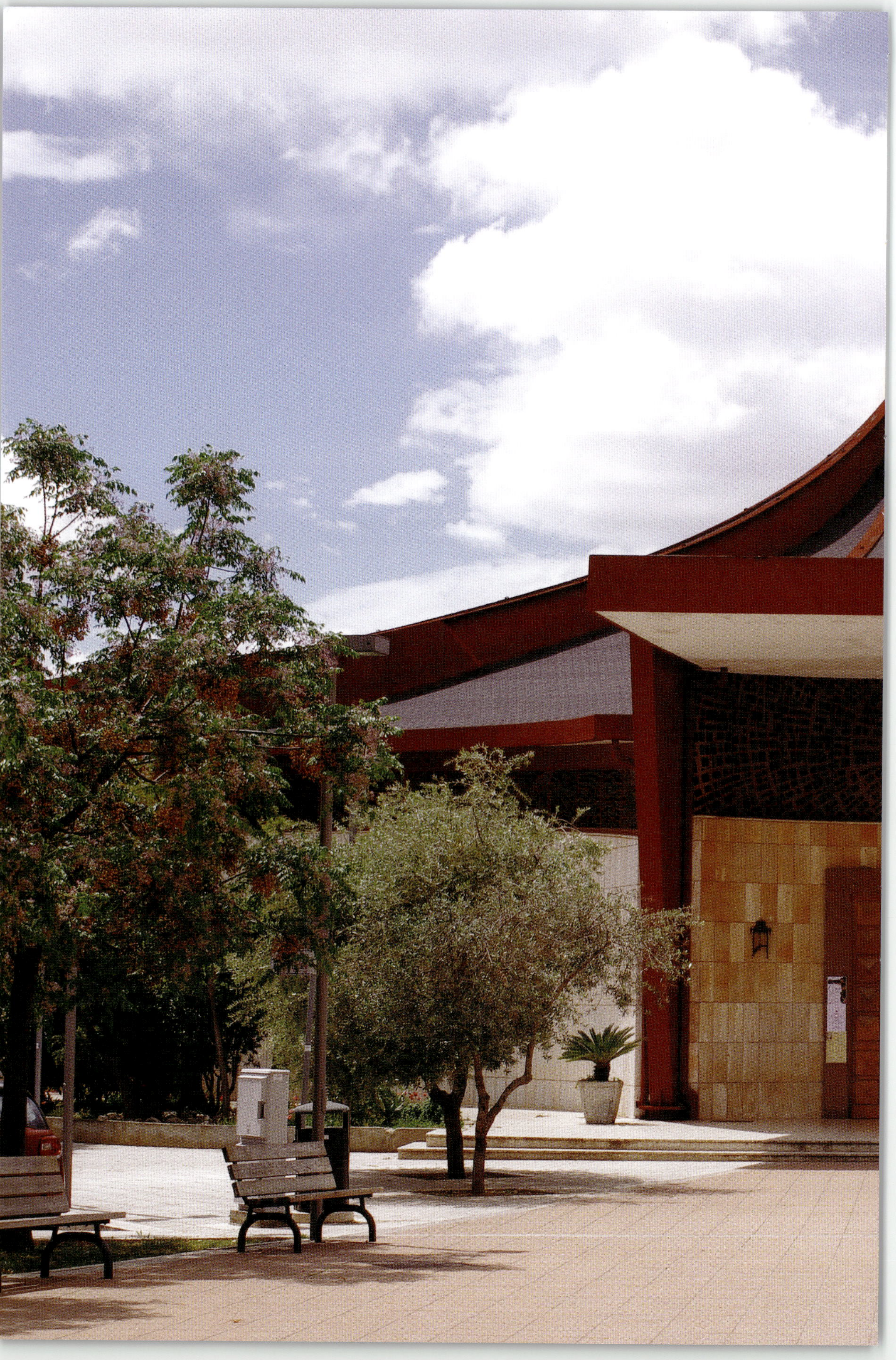

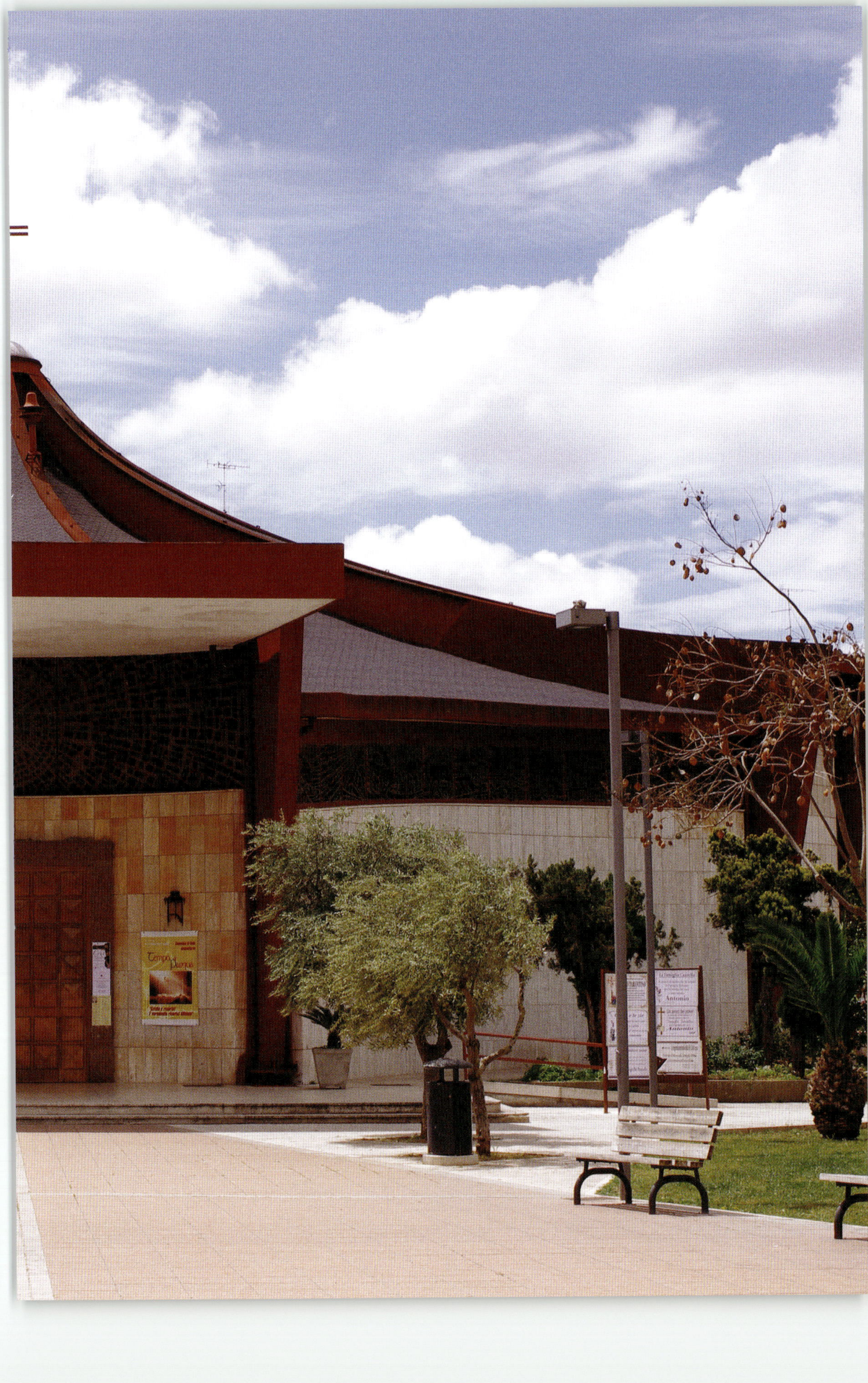

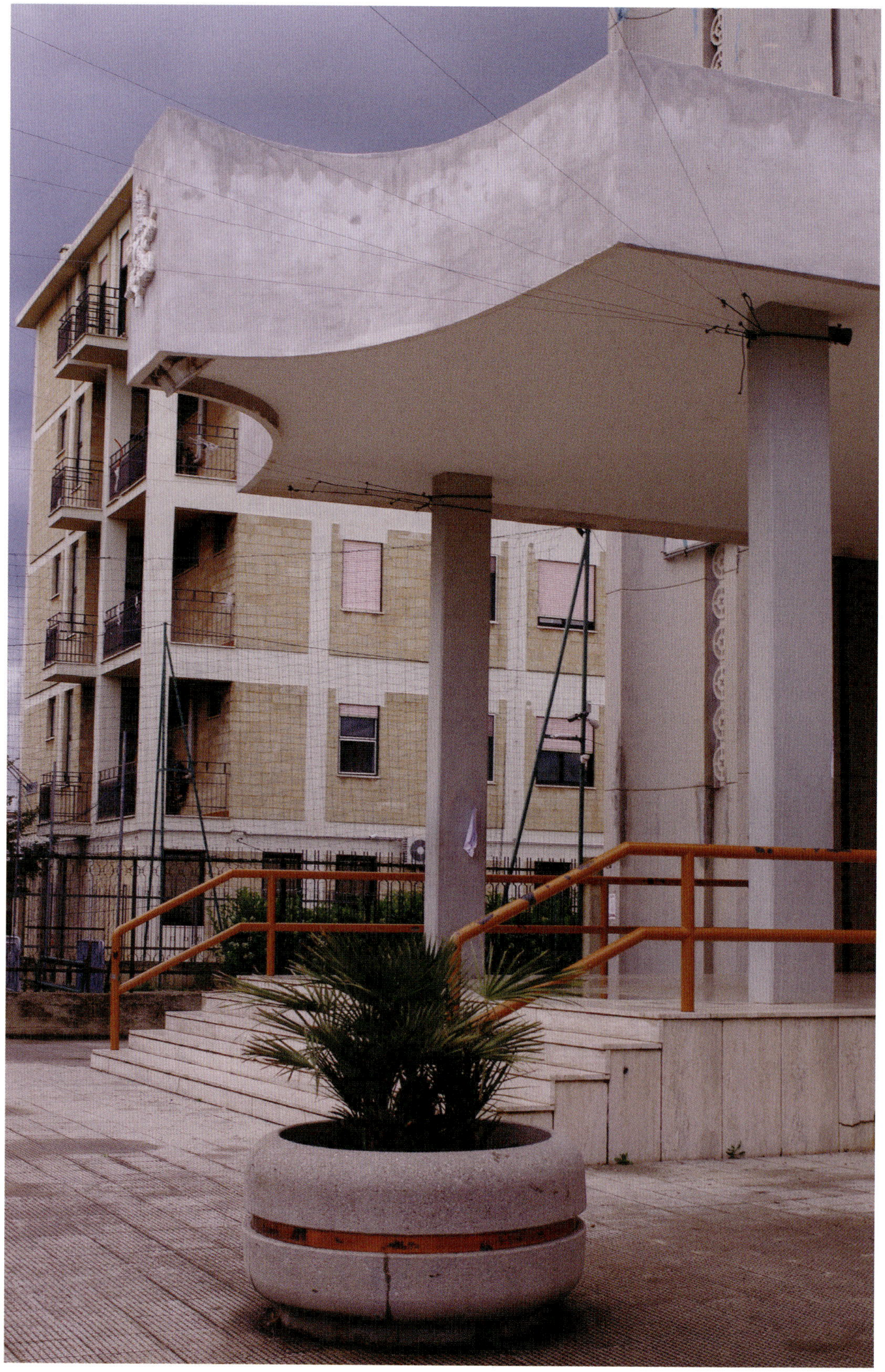

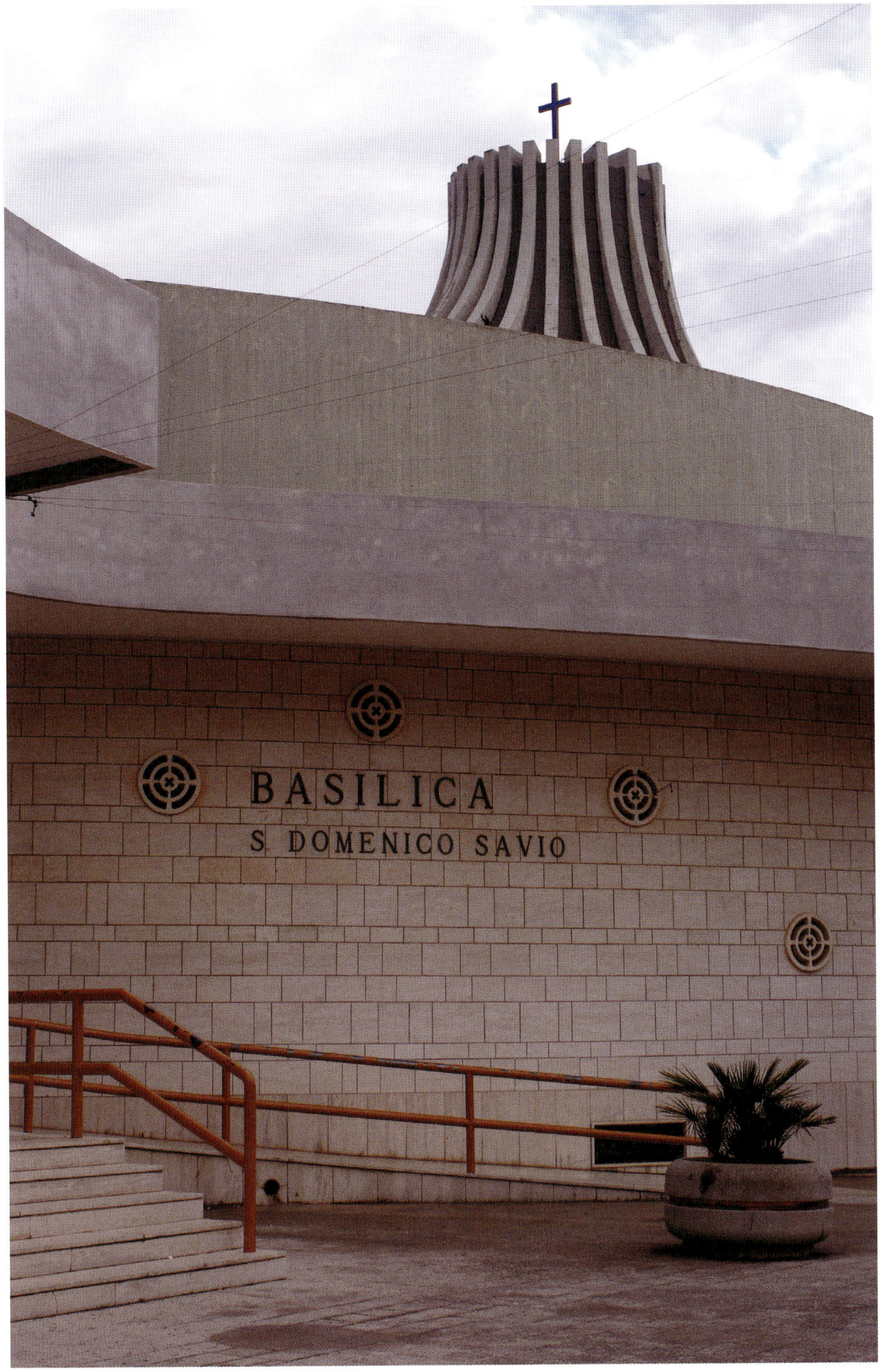
BASILICA
S DOMENICO SAVIO

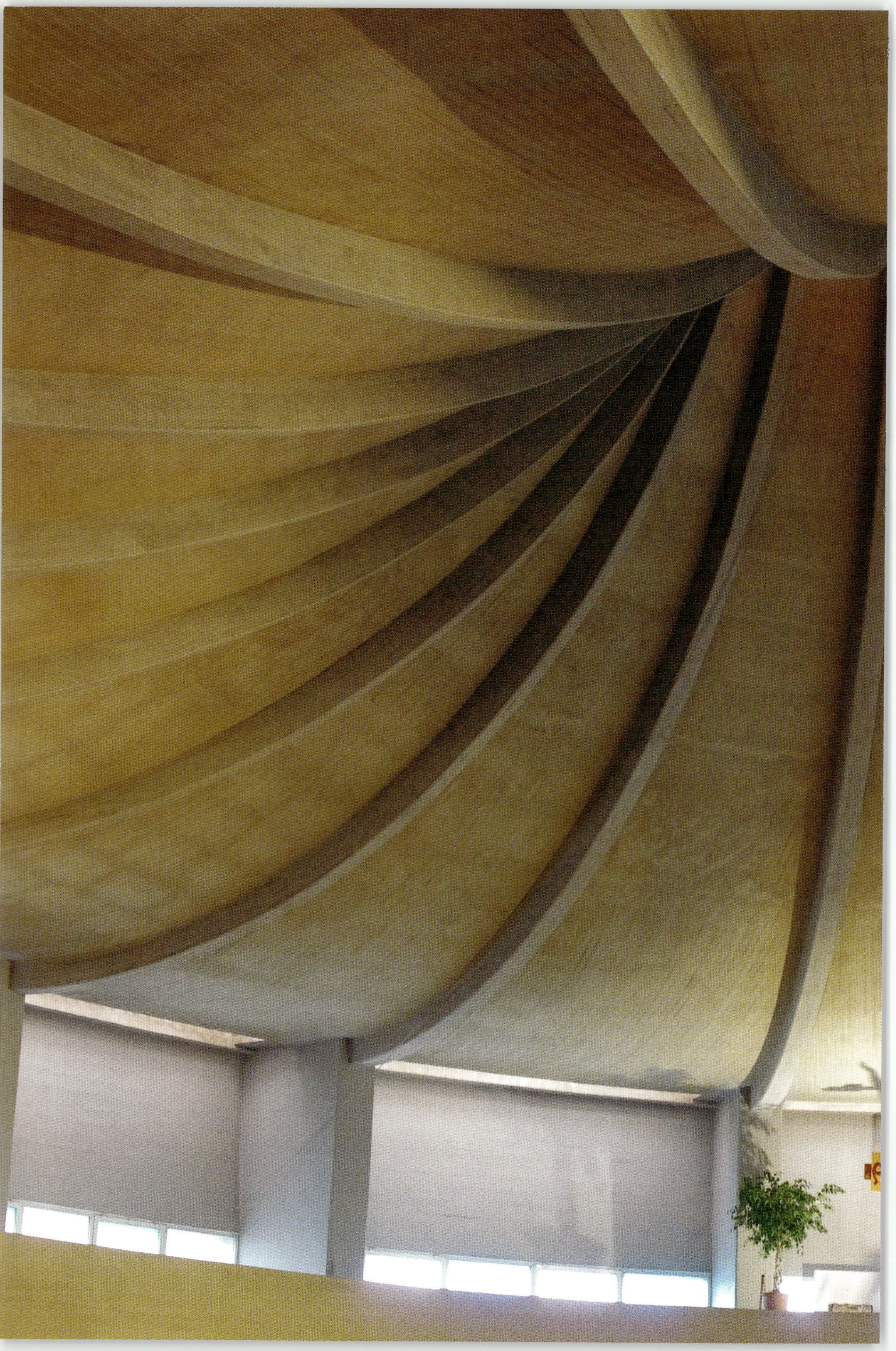

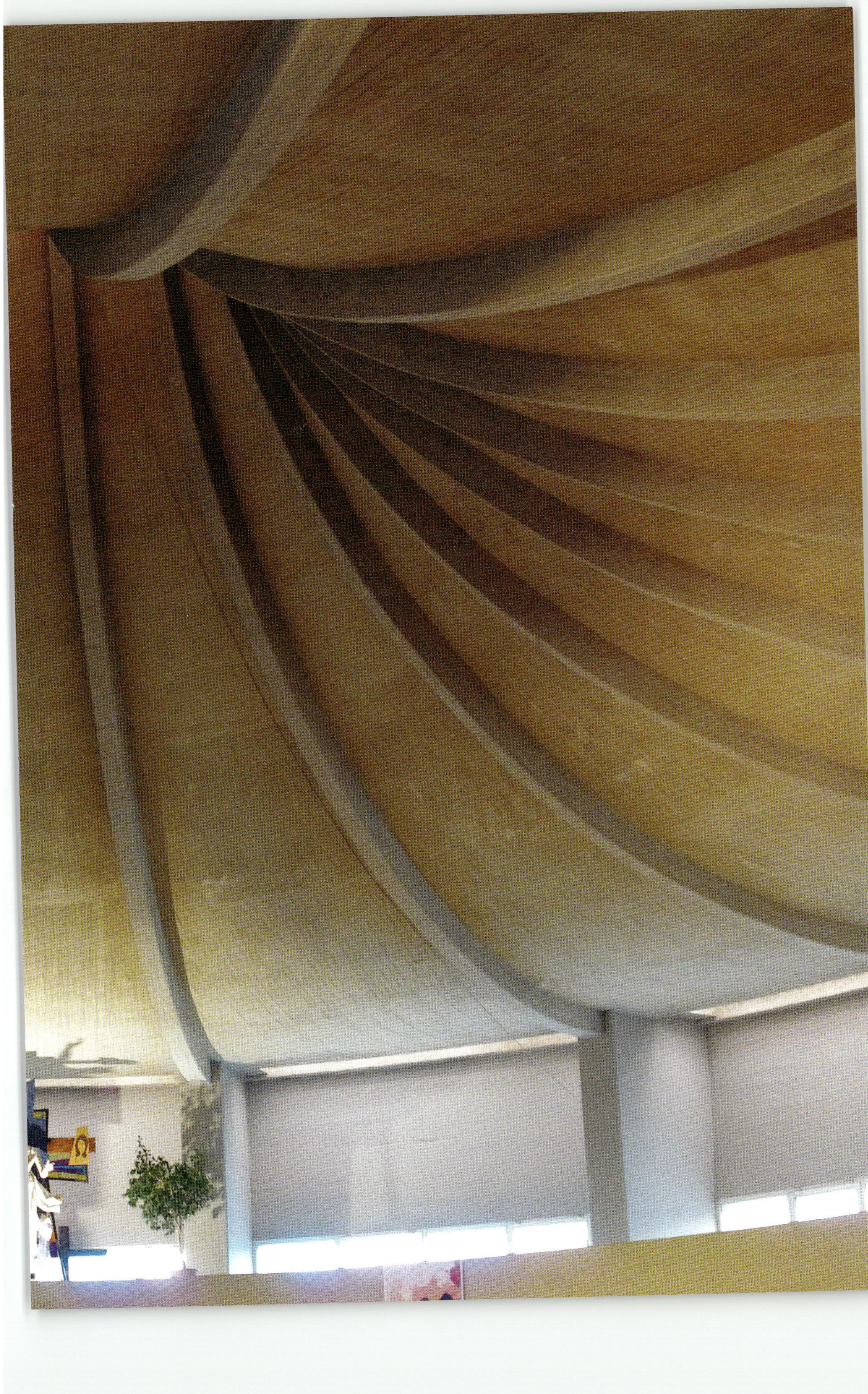

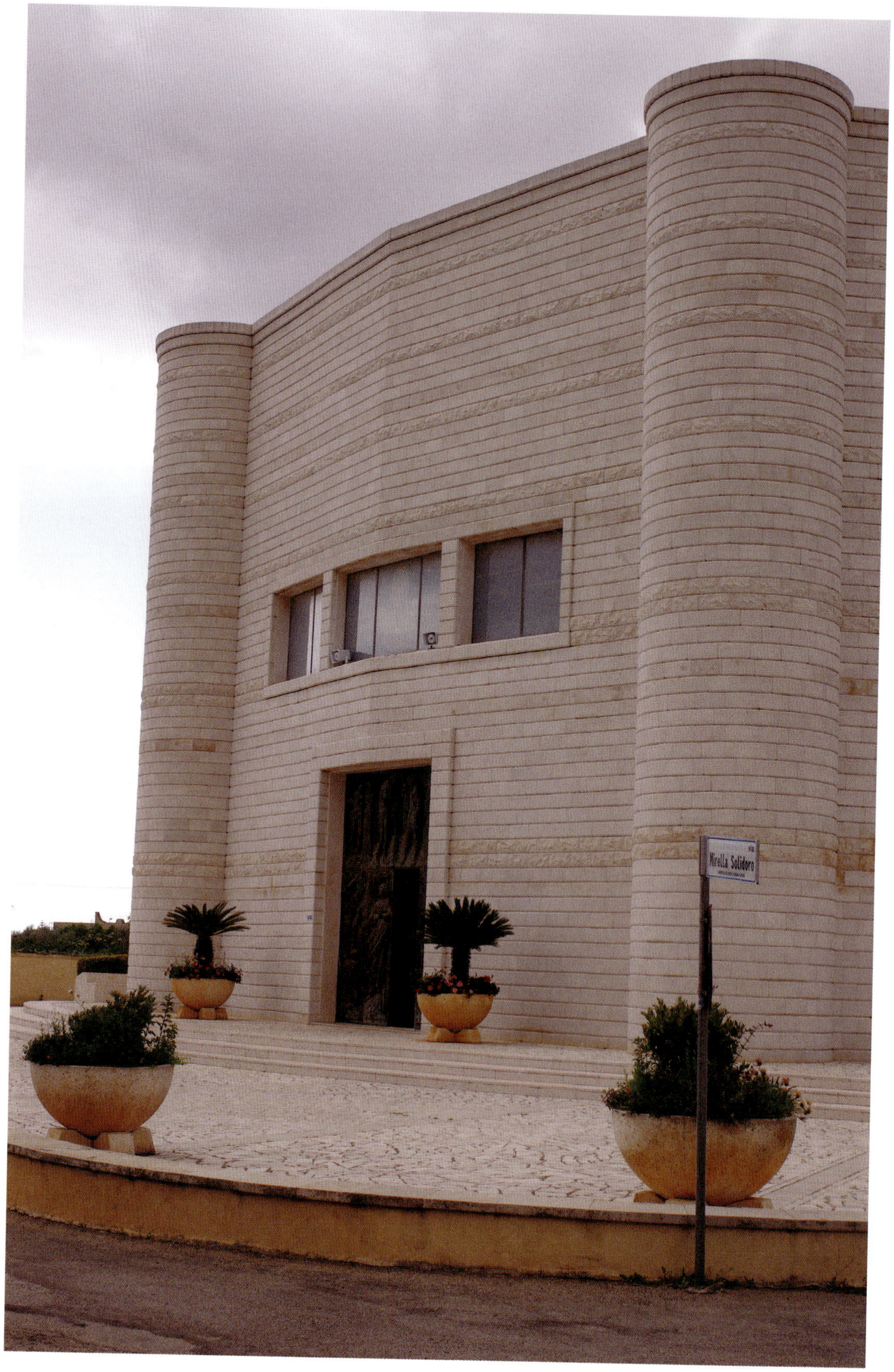
Via
Mirella Solidoro

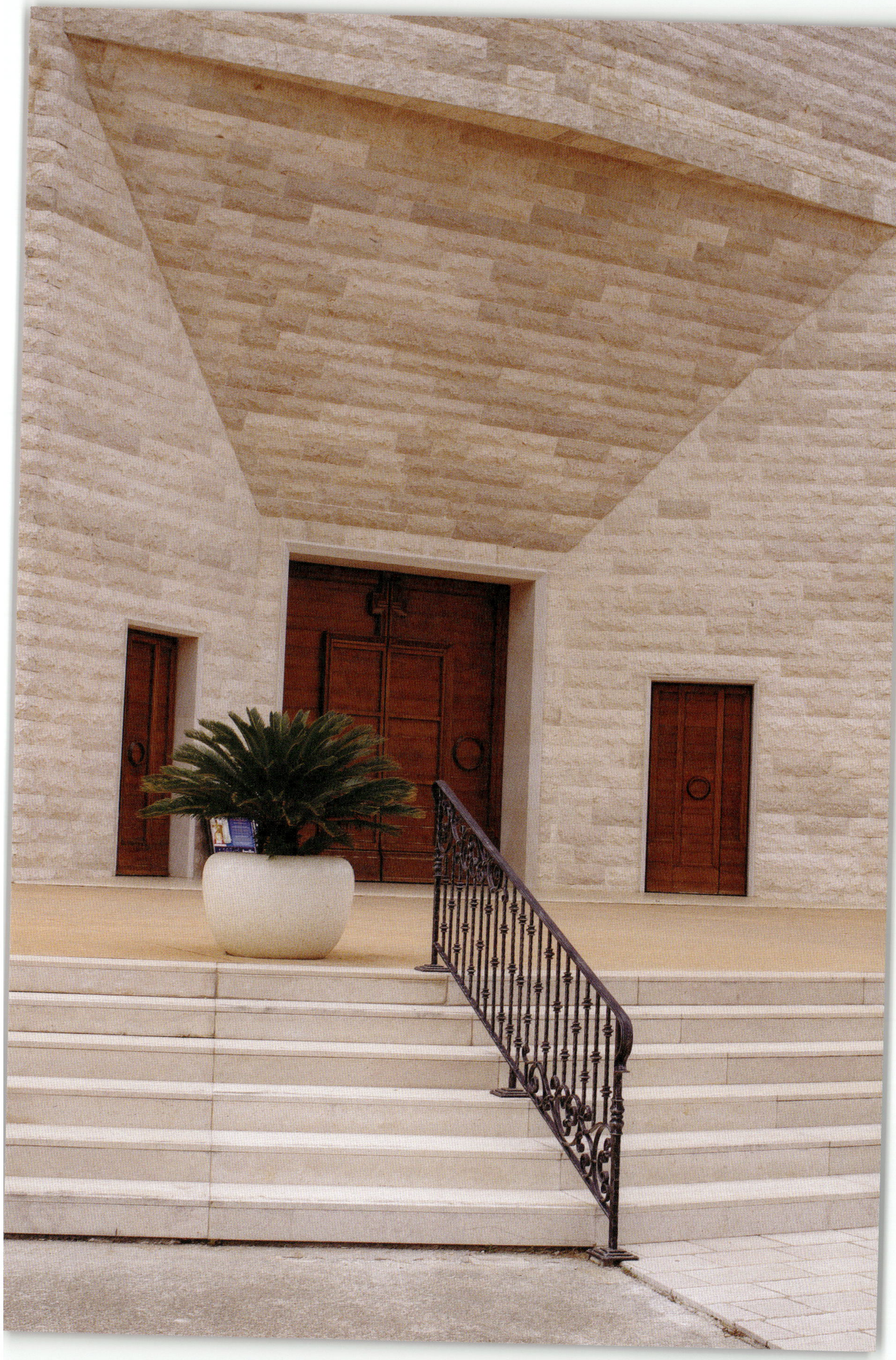

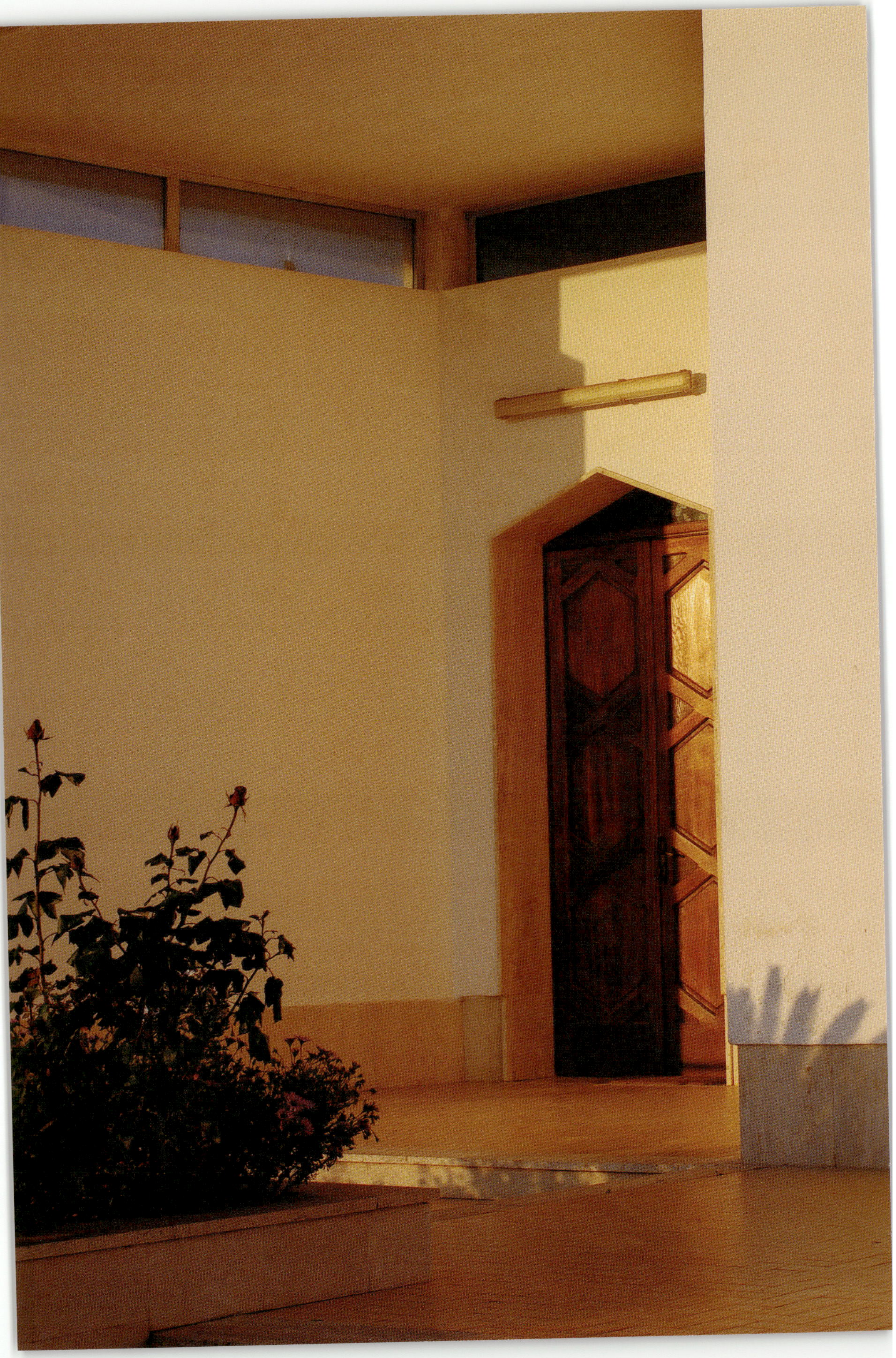

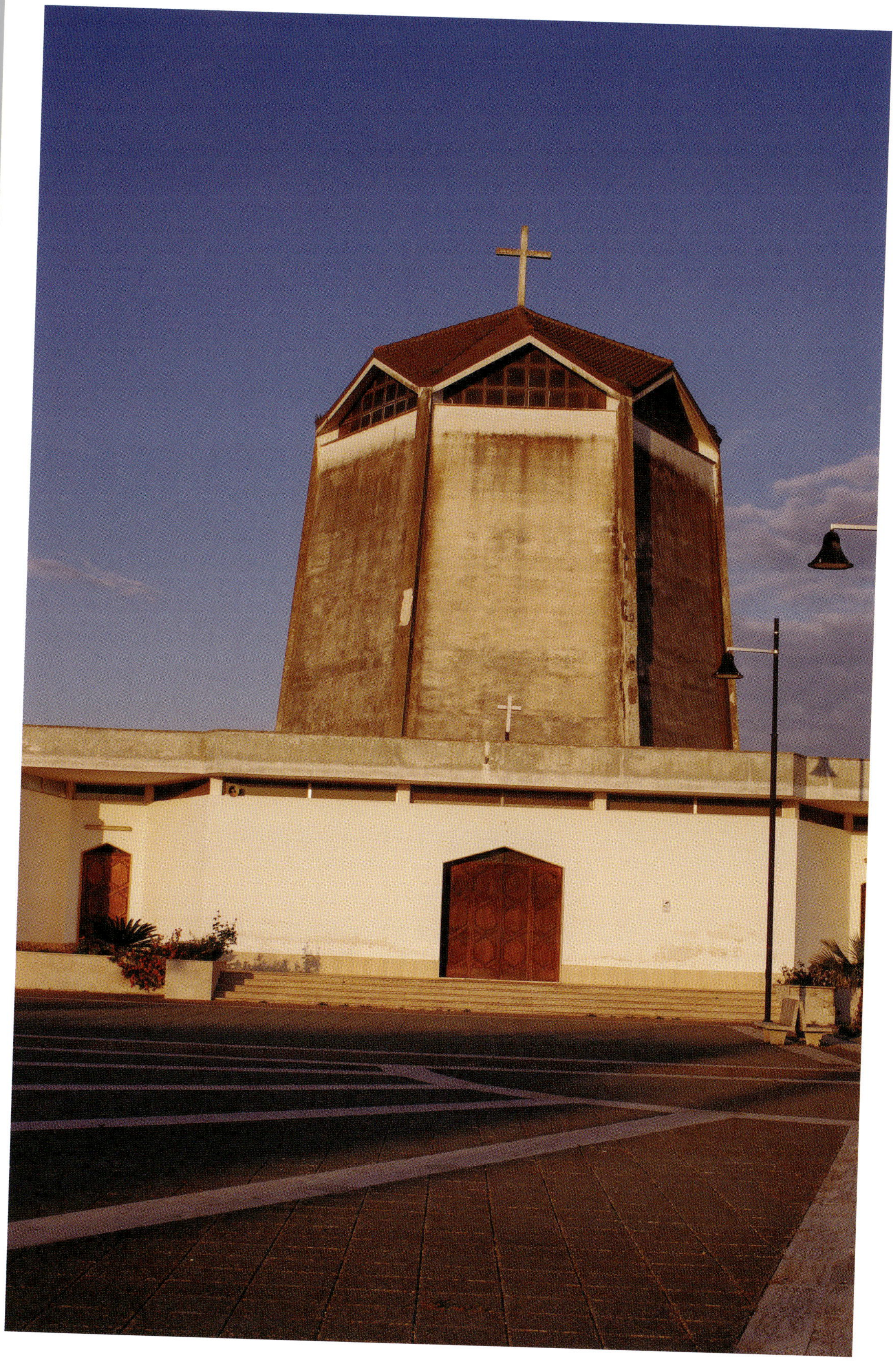

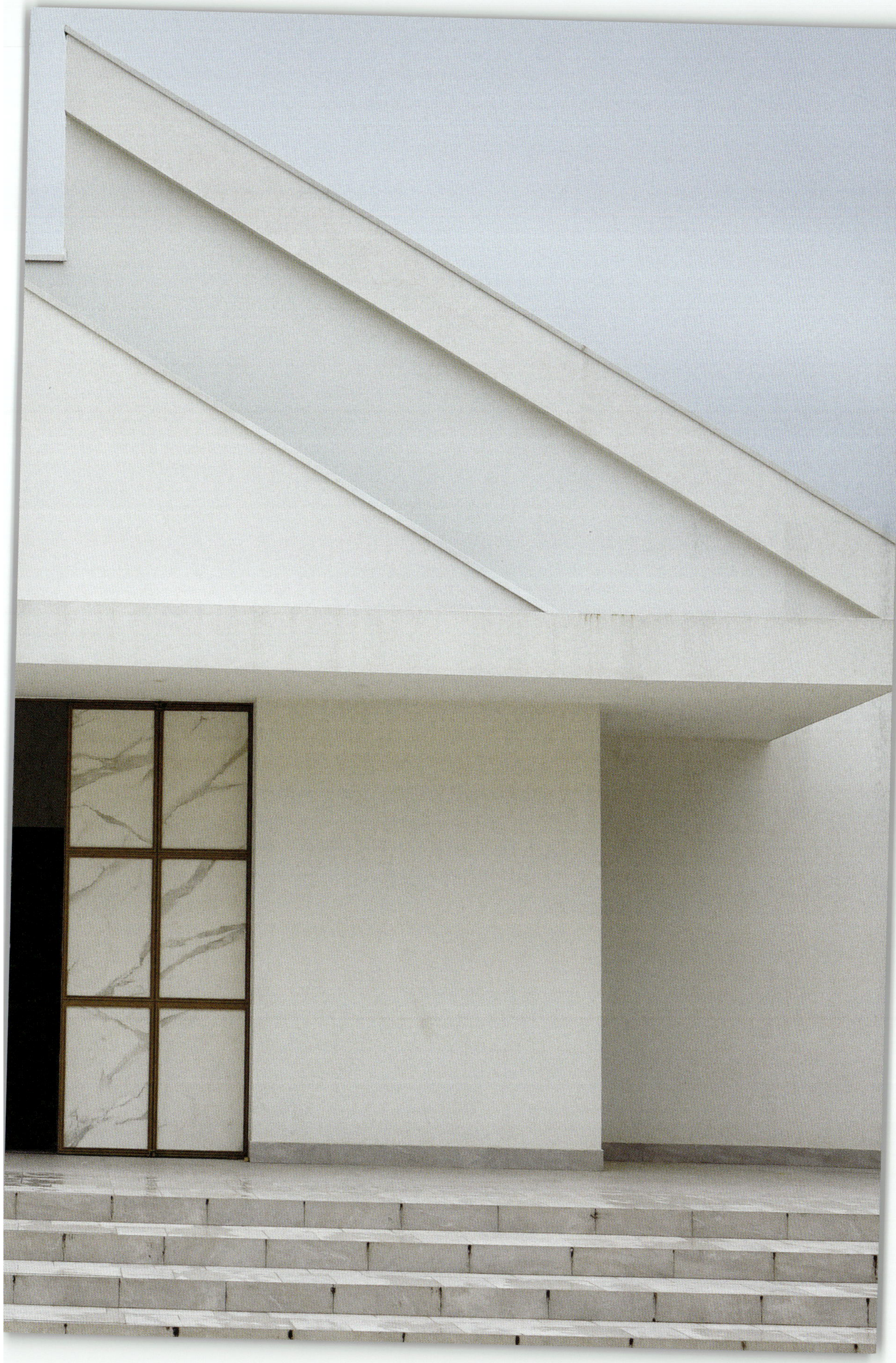

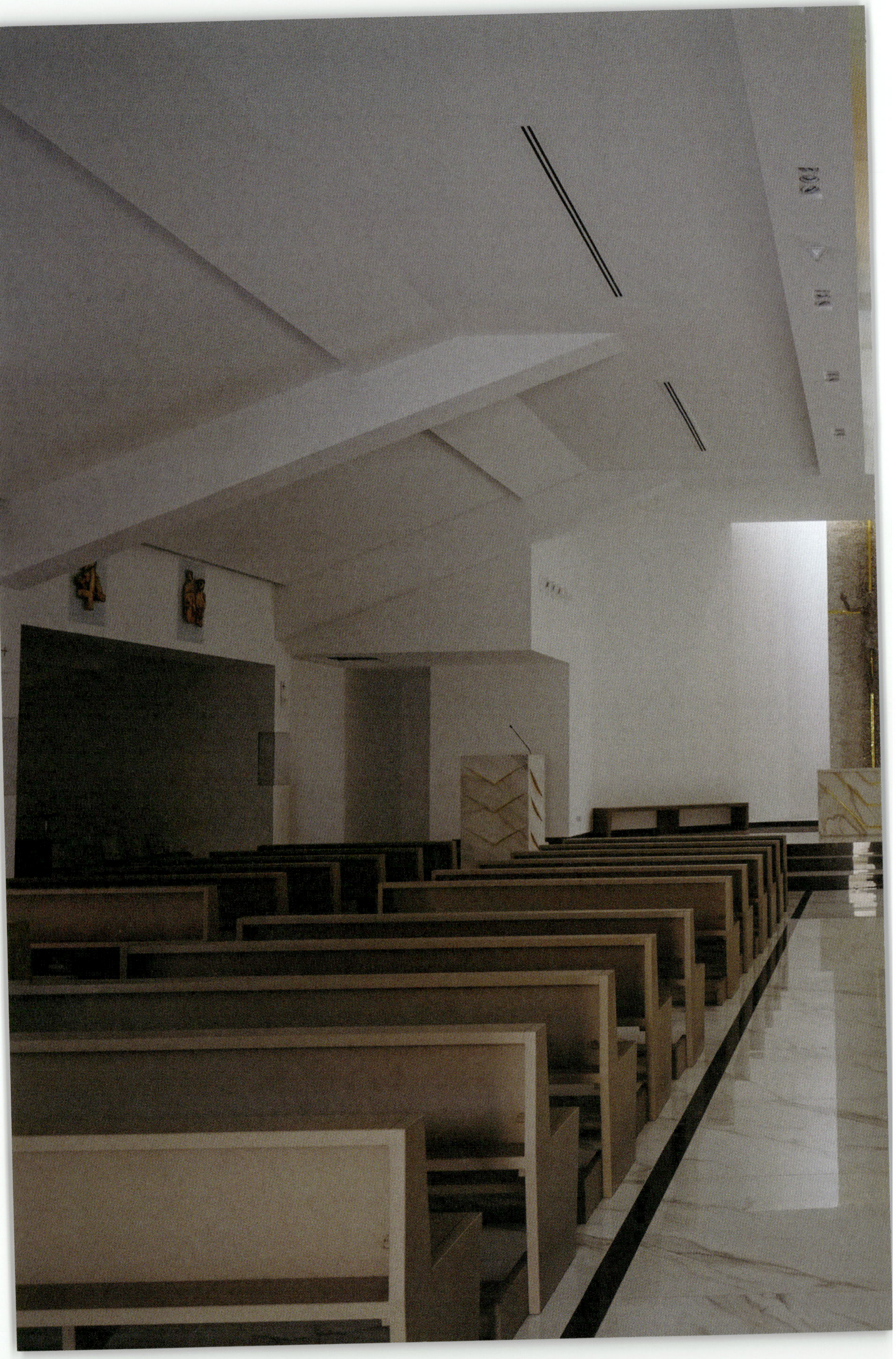

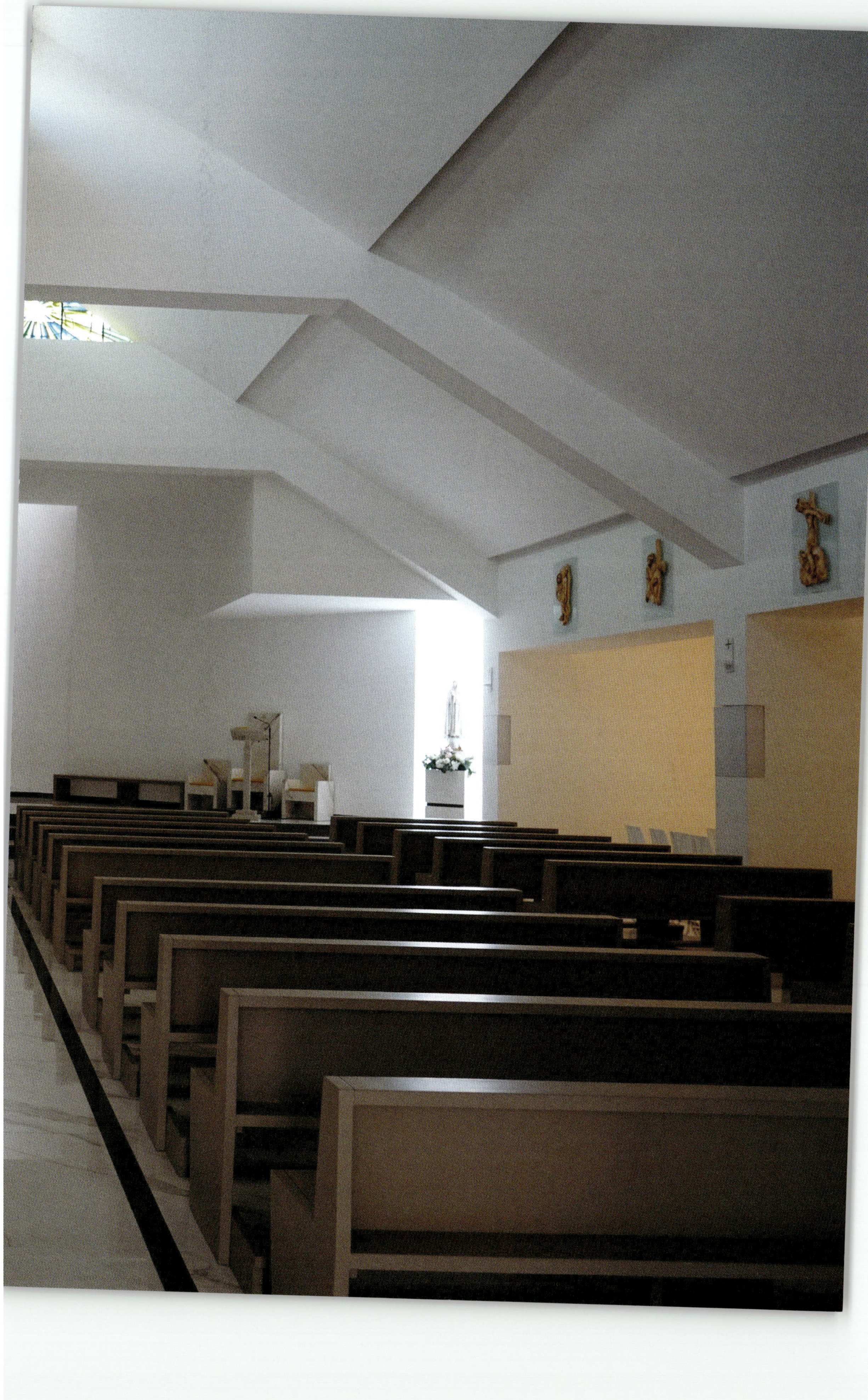

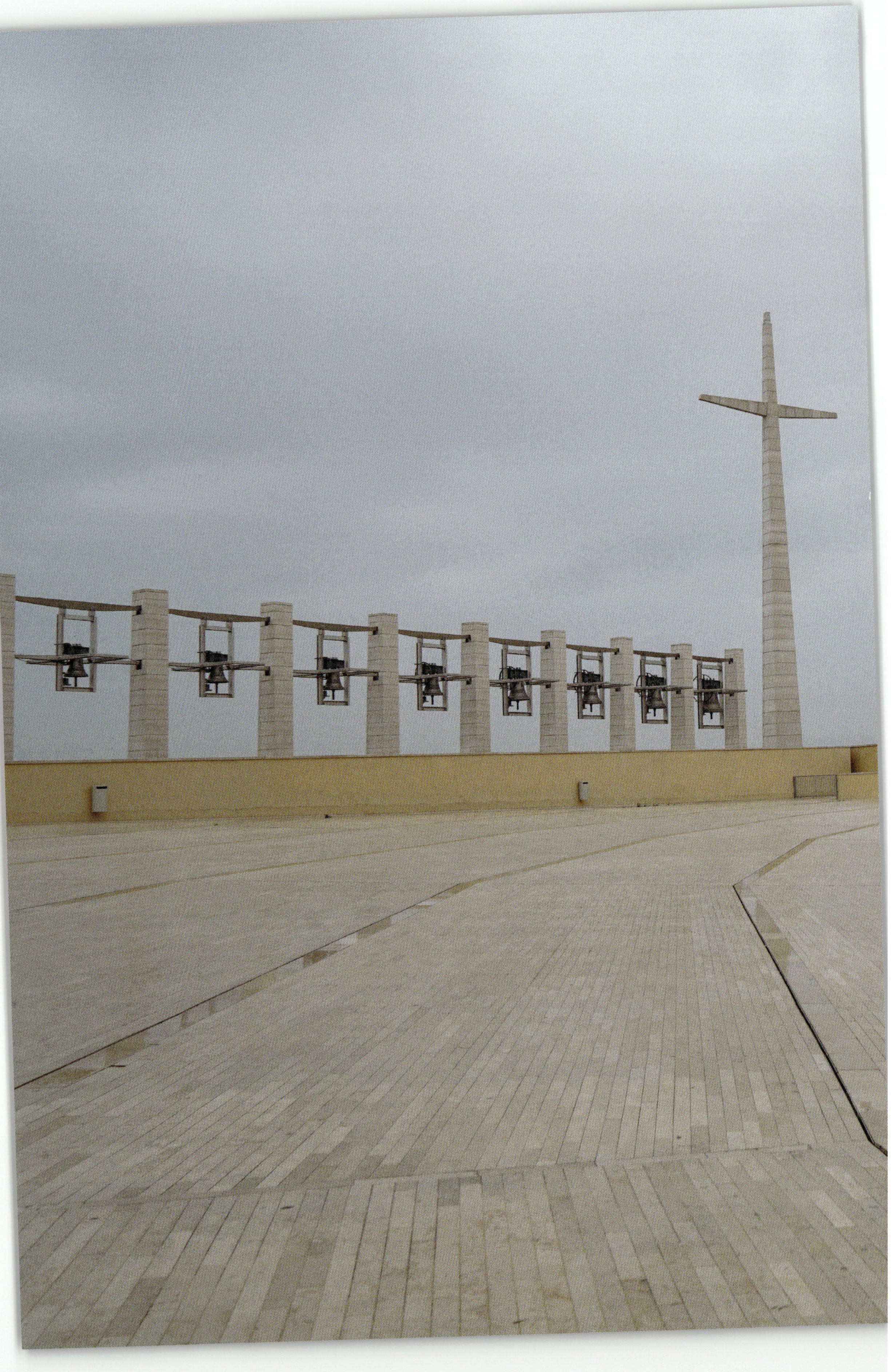

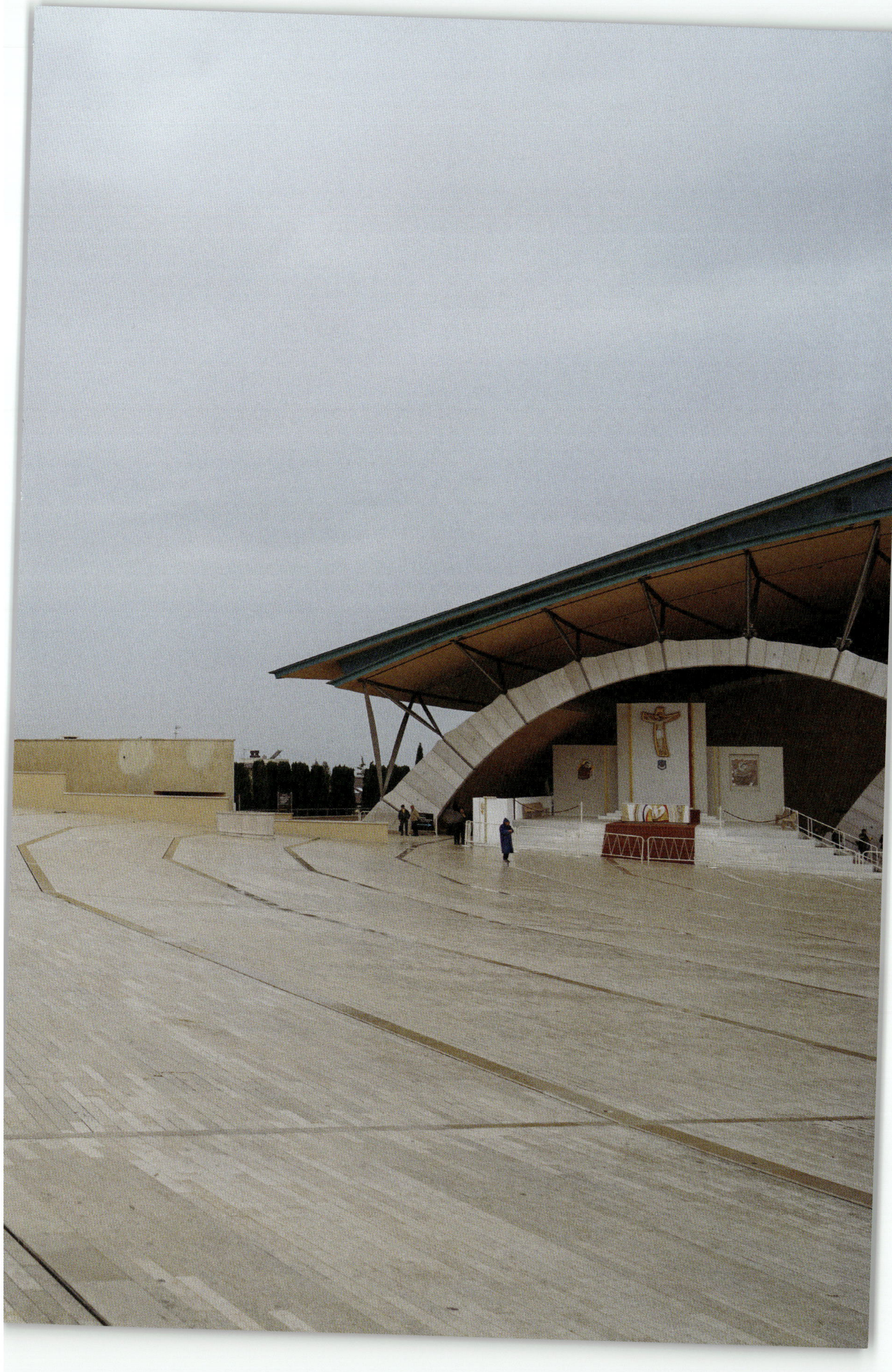

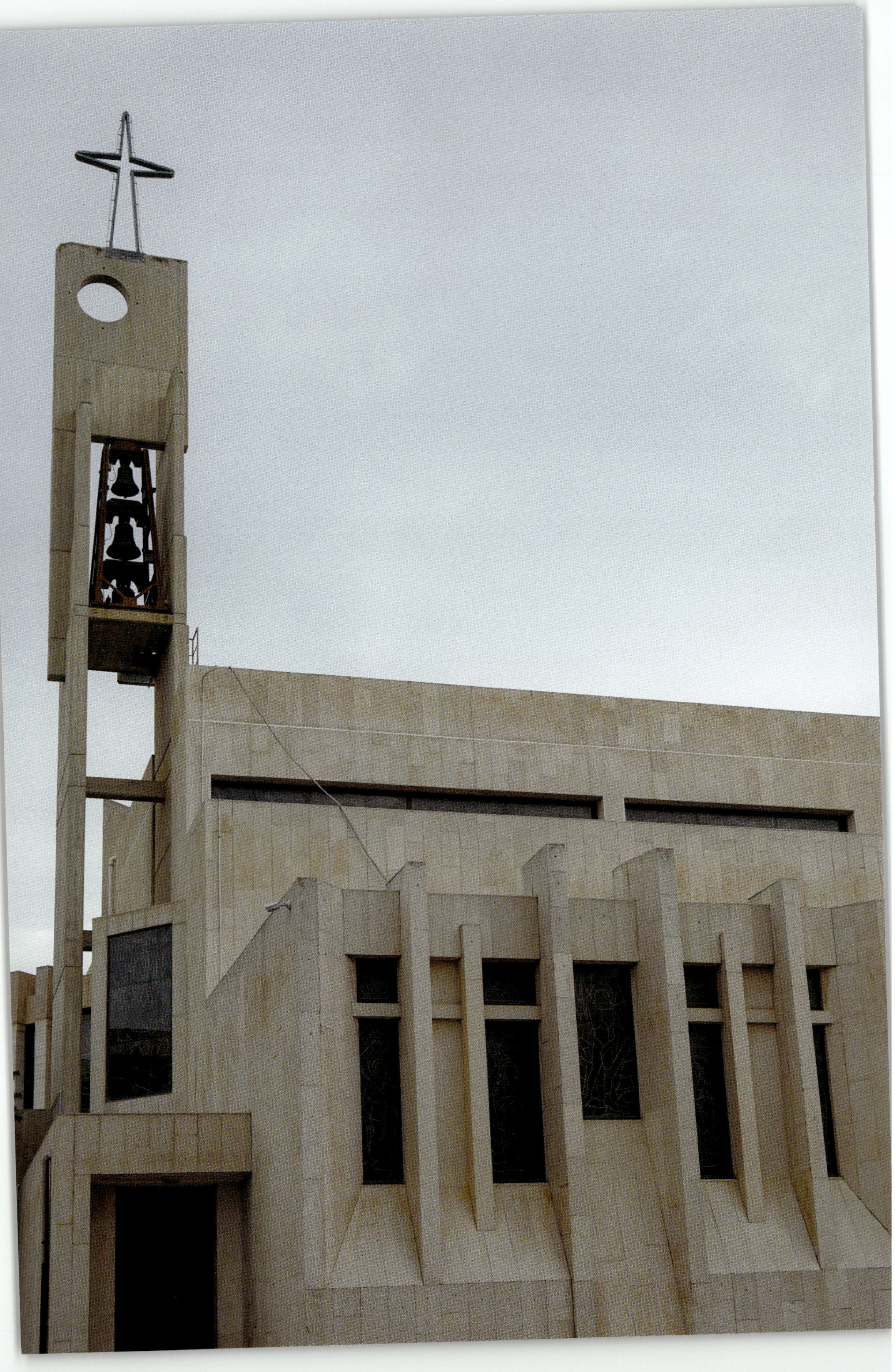

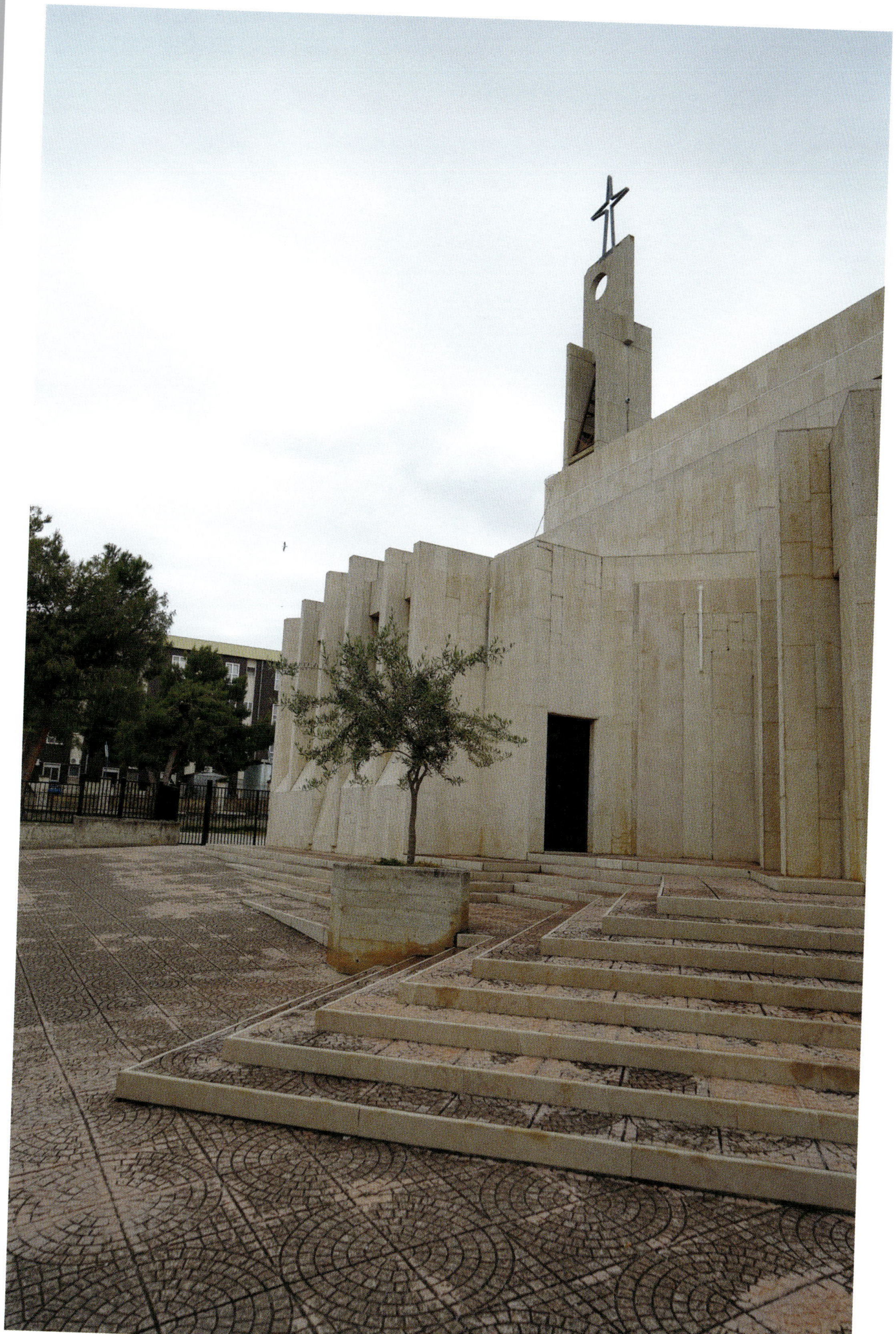

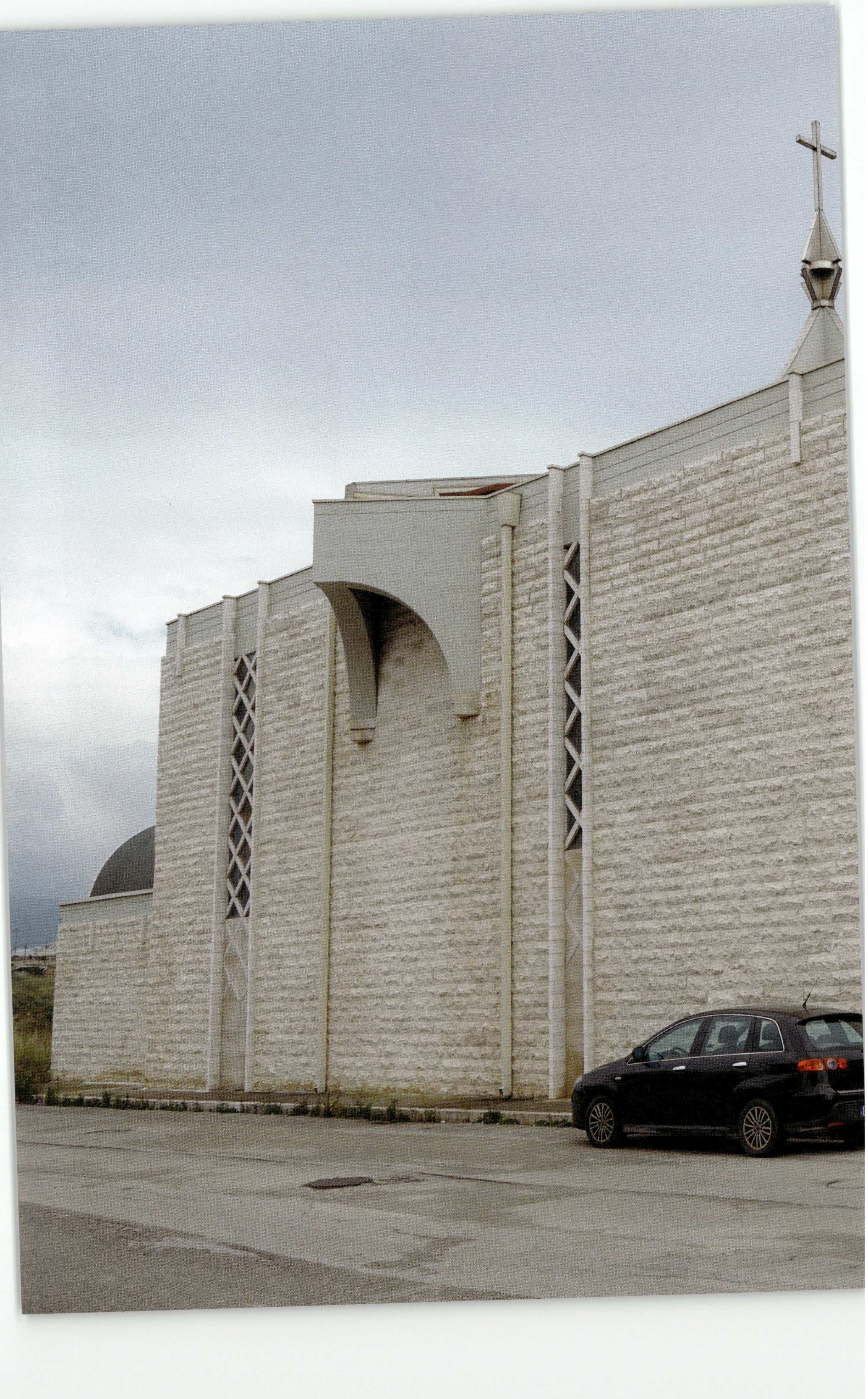

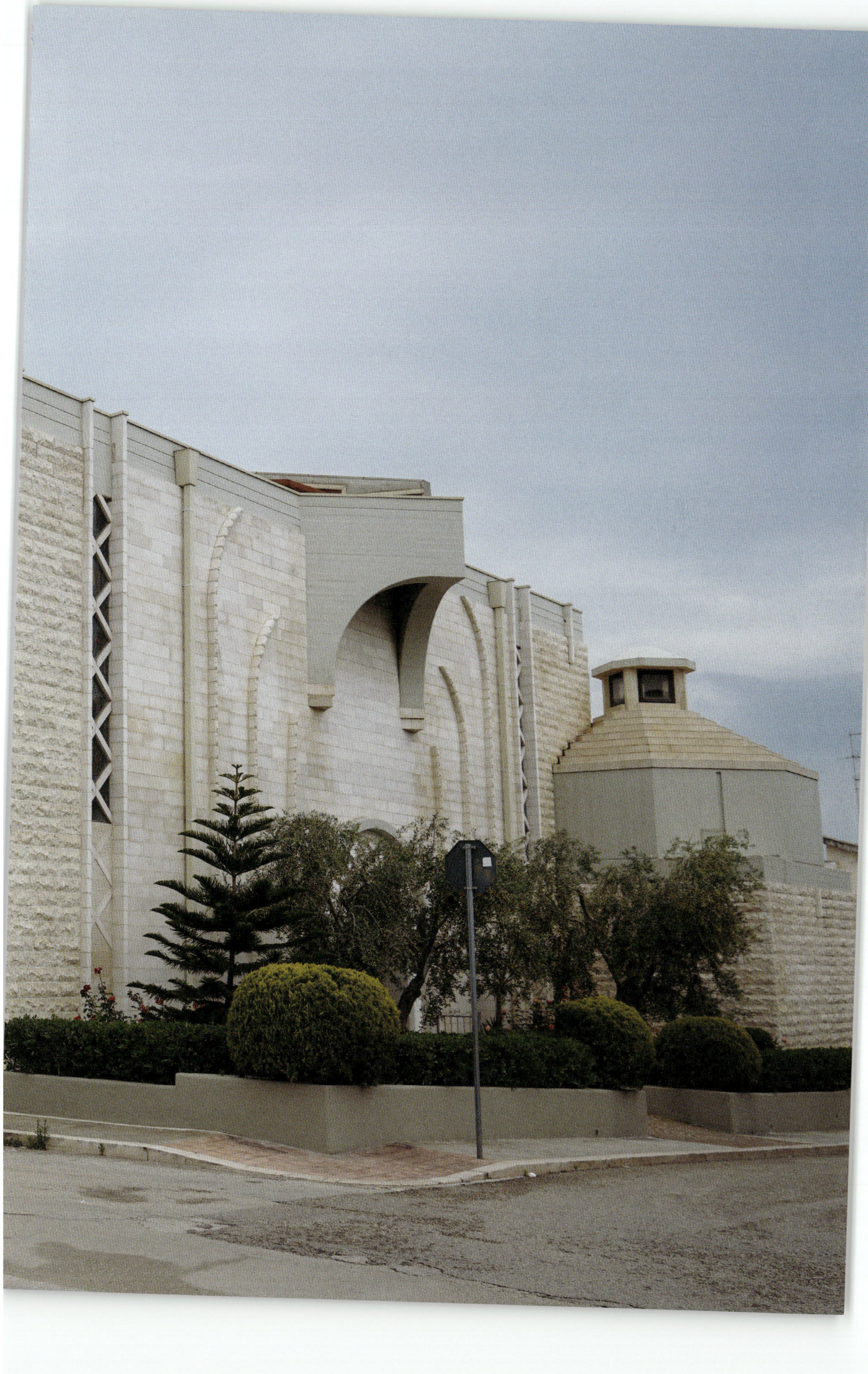

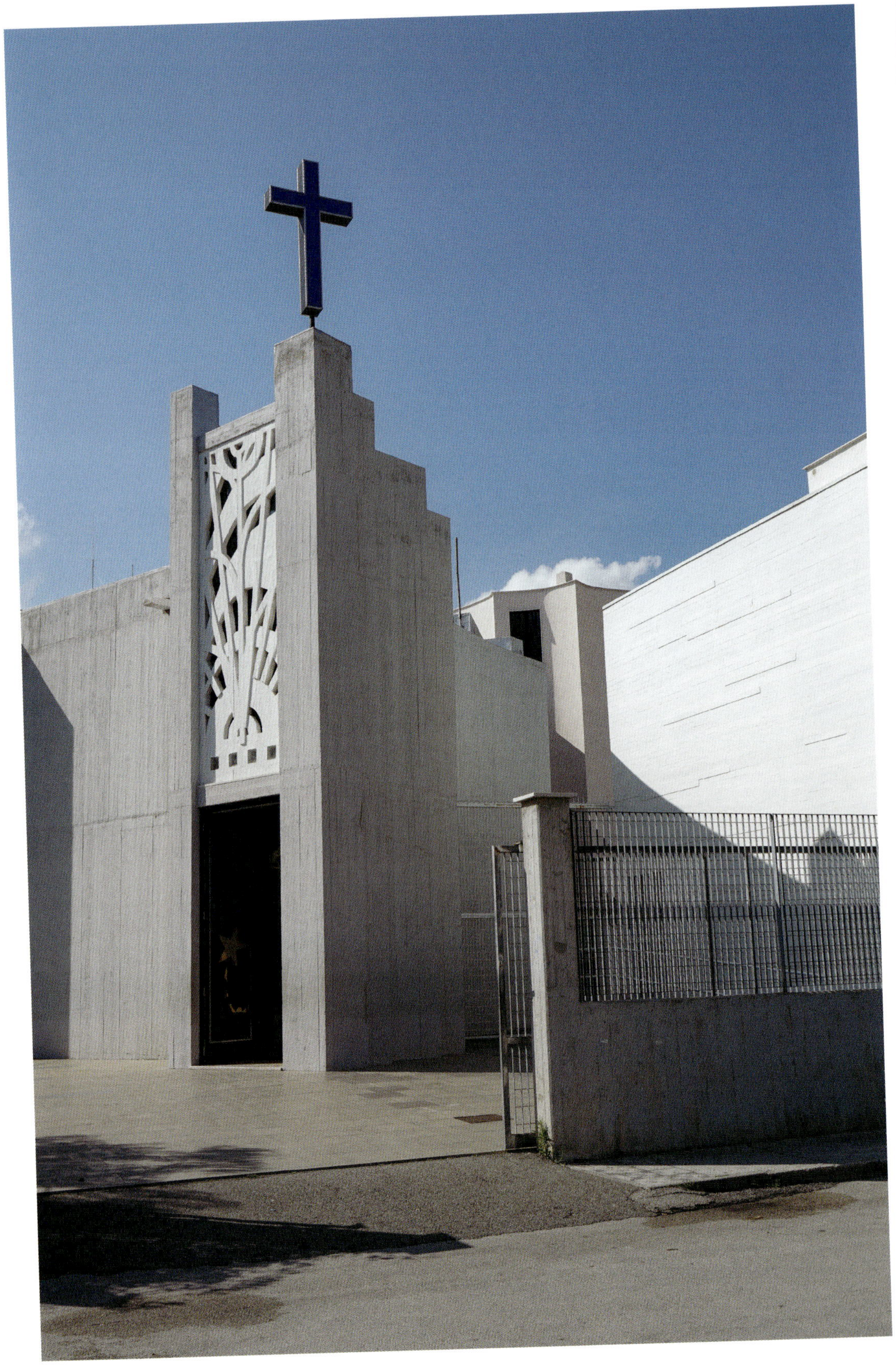

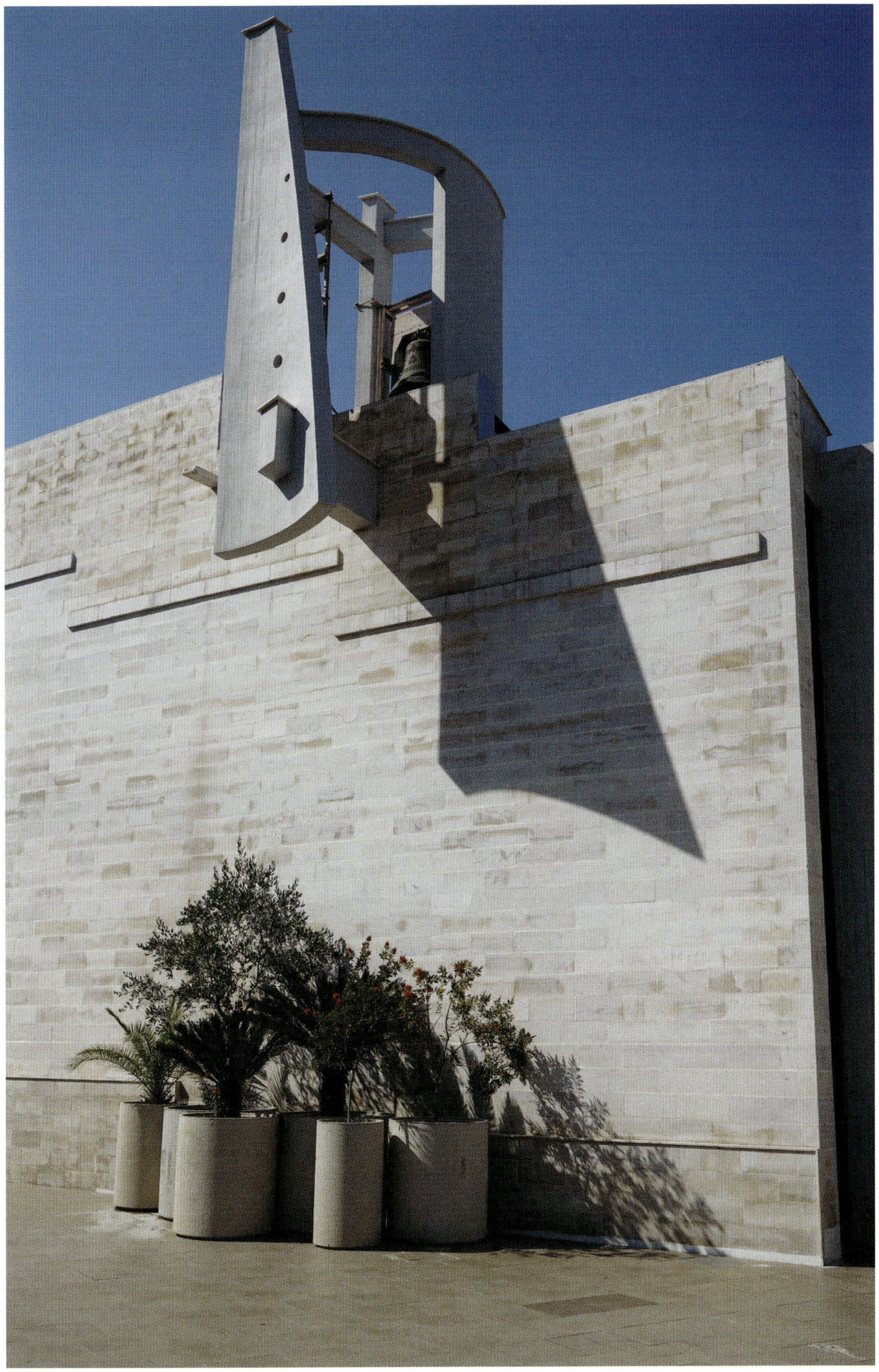

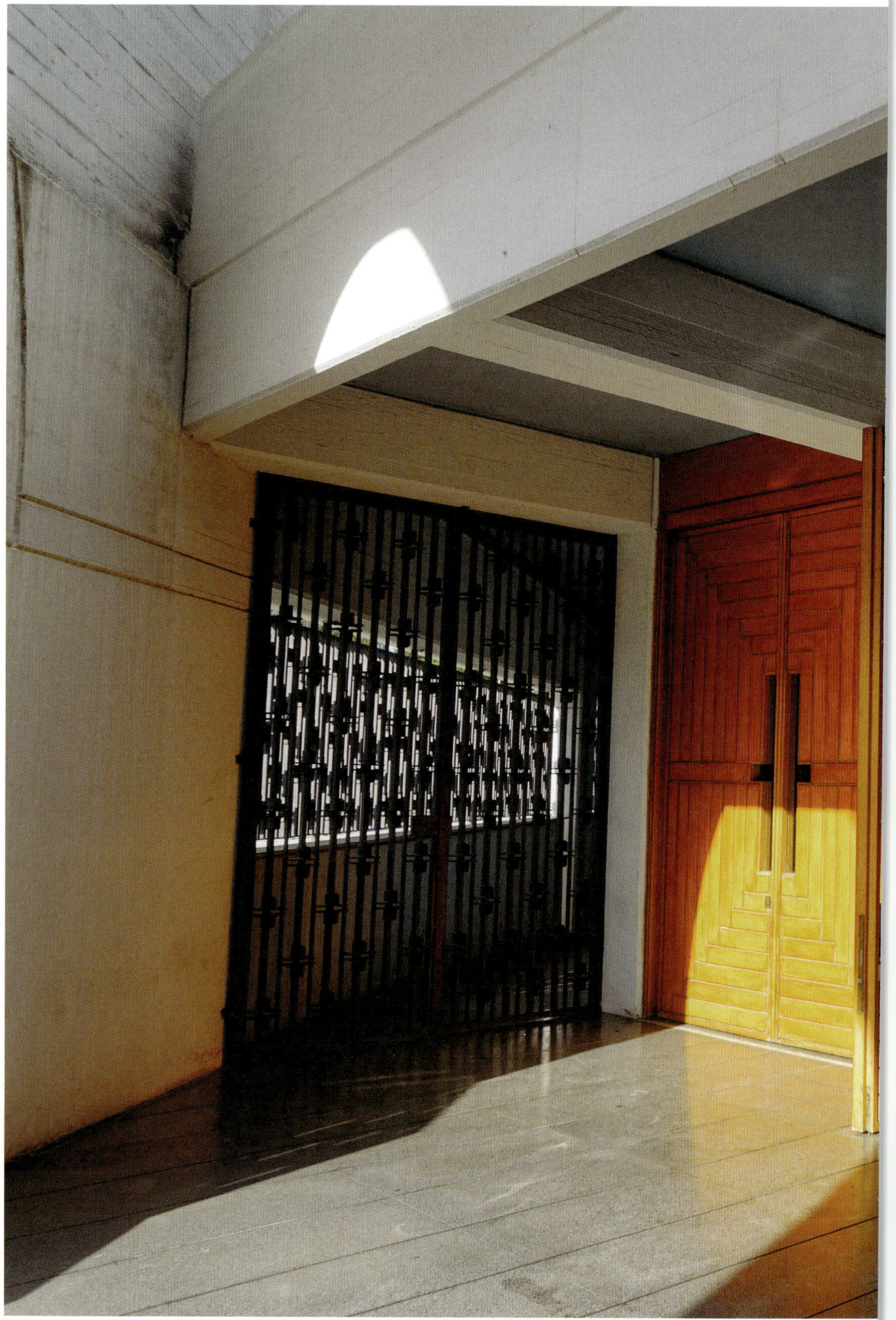

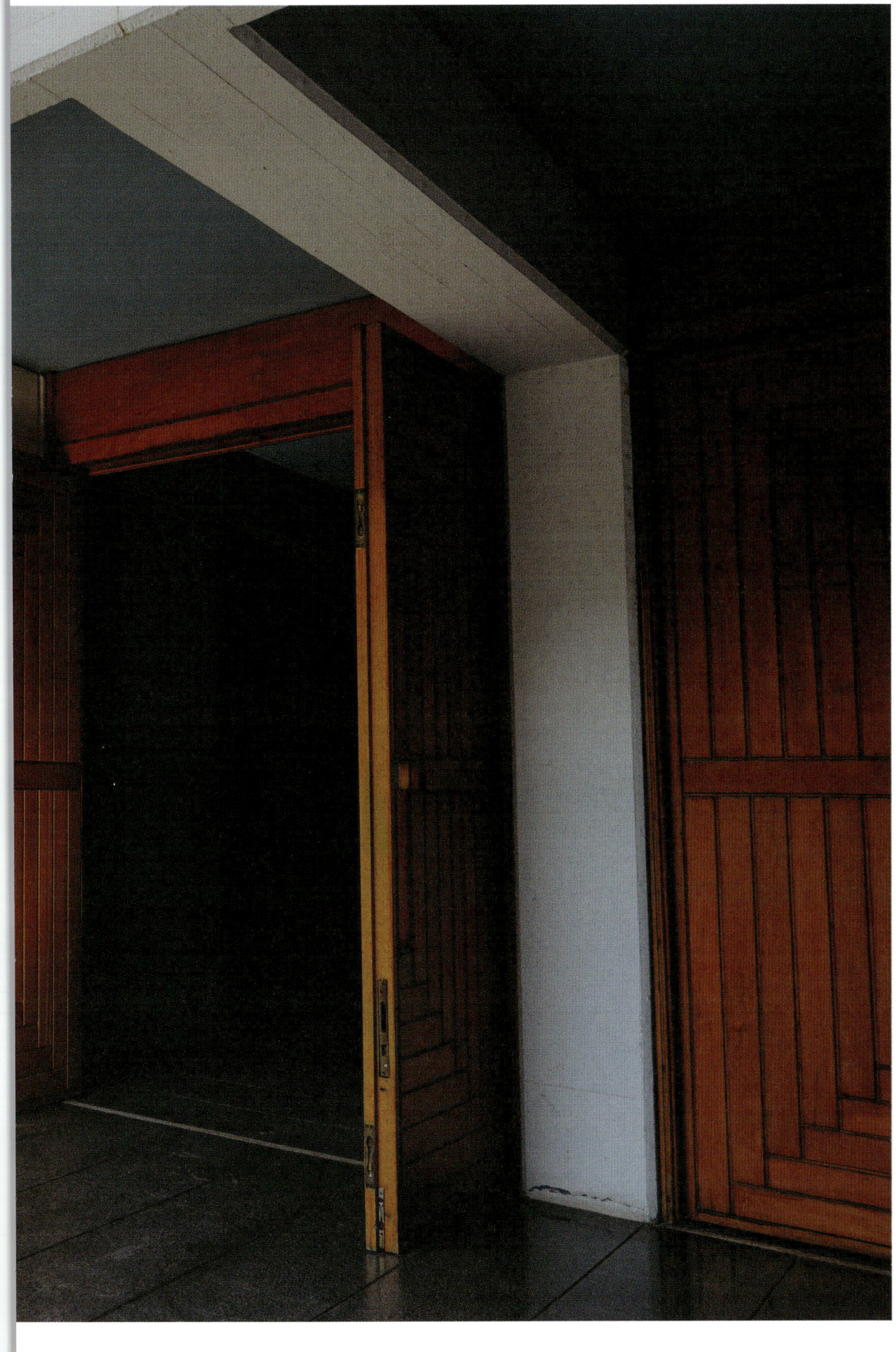

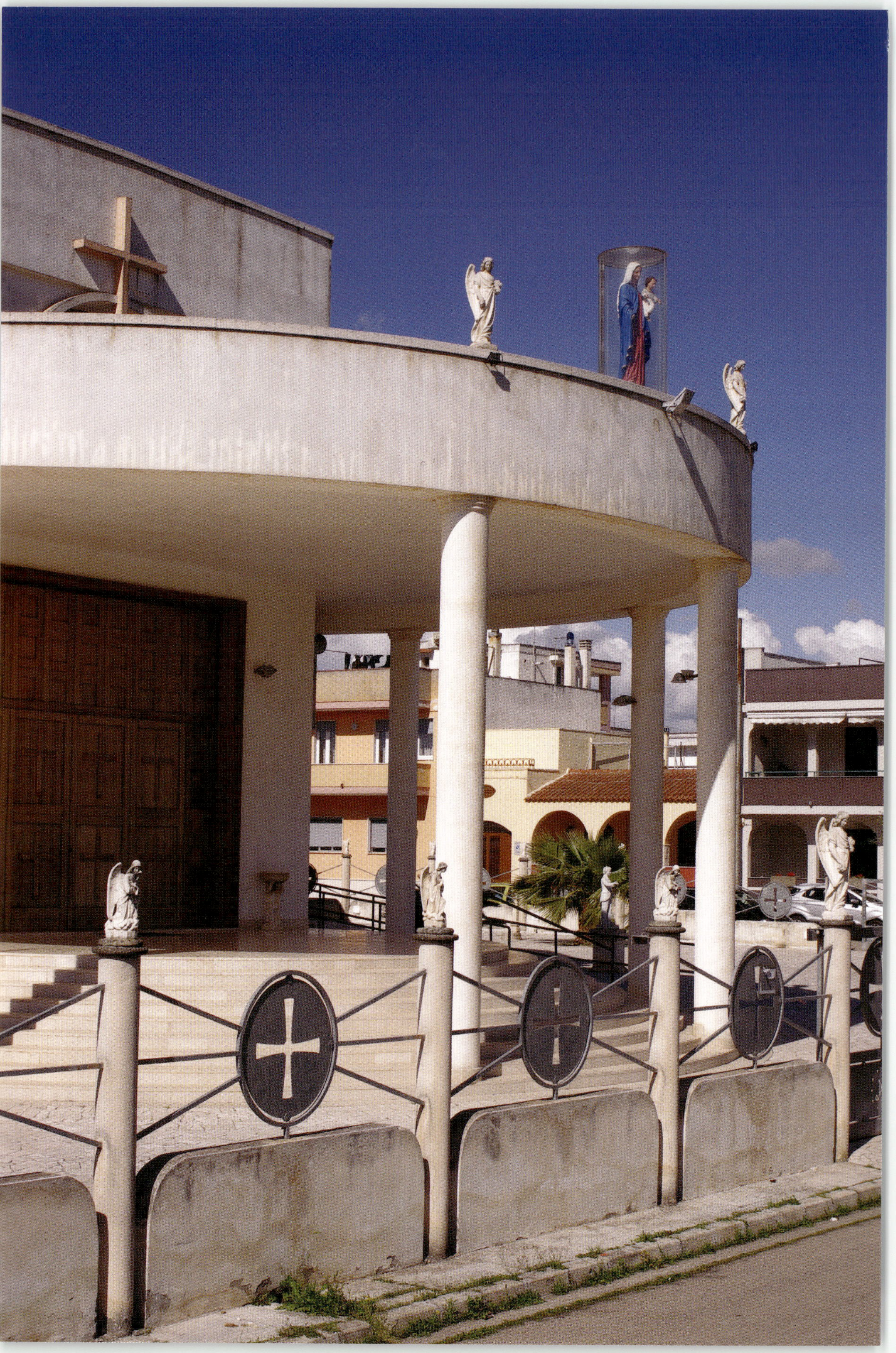

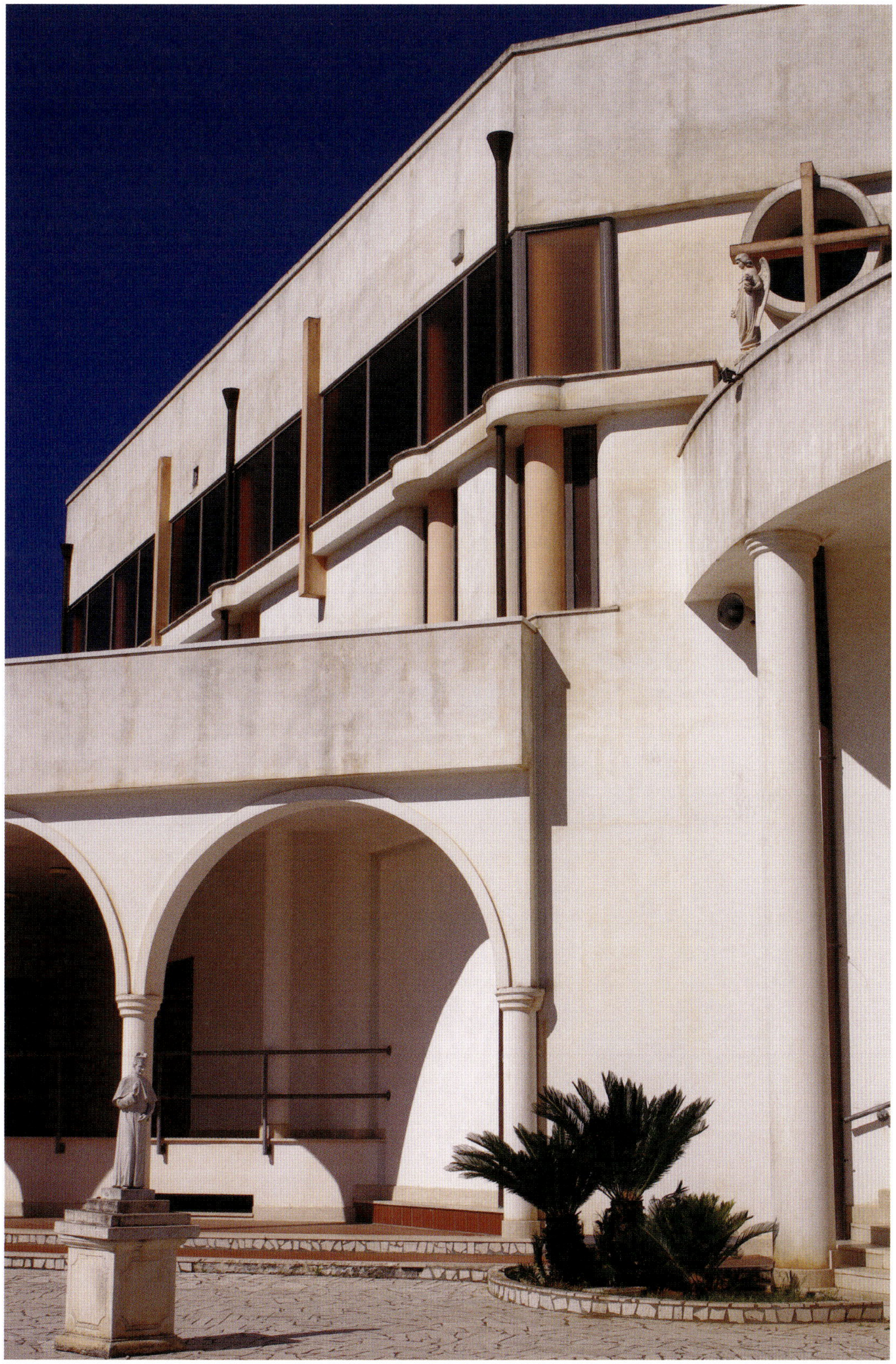

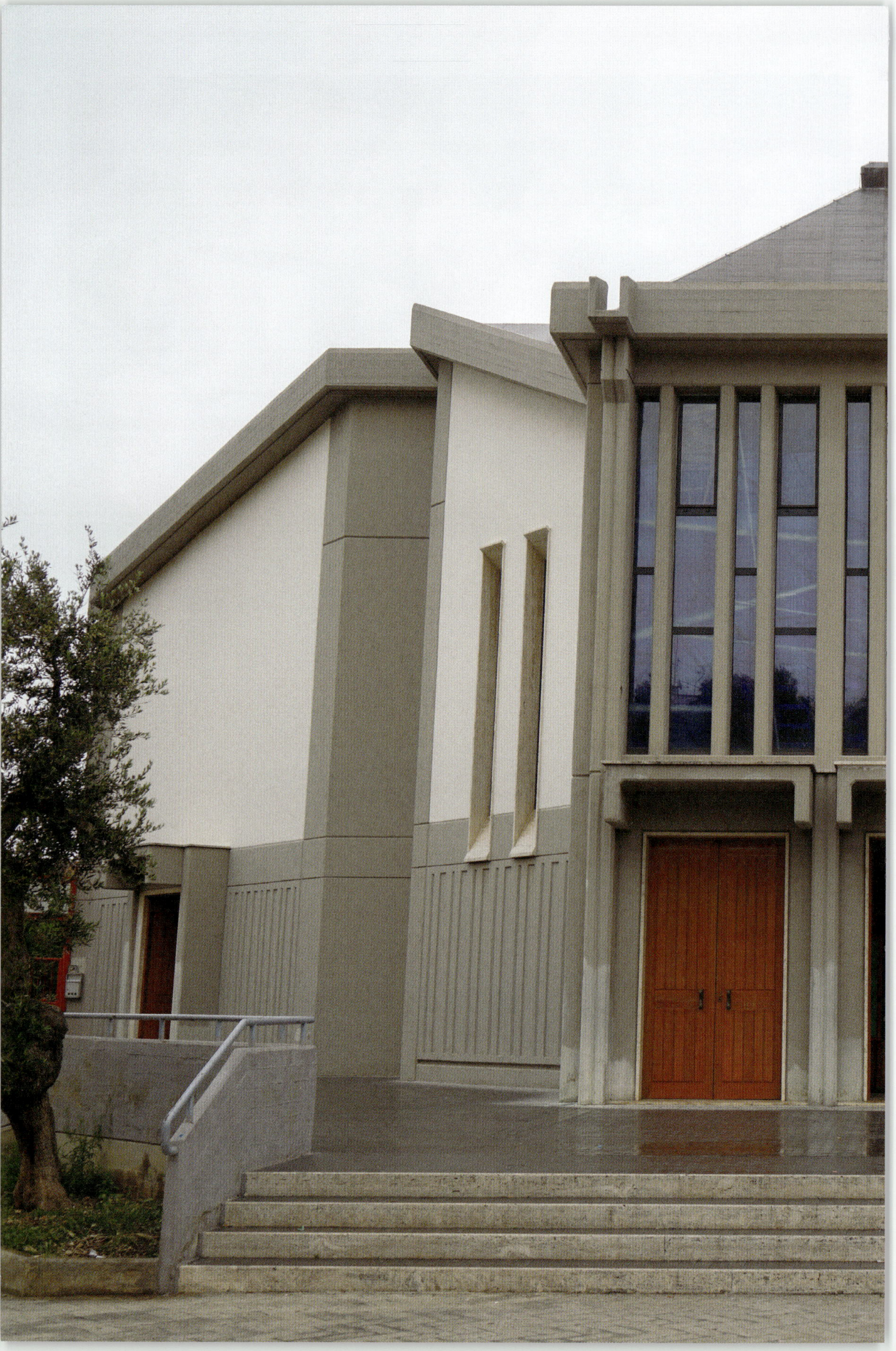

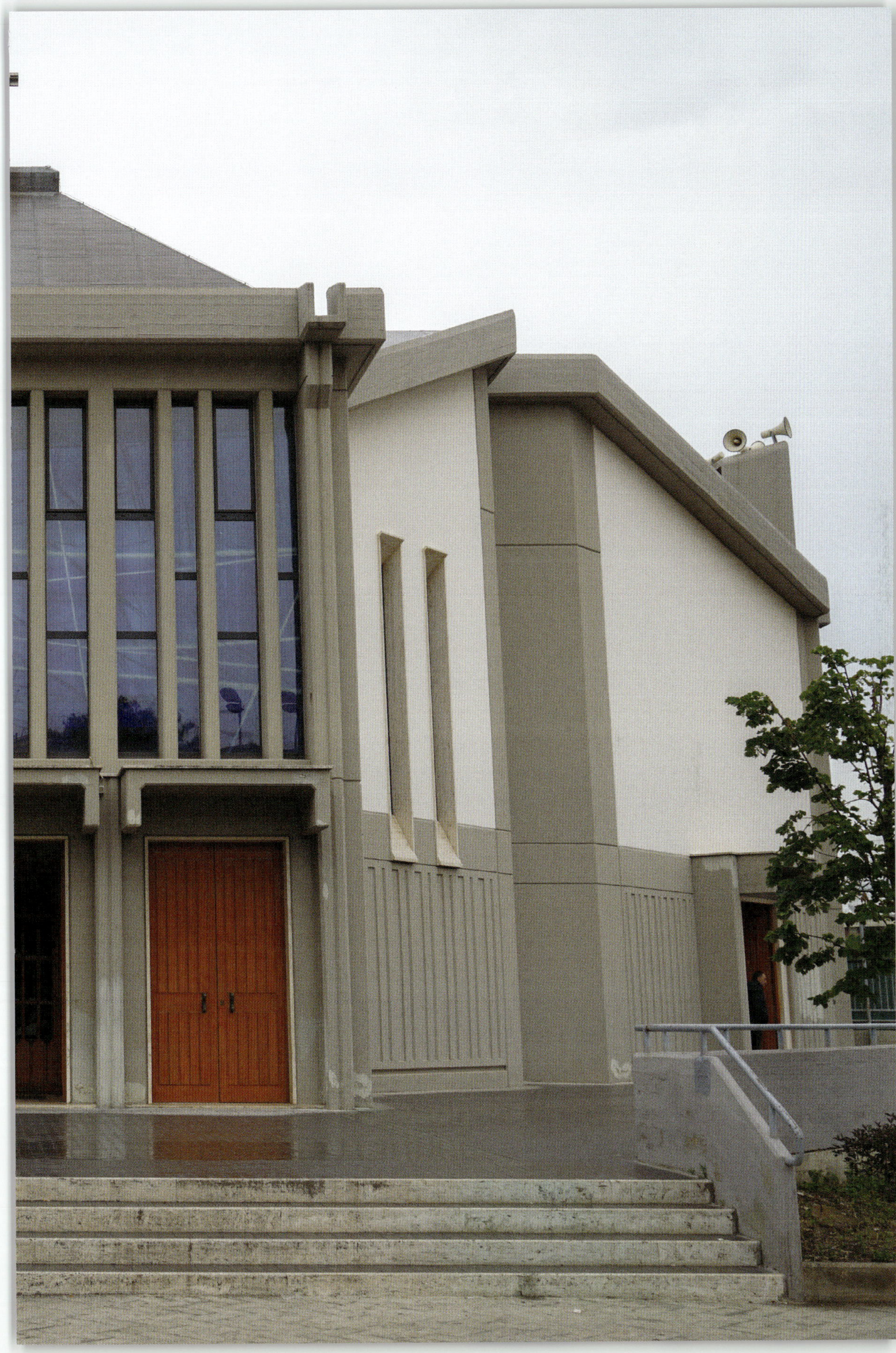

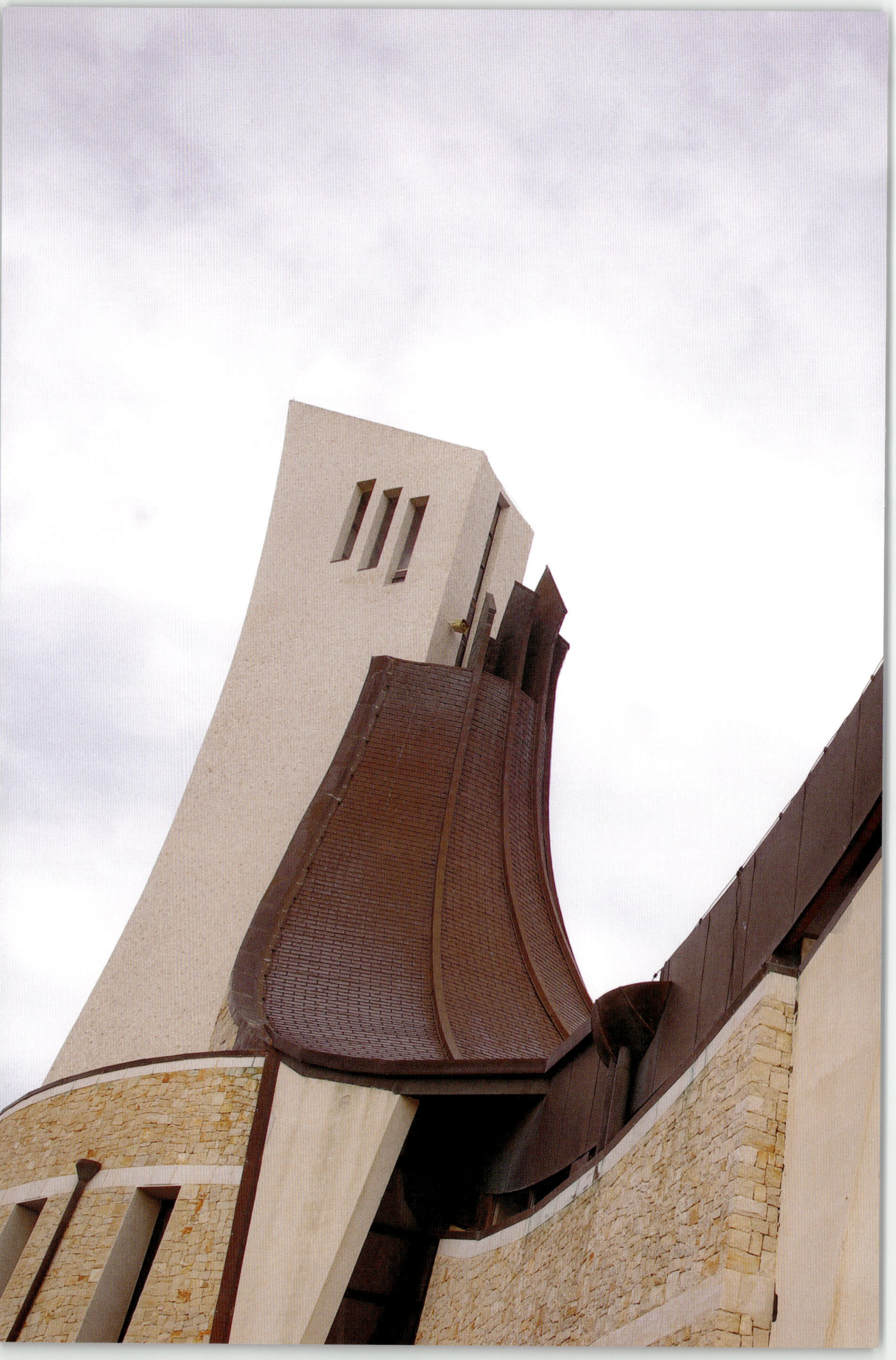

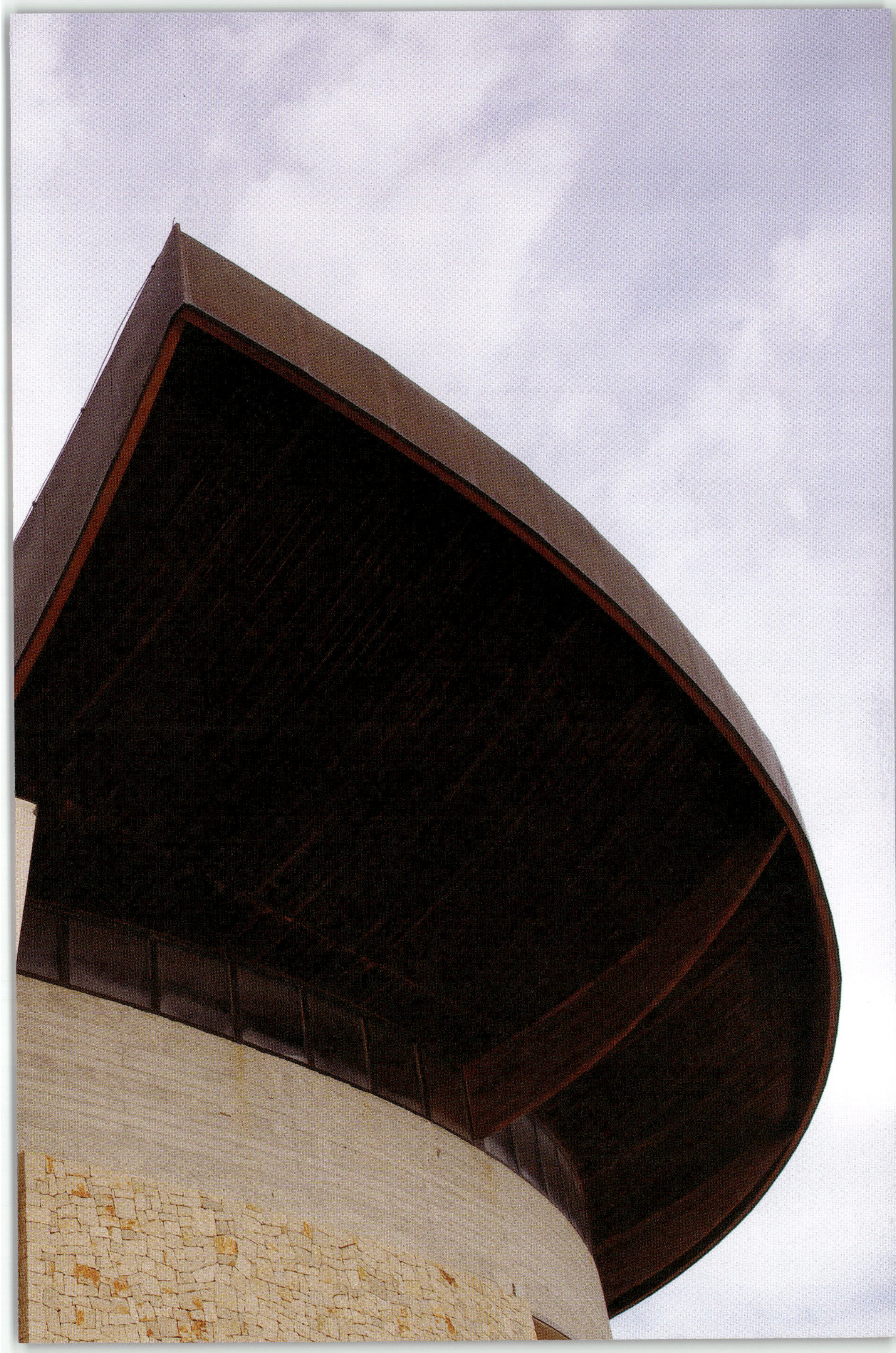

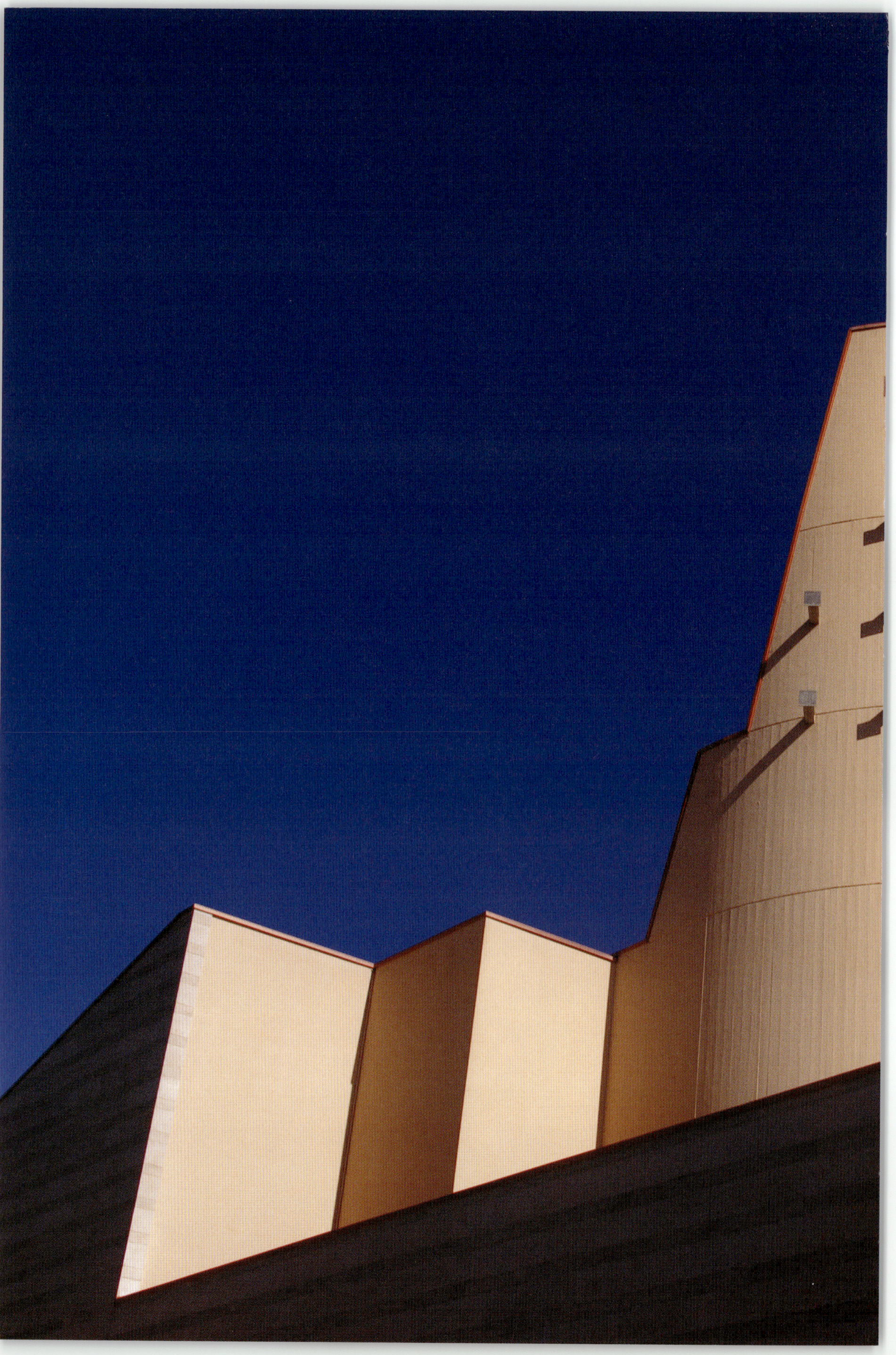

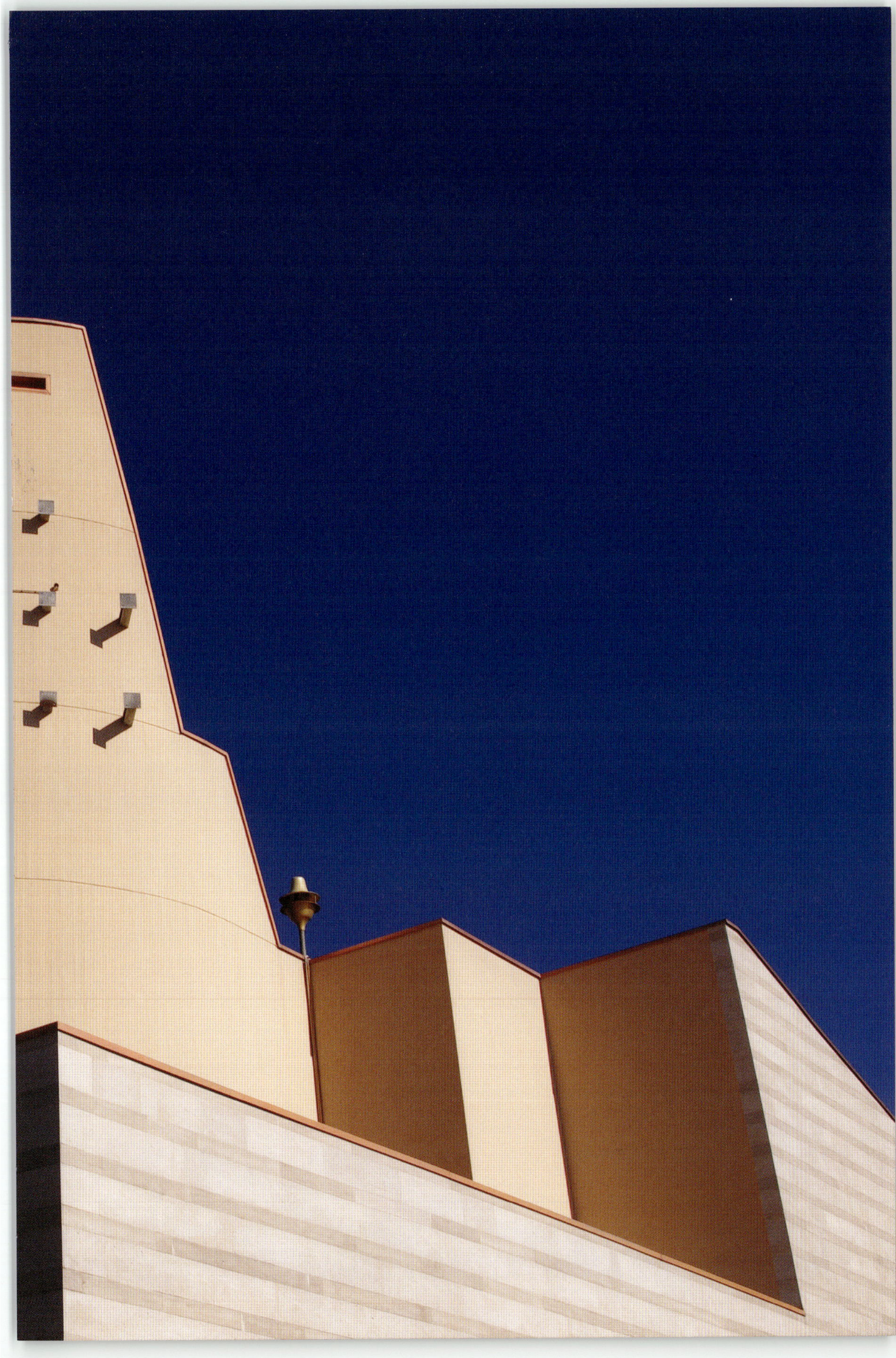

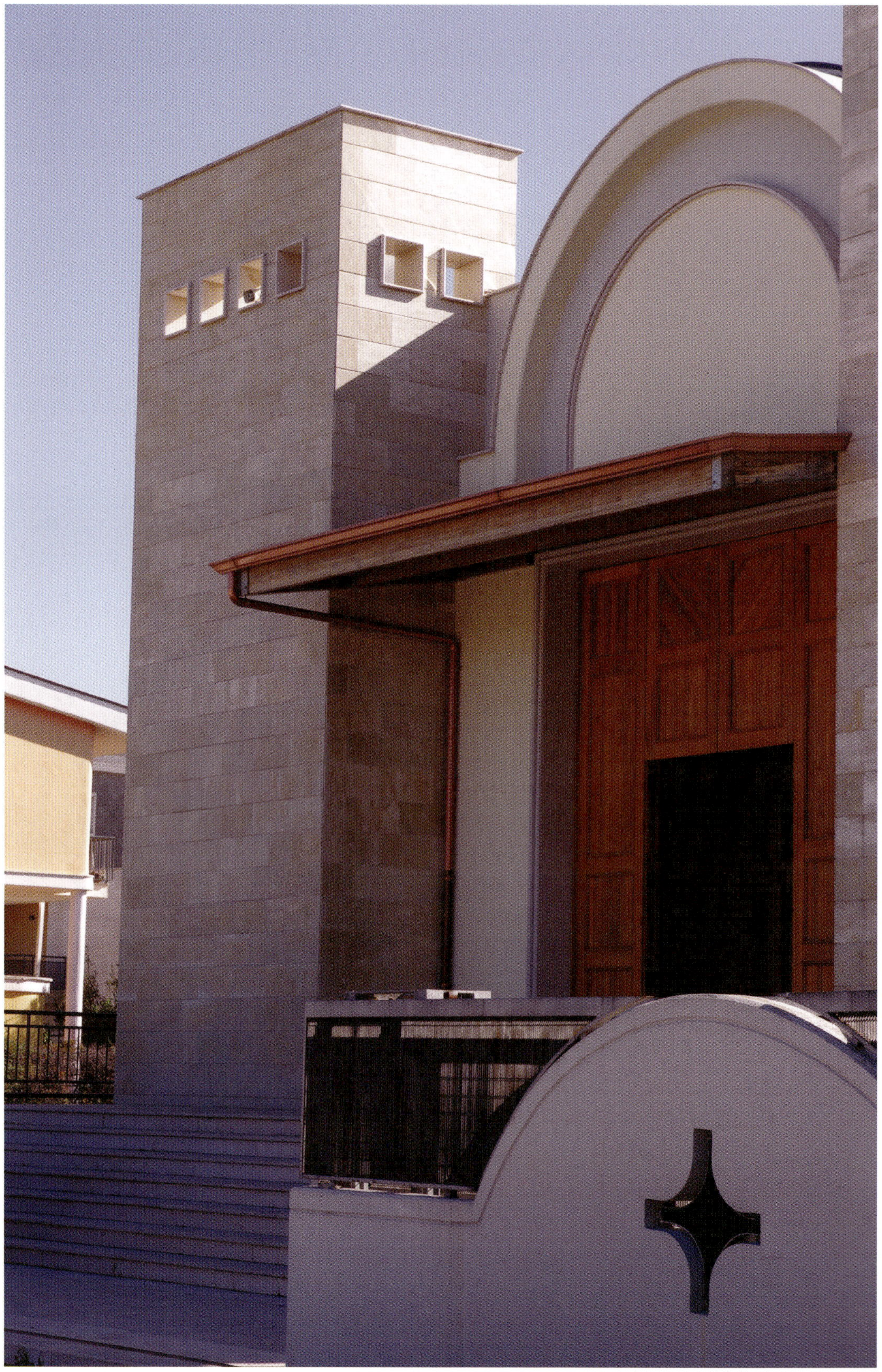

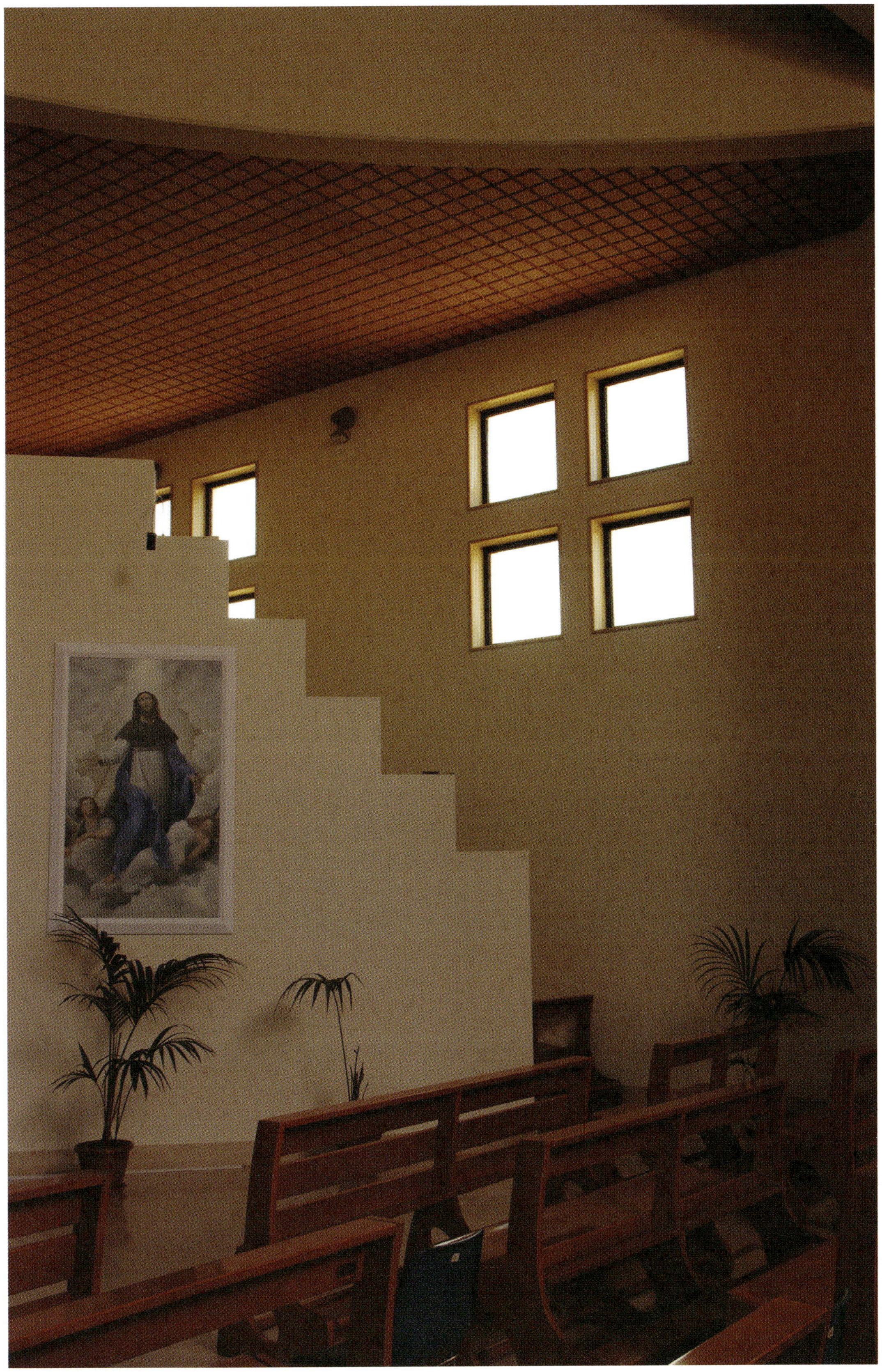

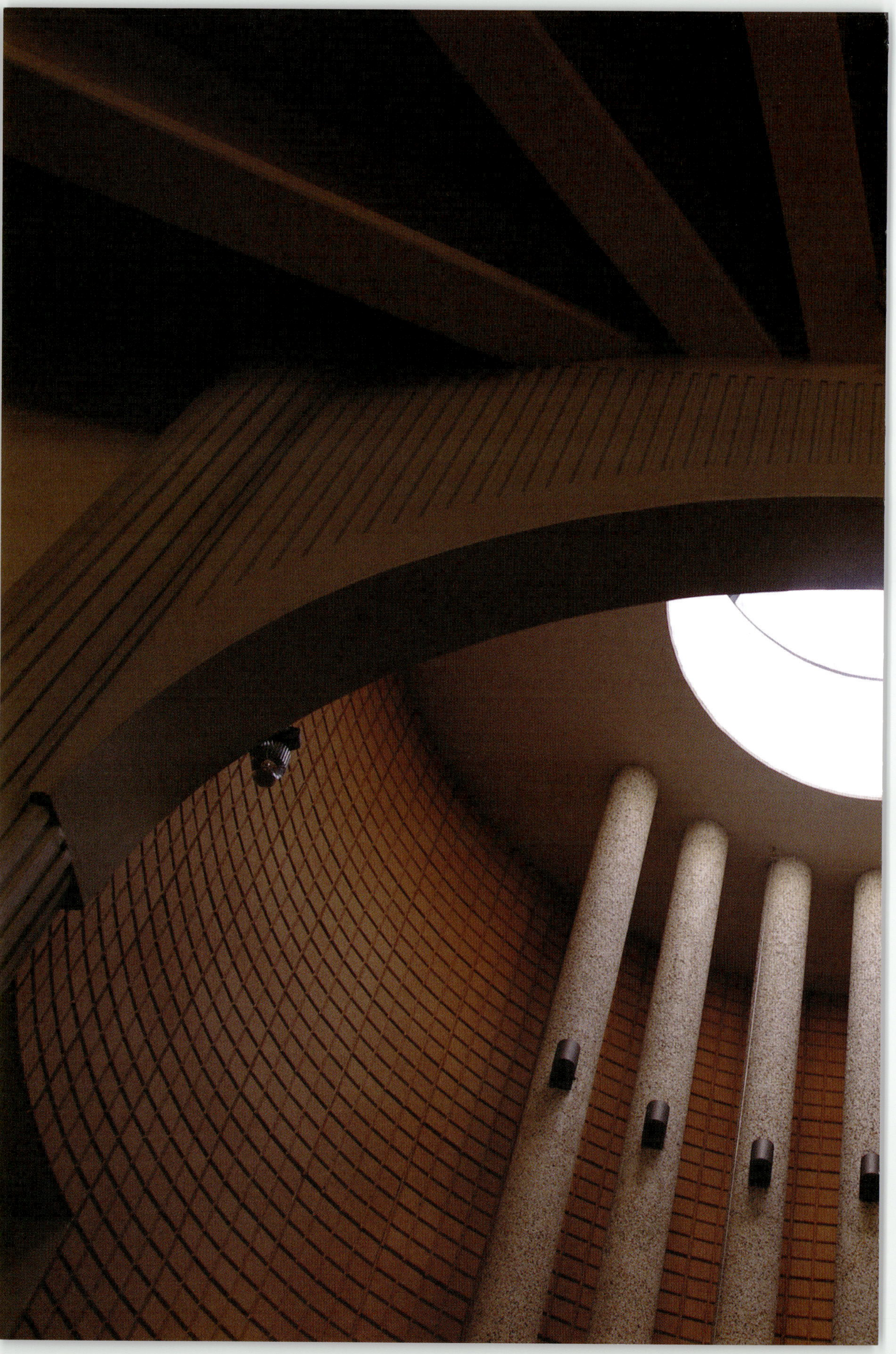

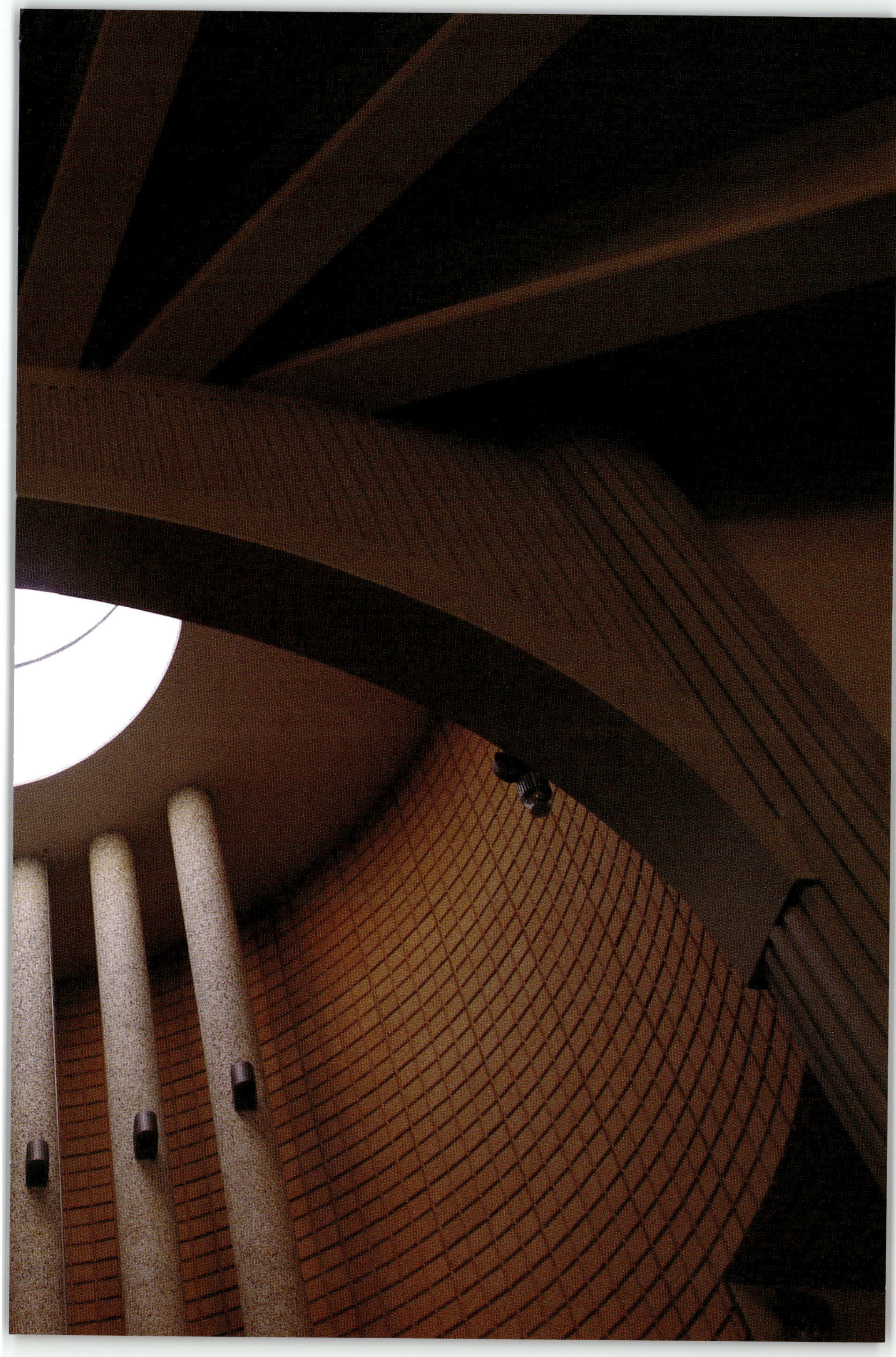

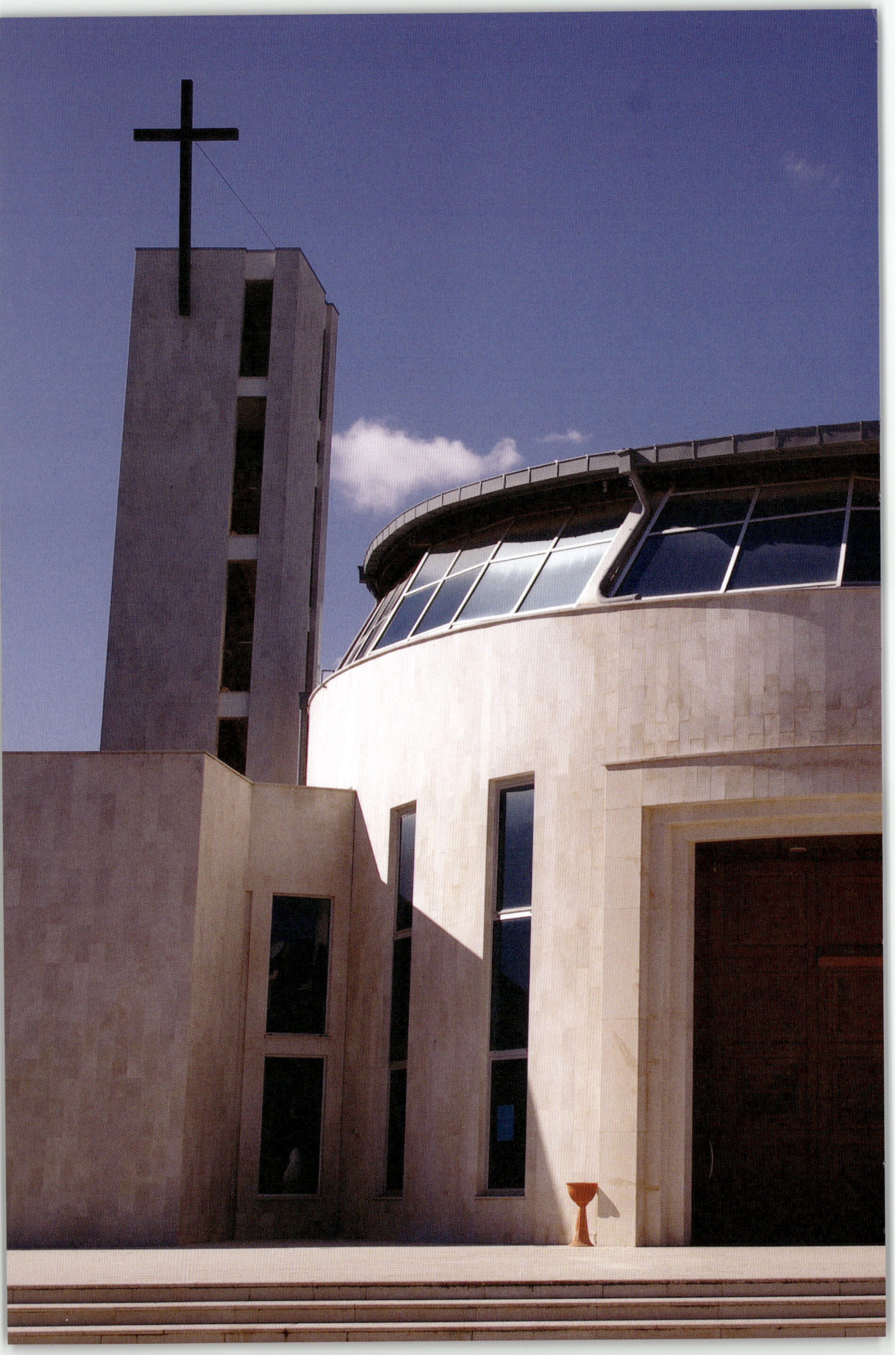

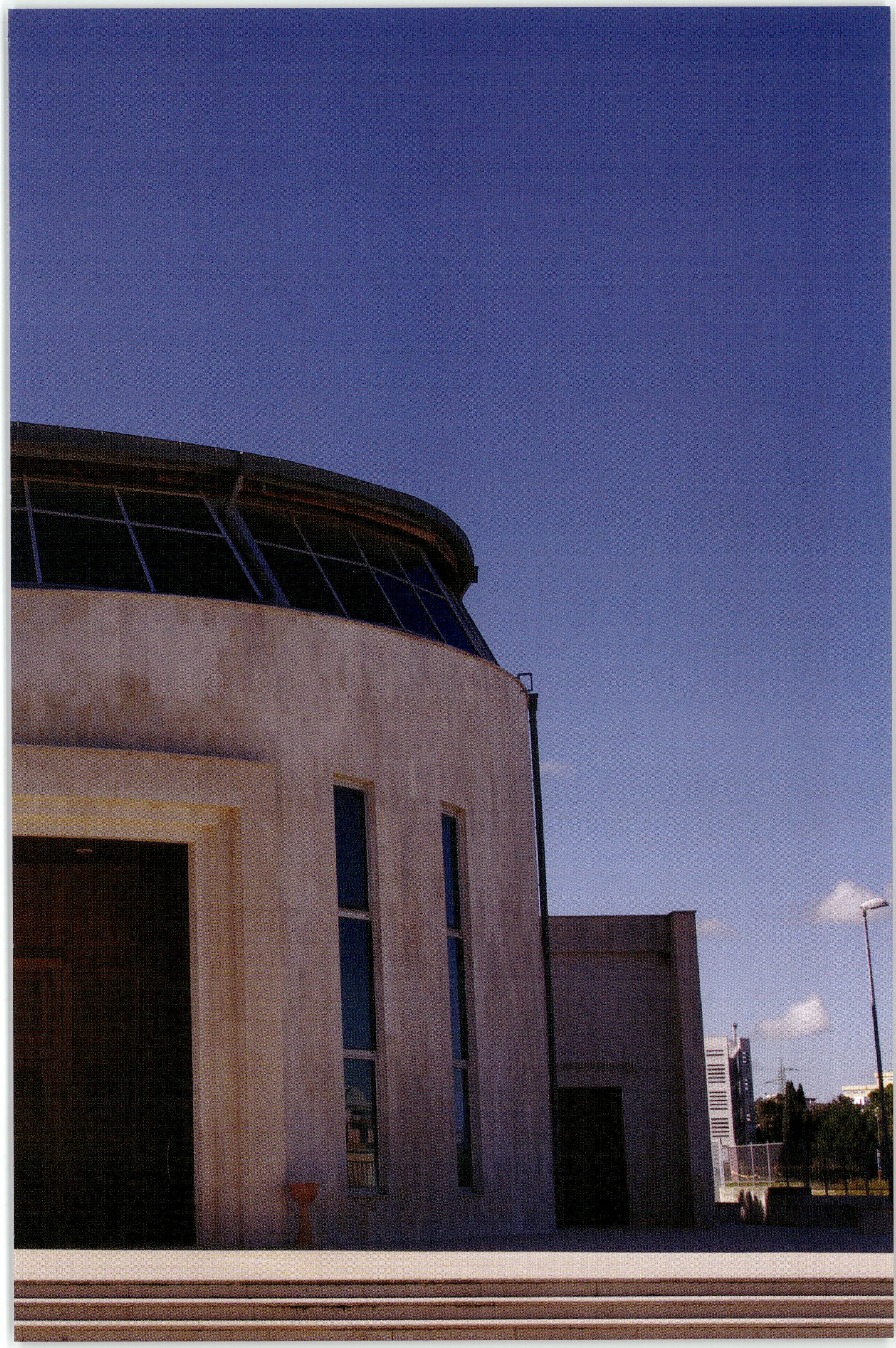

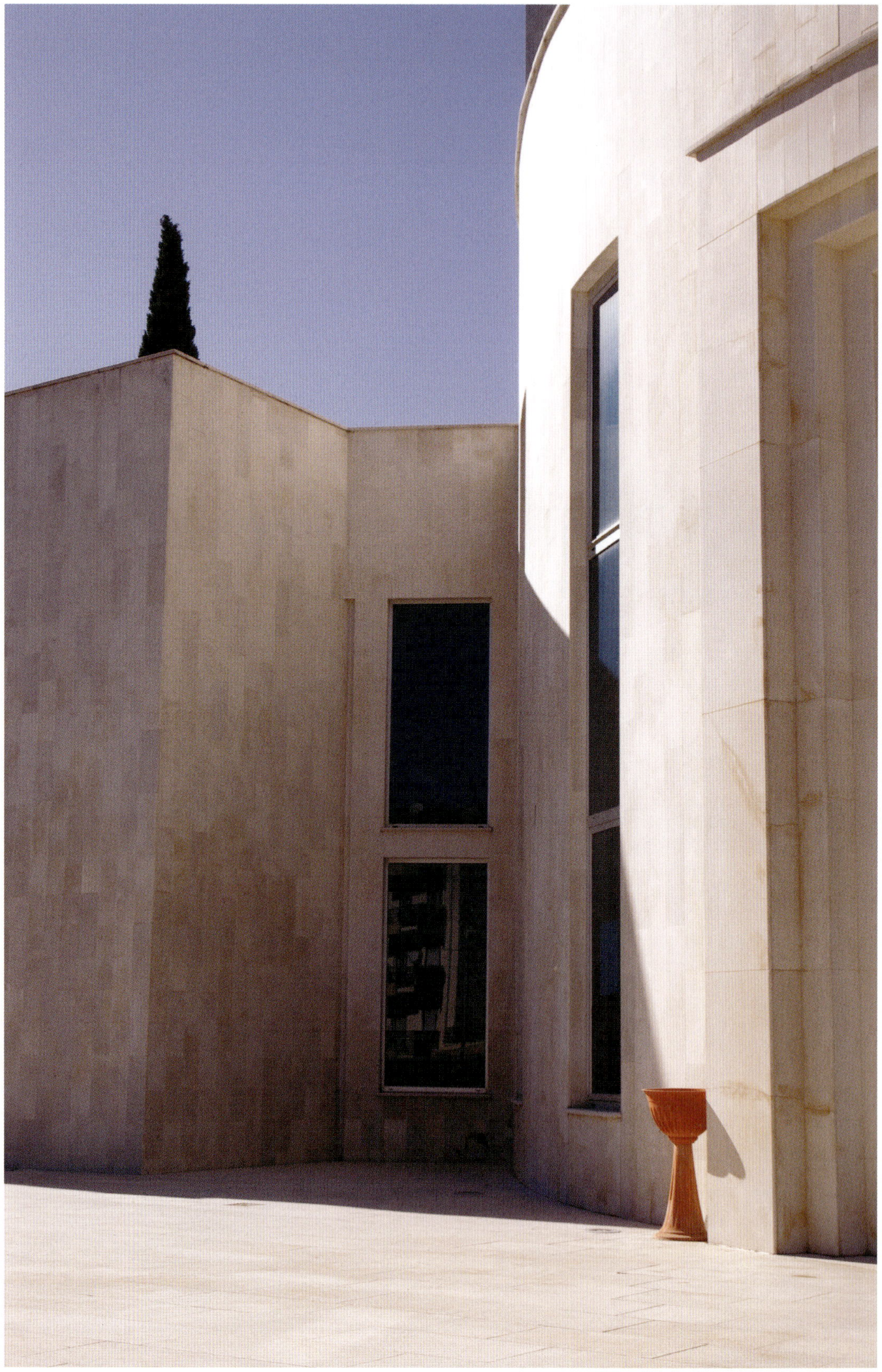

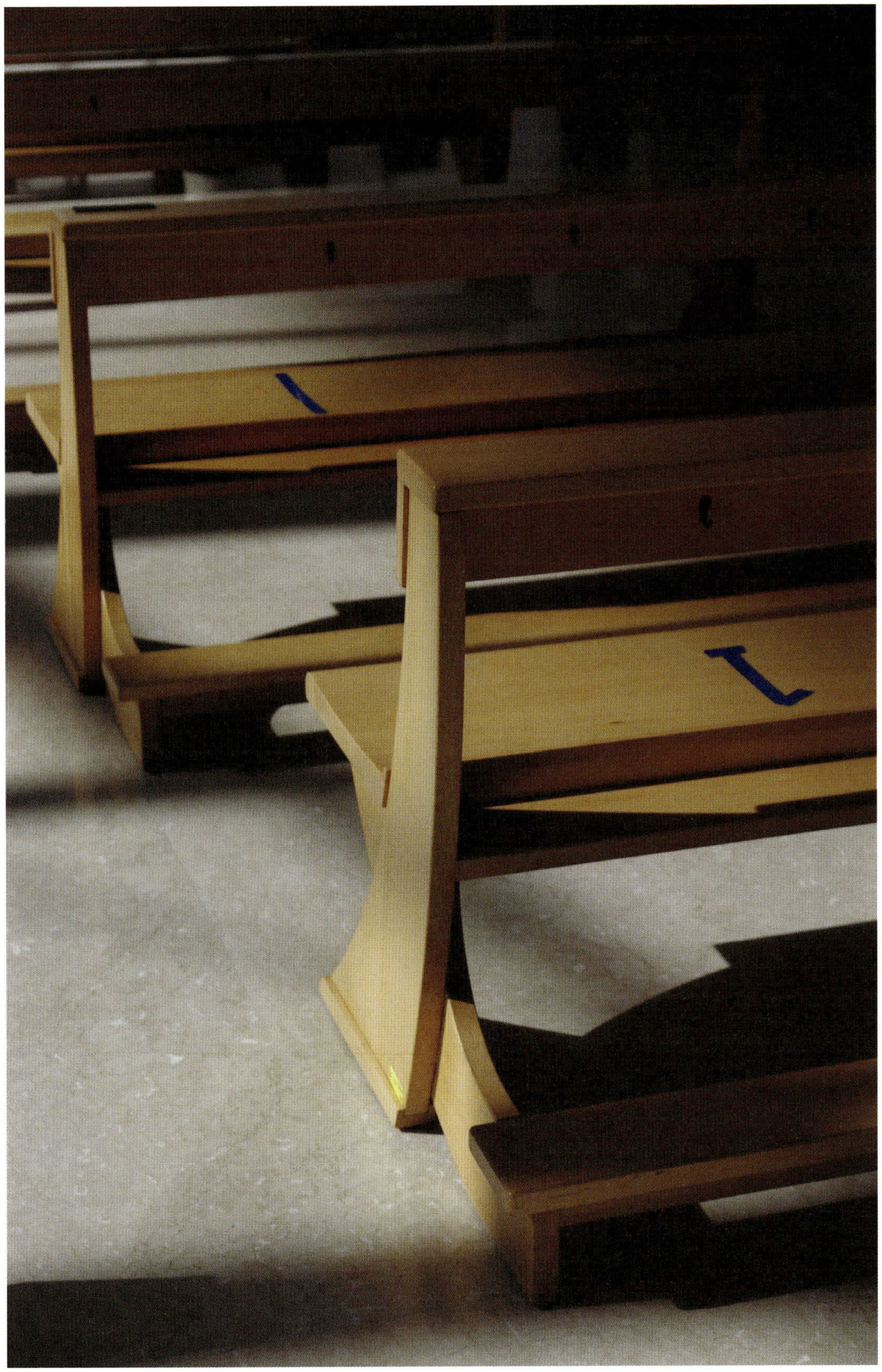

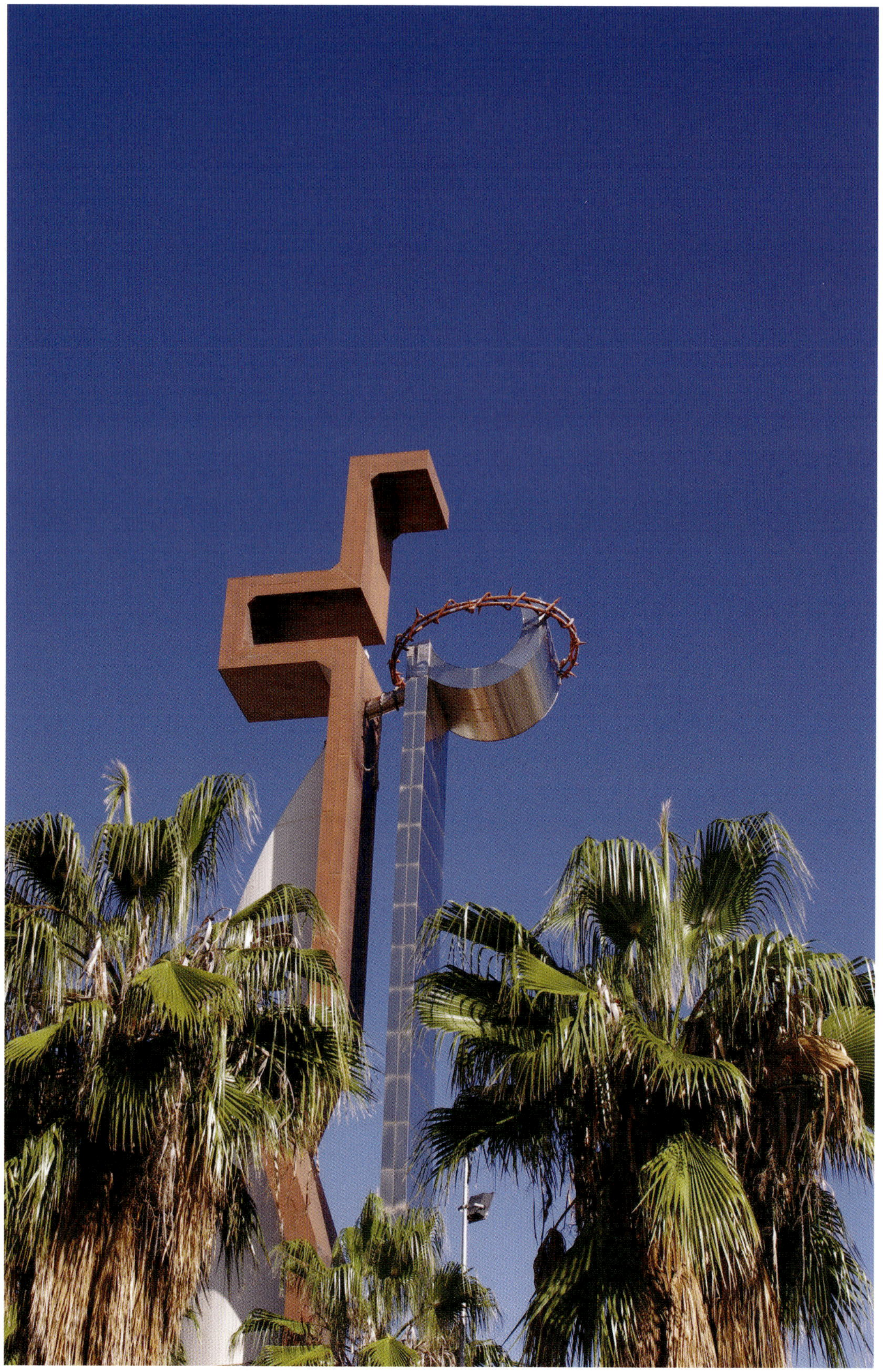

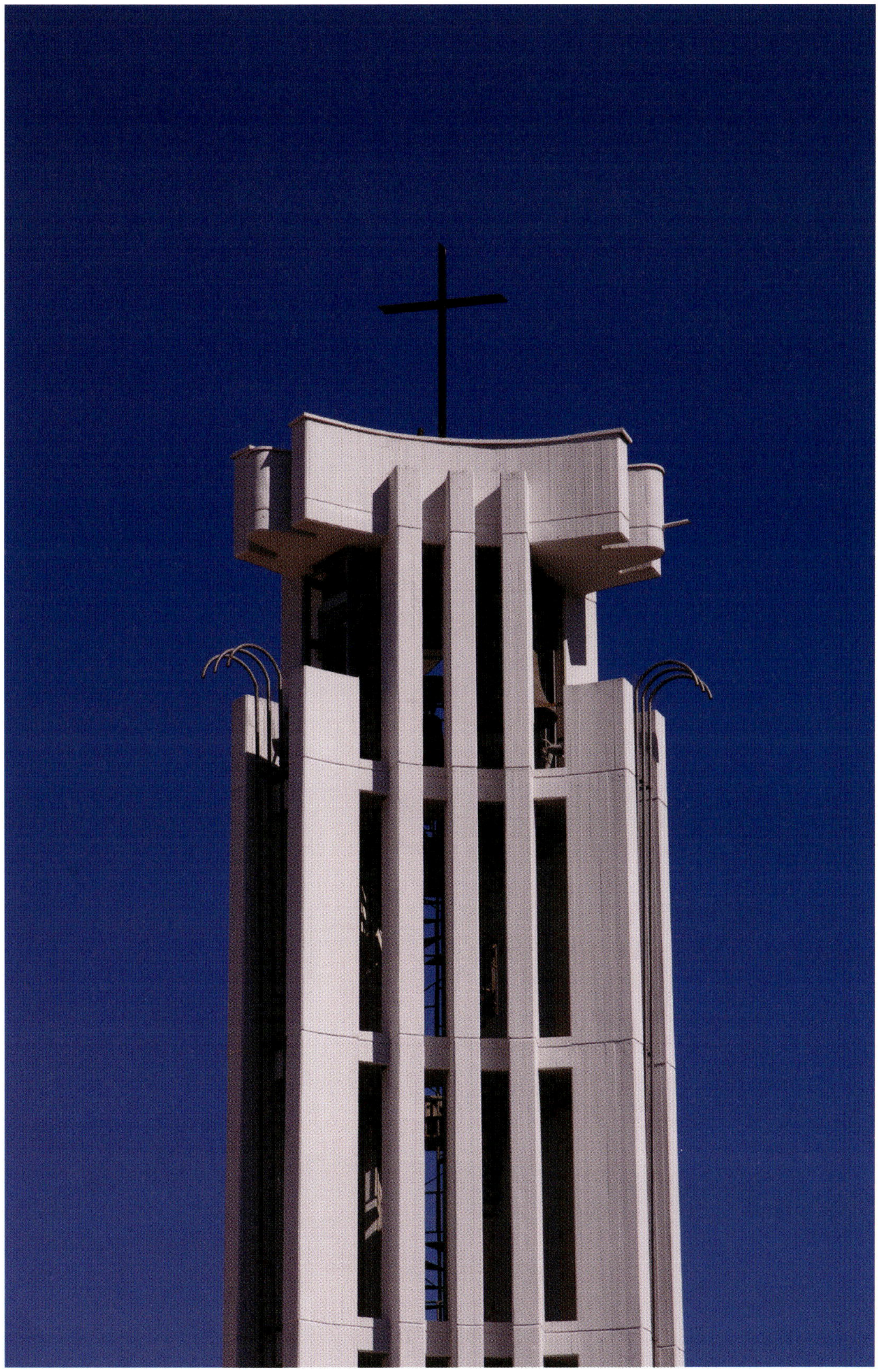

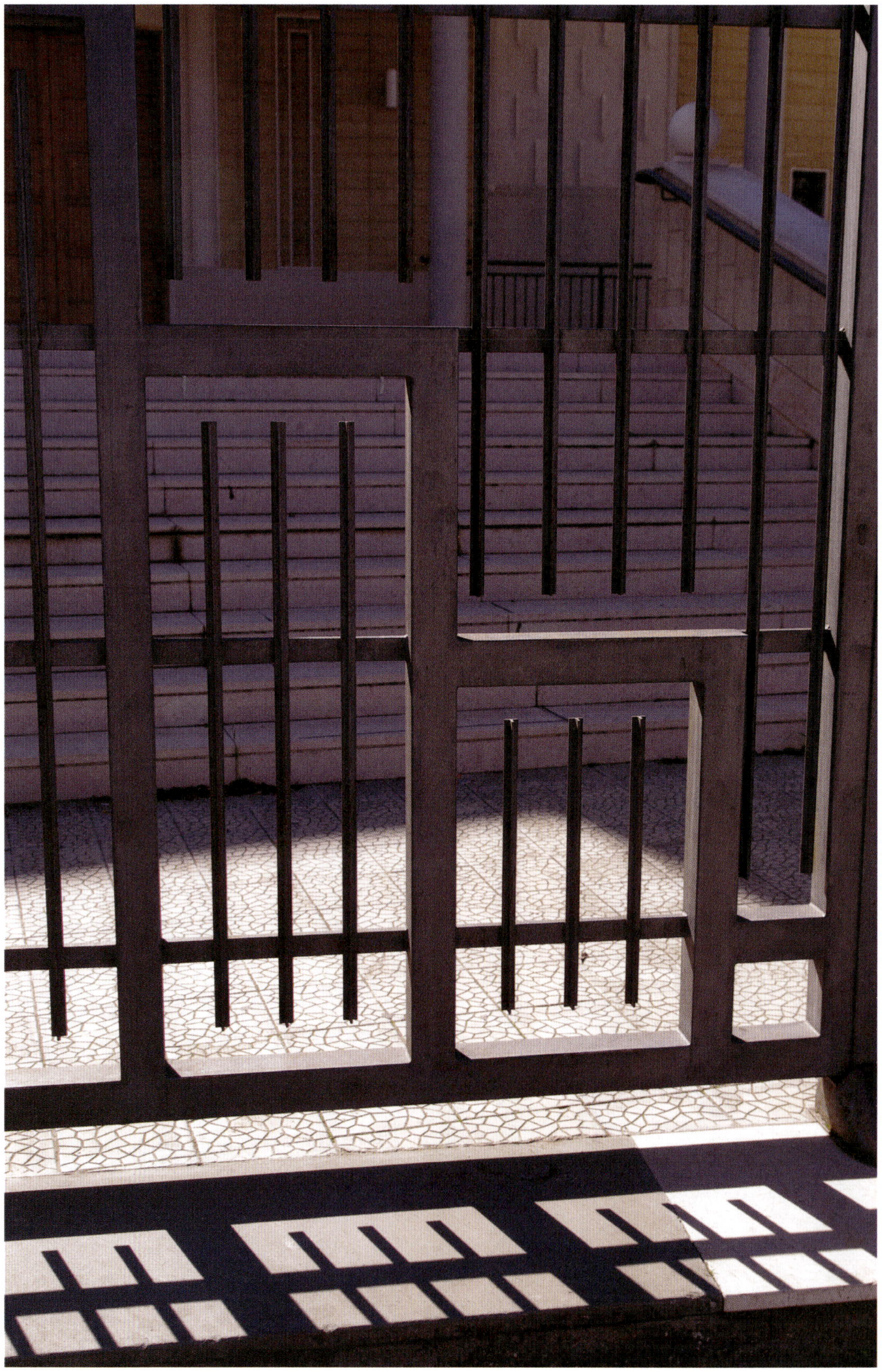

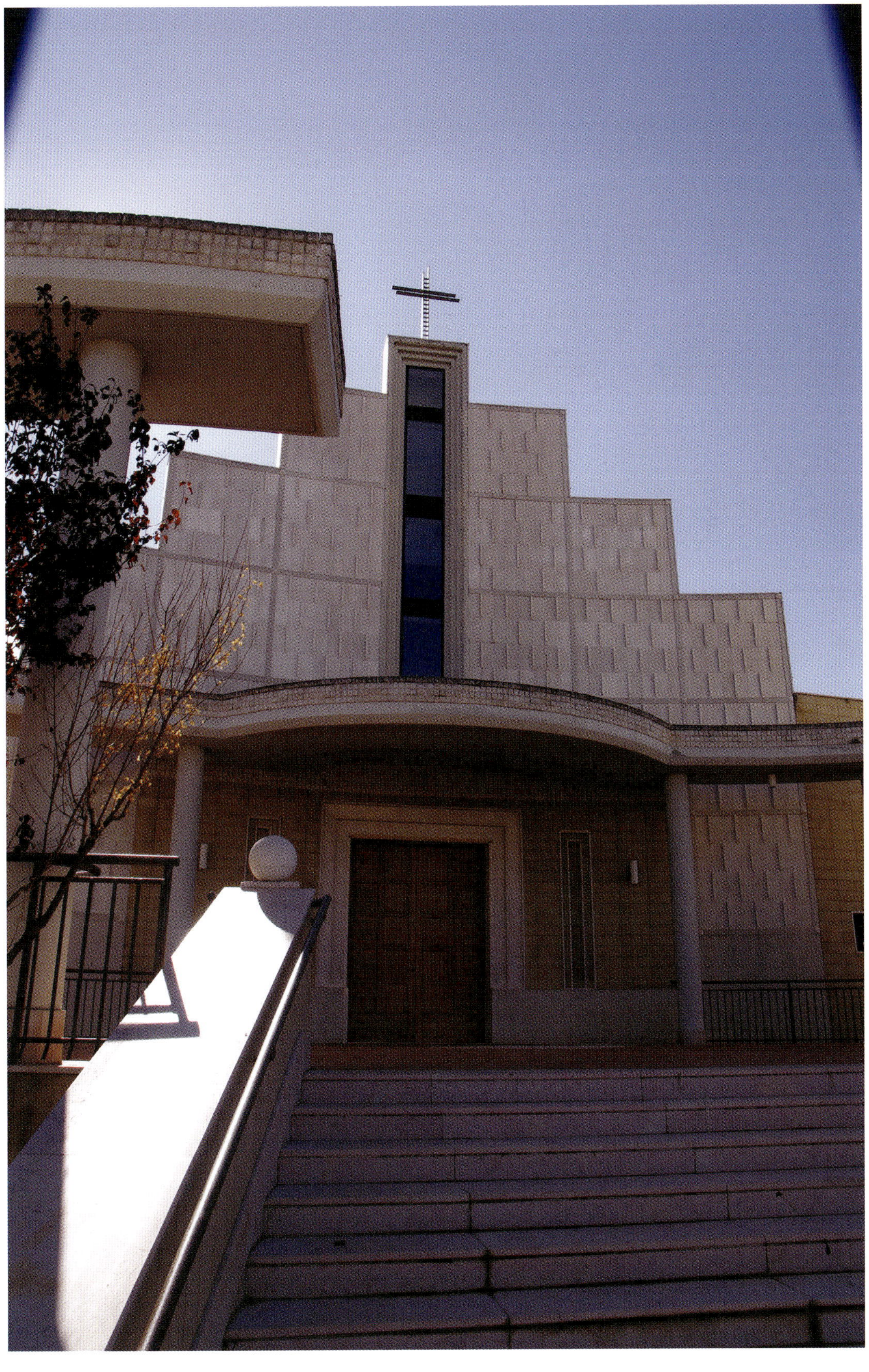

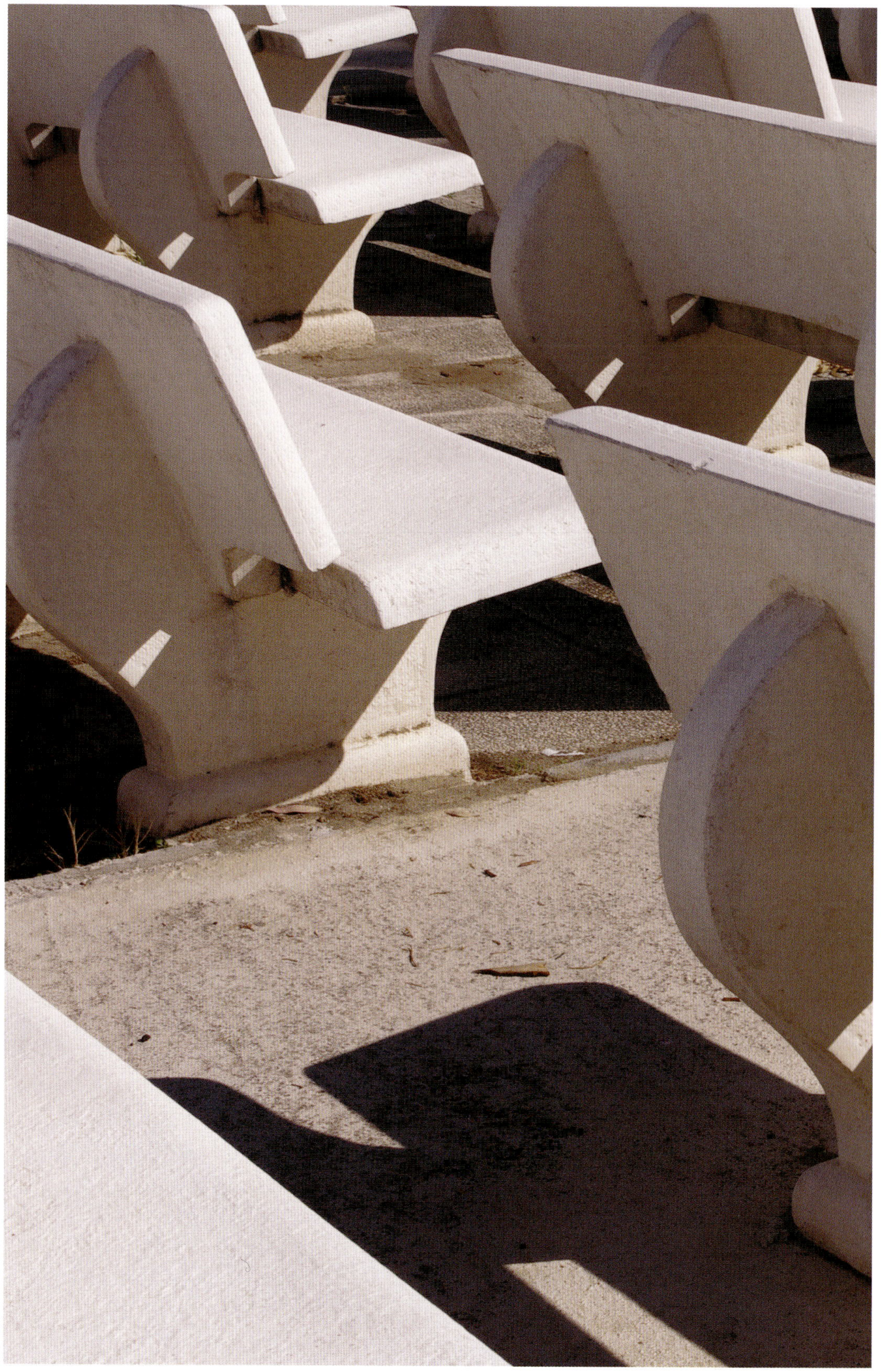

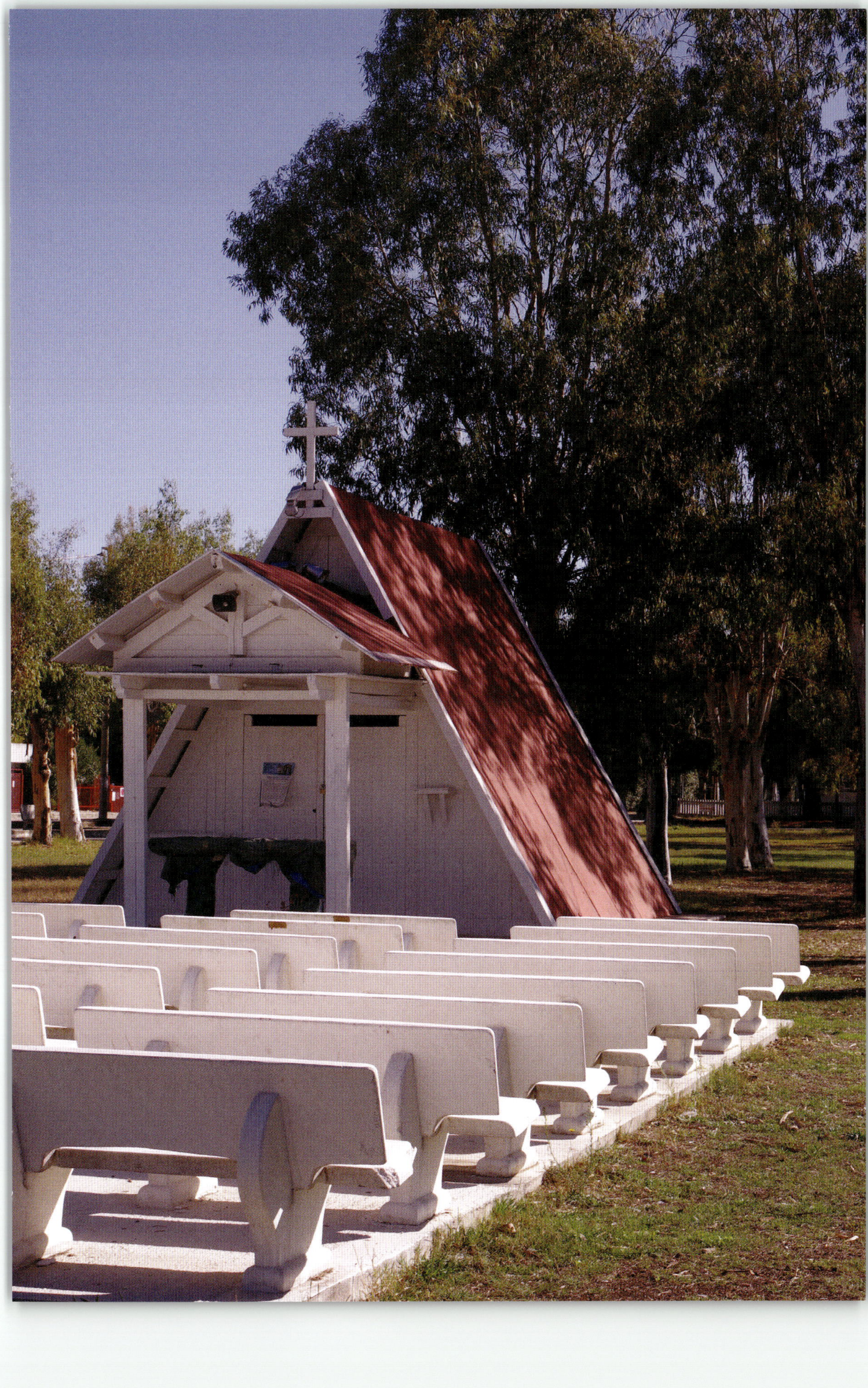

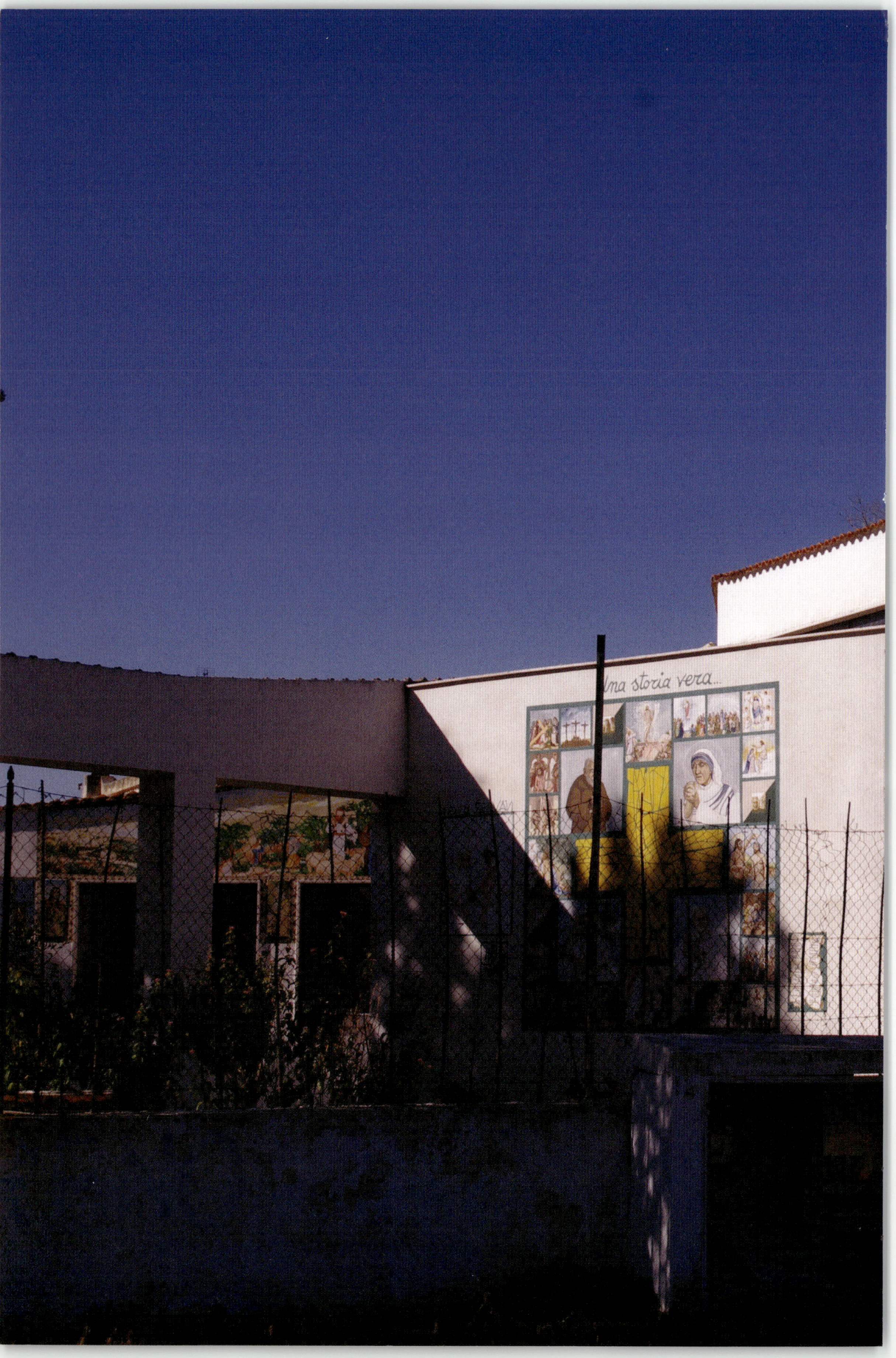
na storia vera...

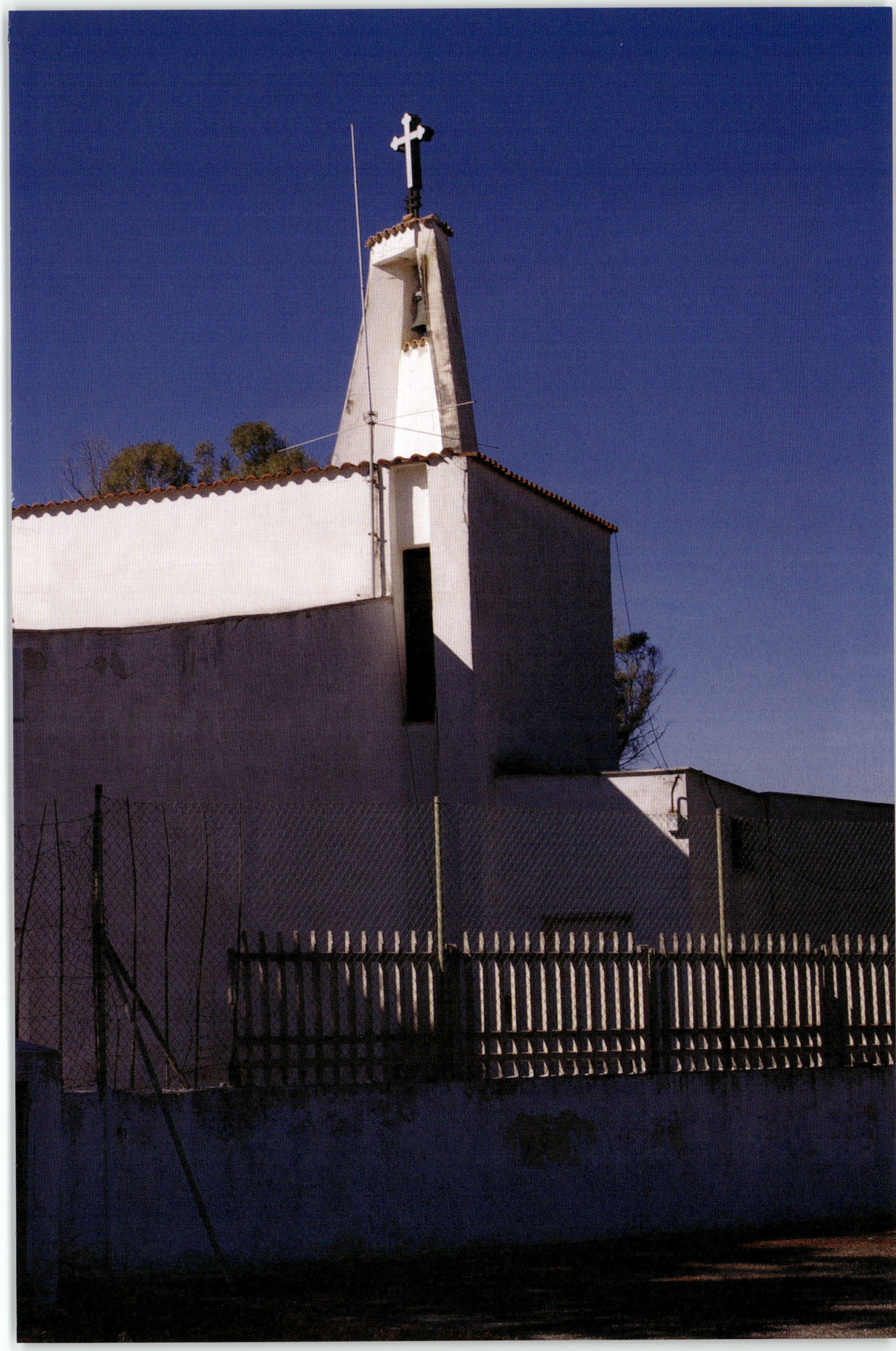

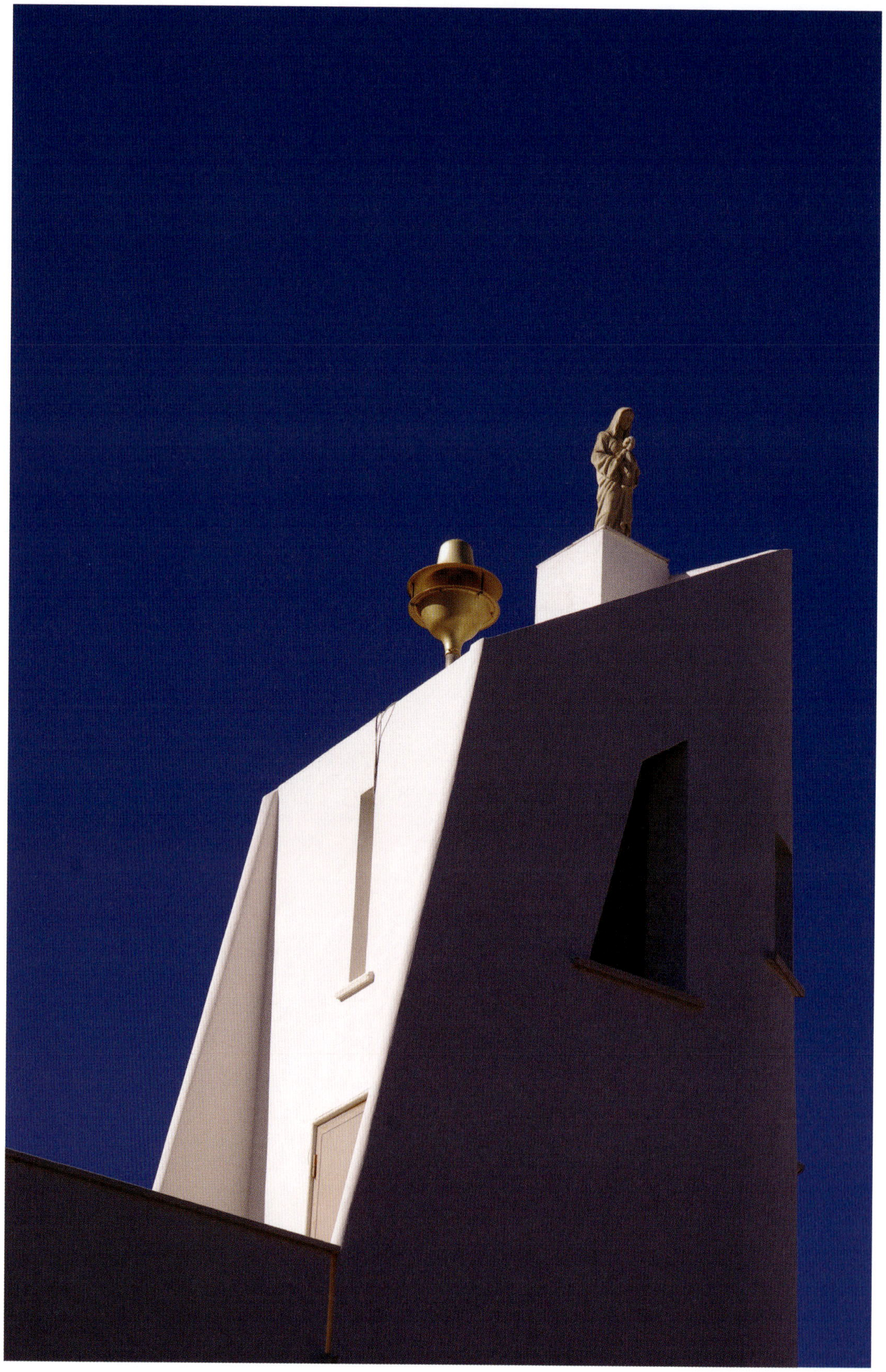

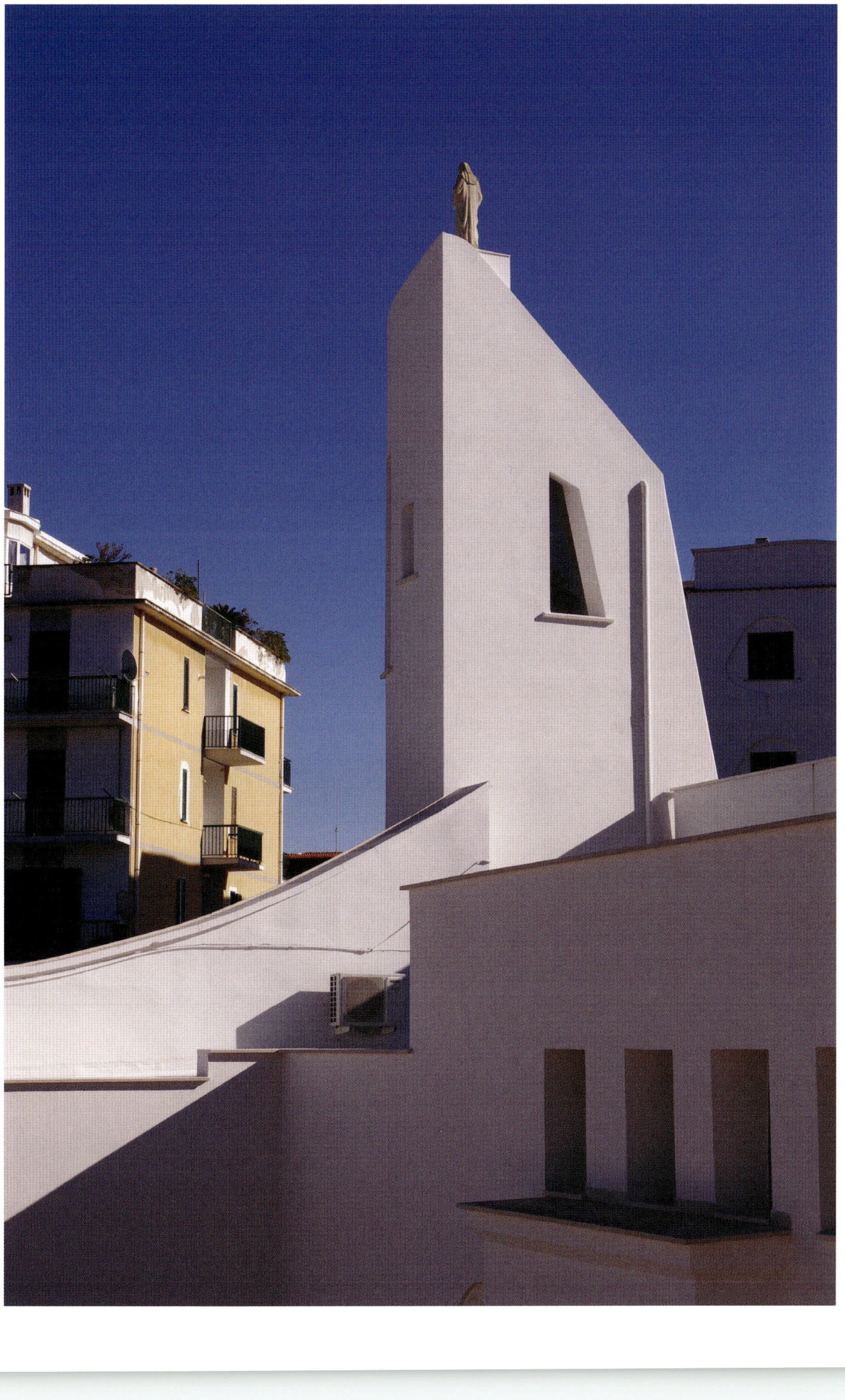

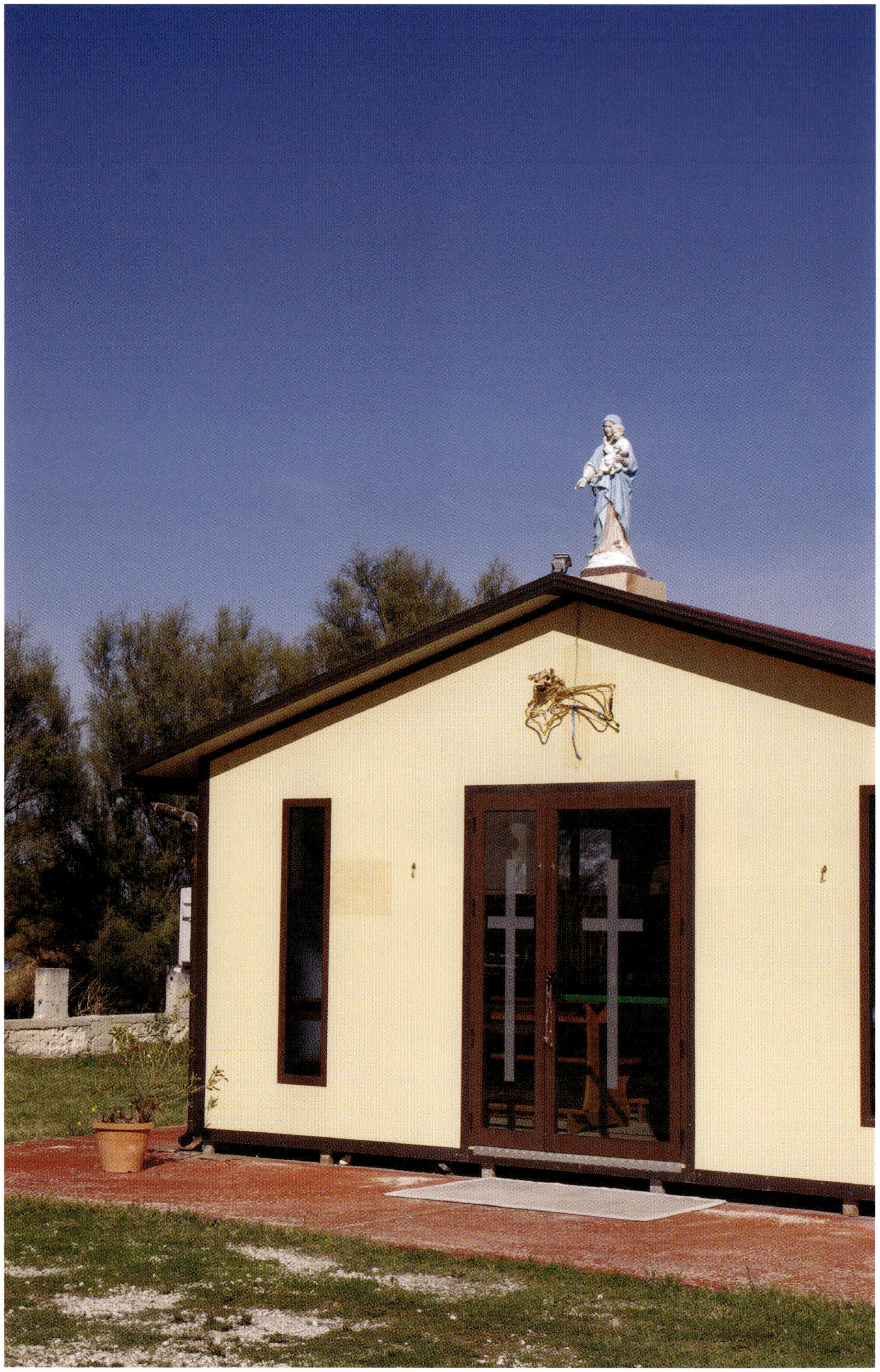

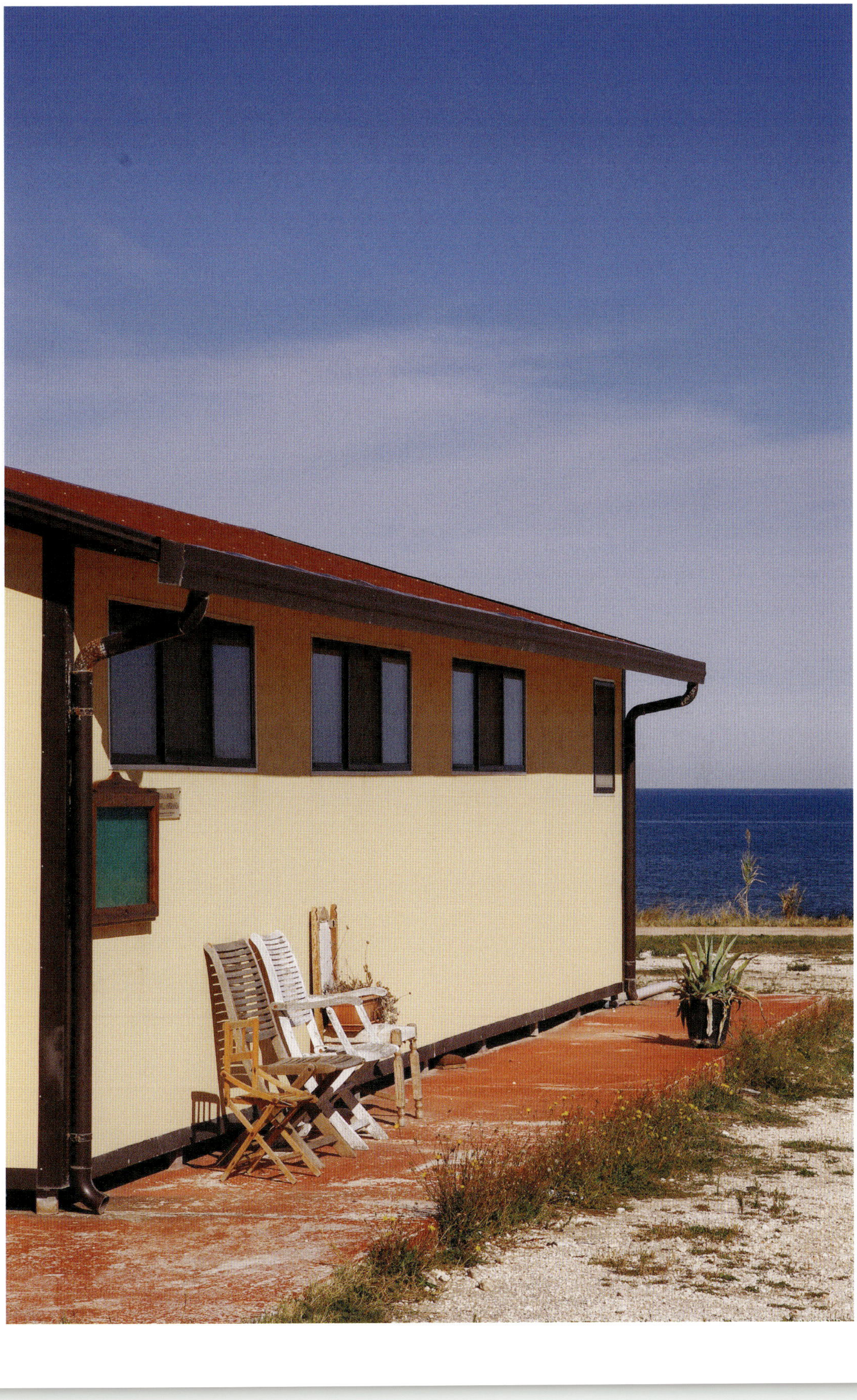

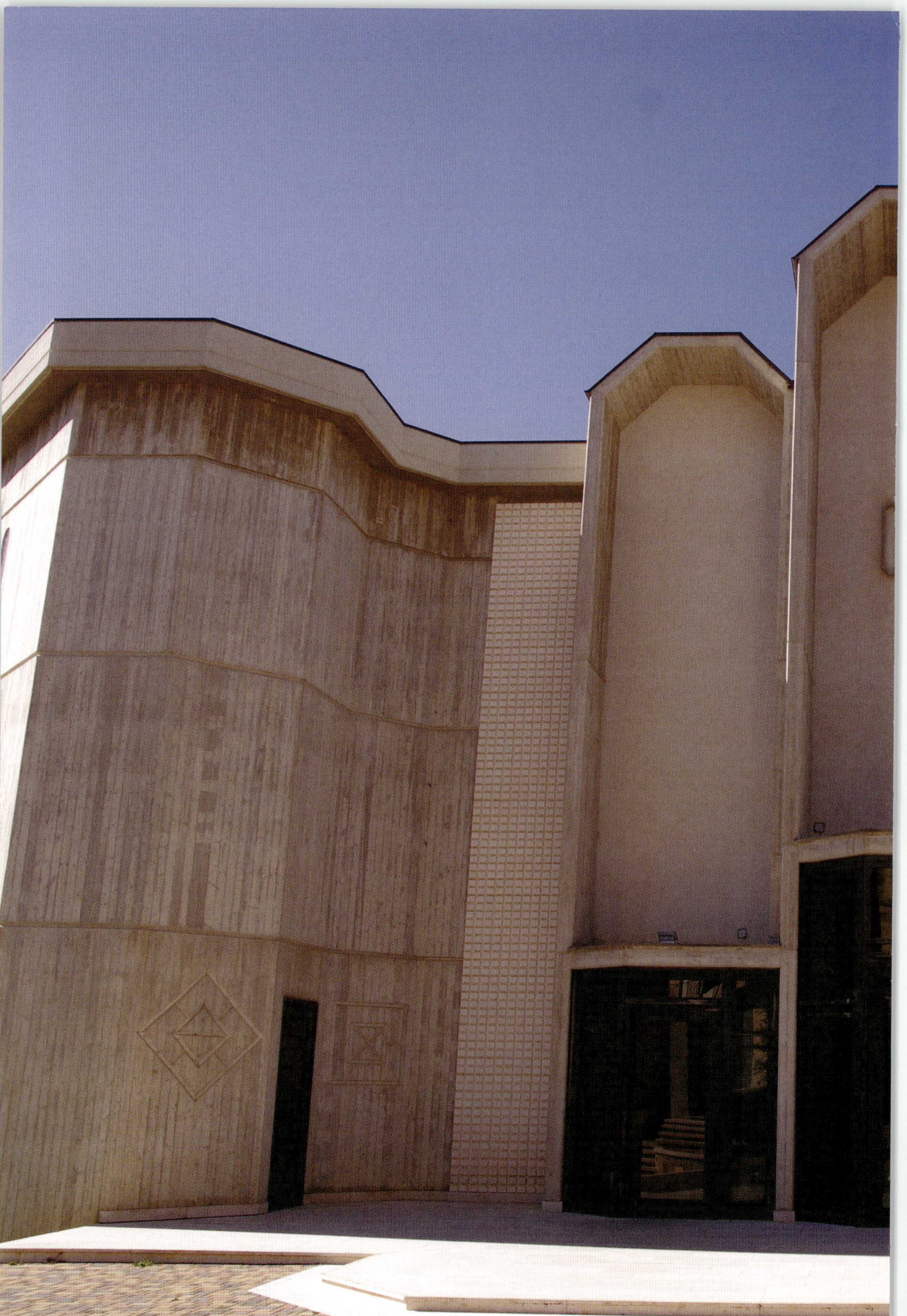

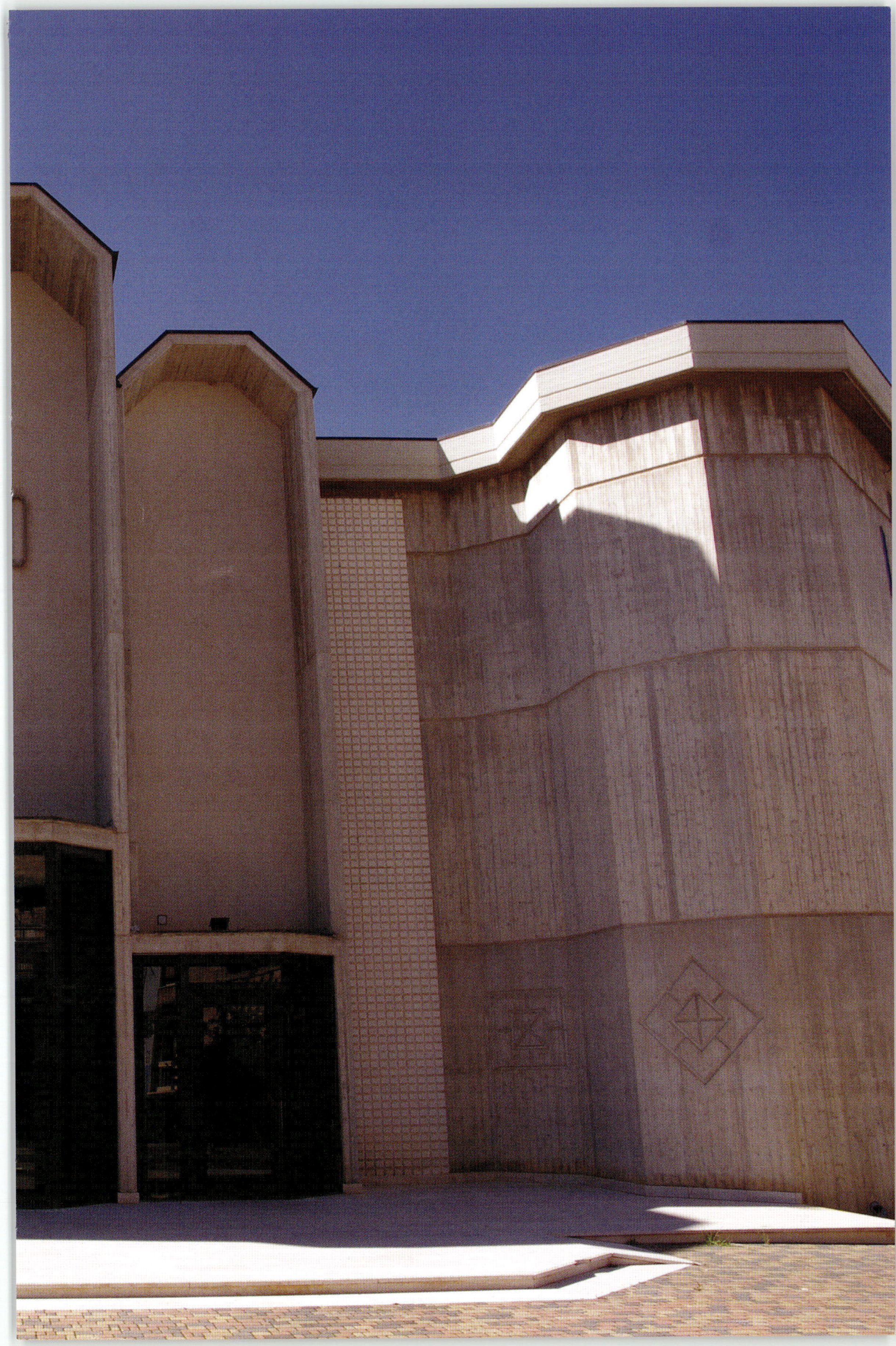

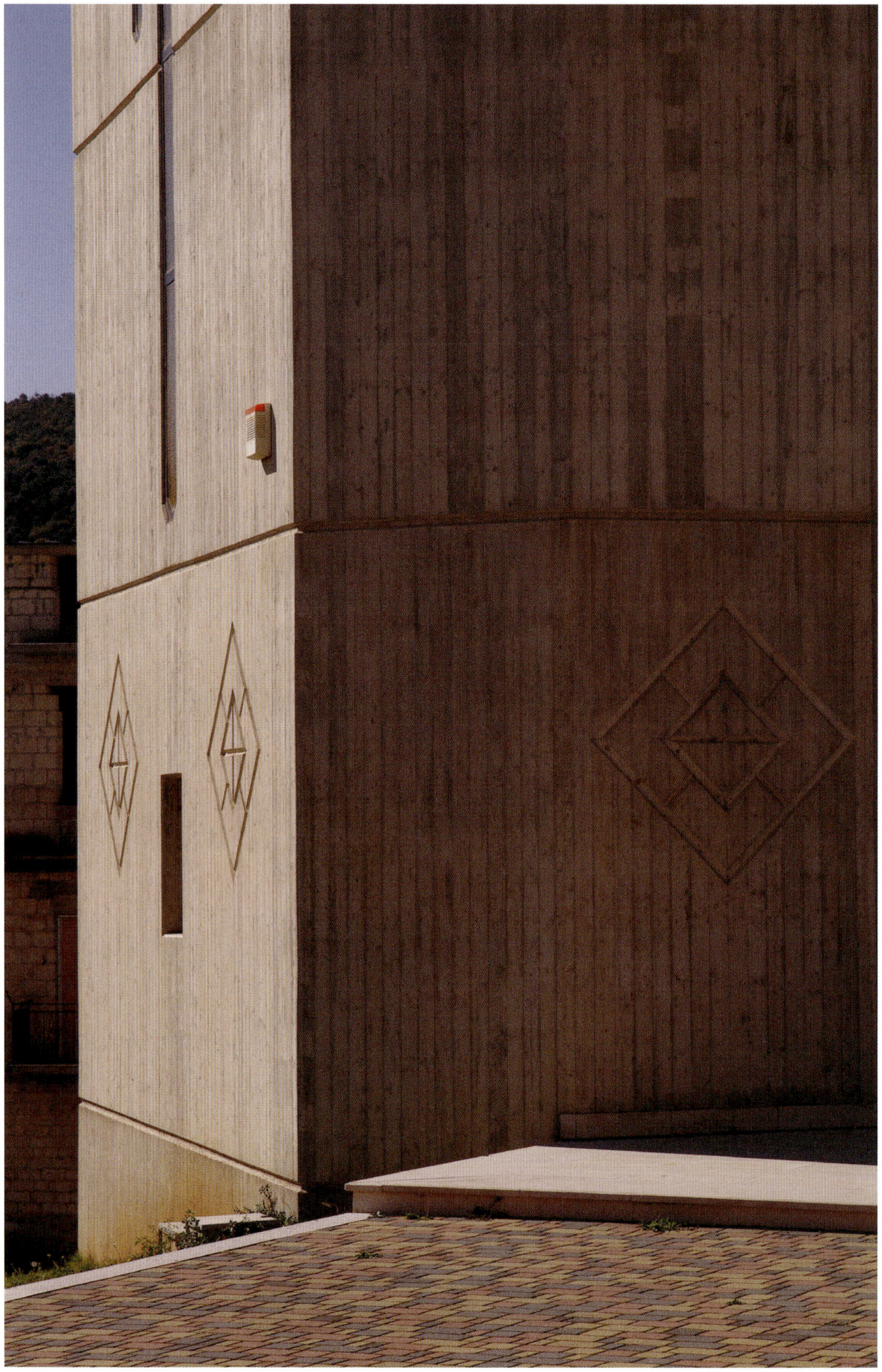

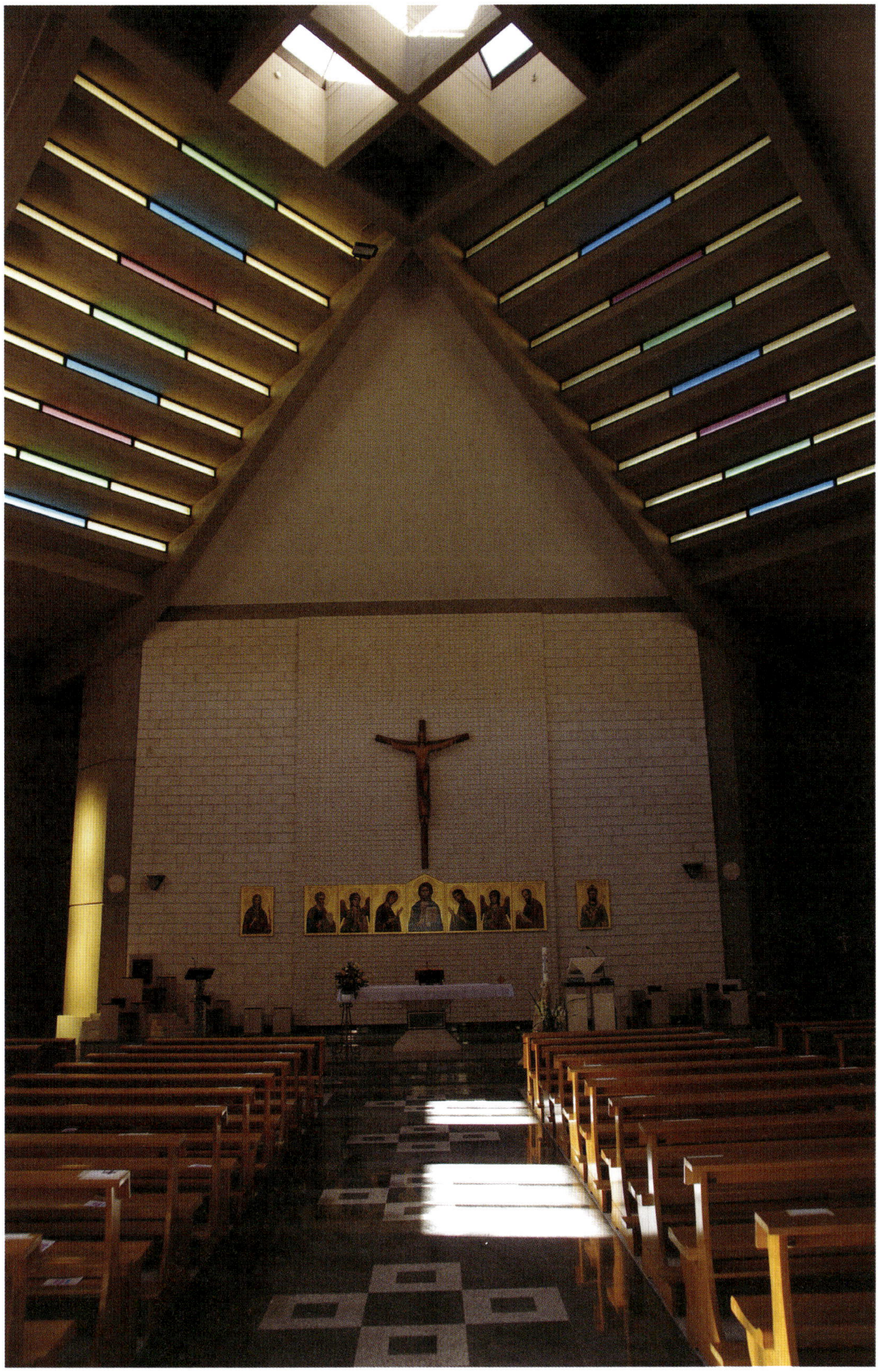

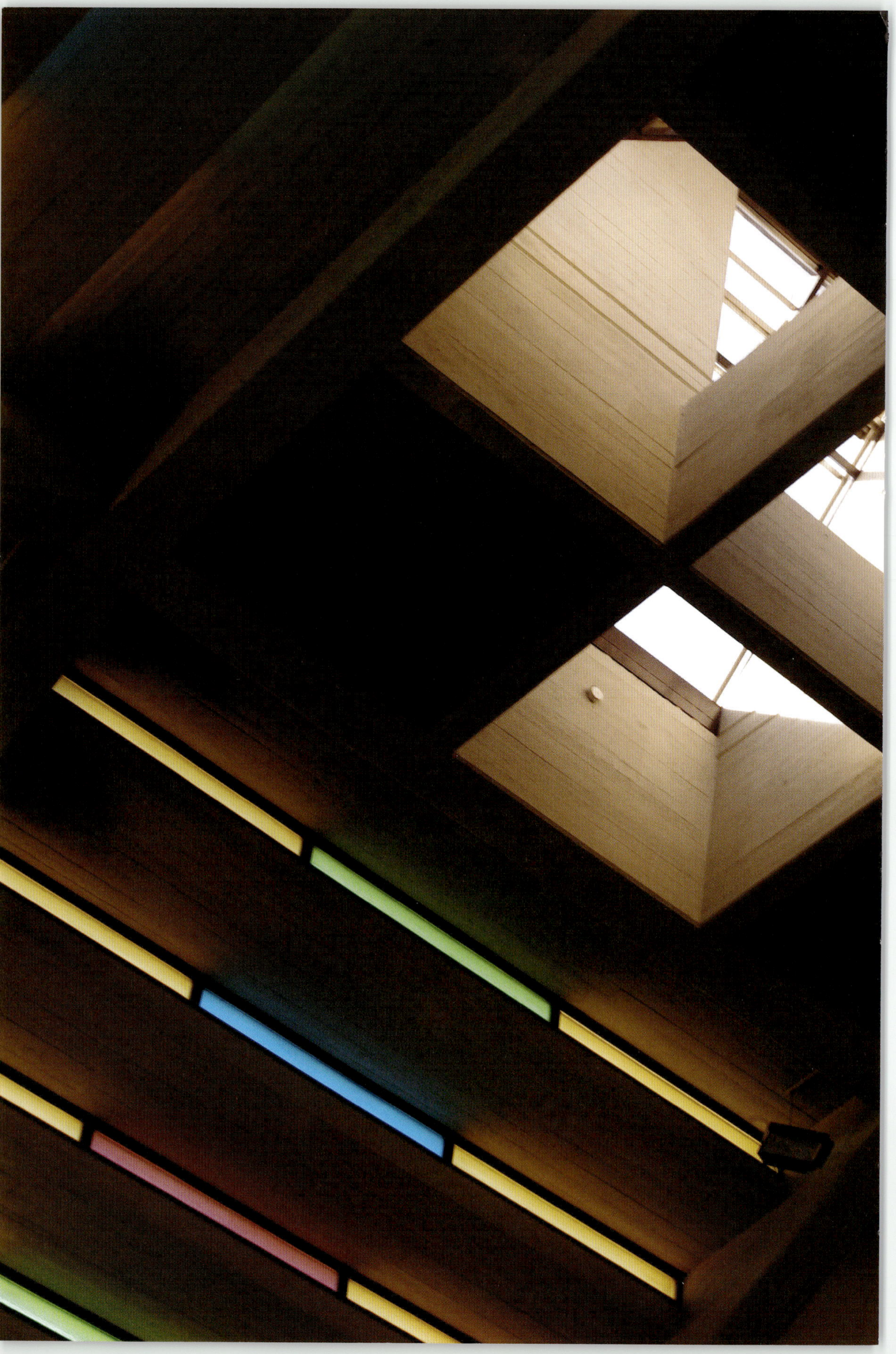

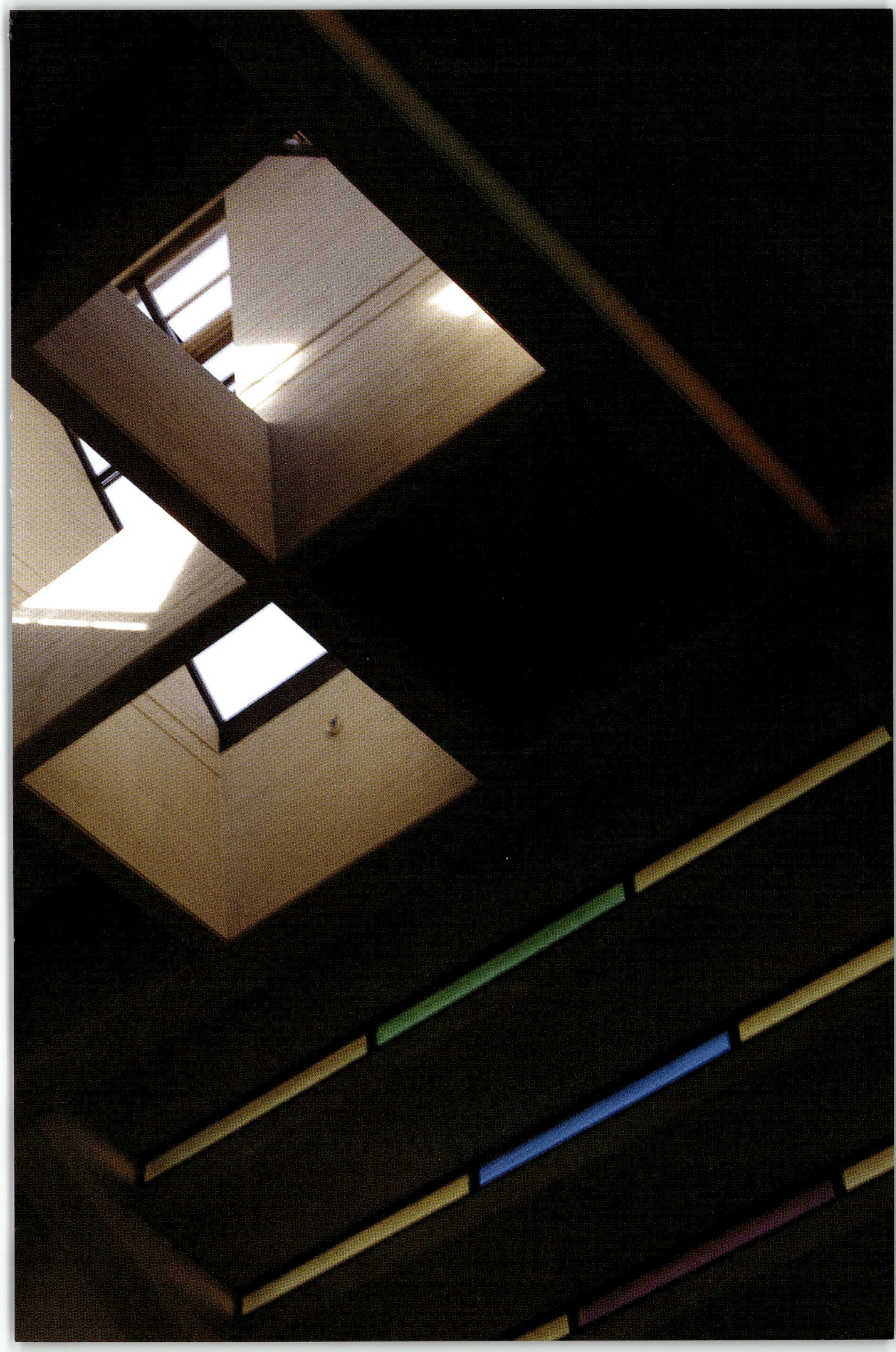

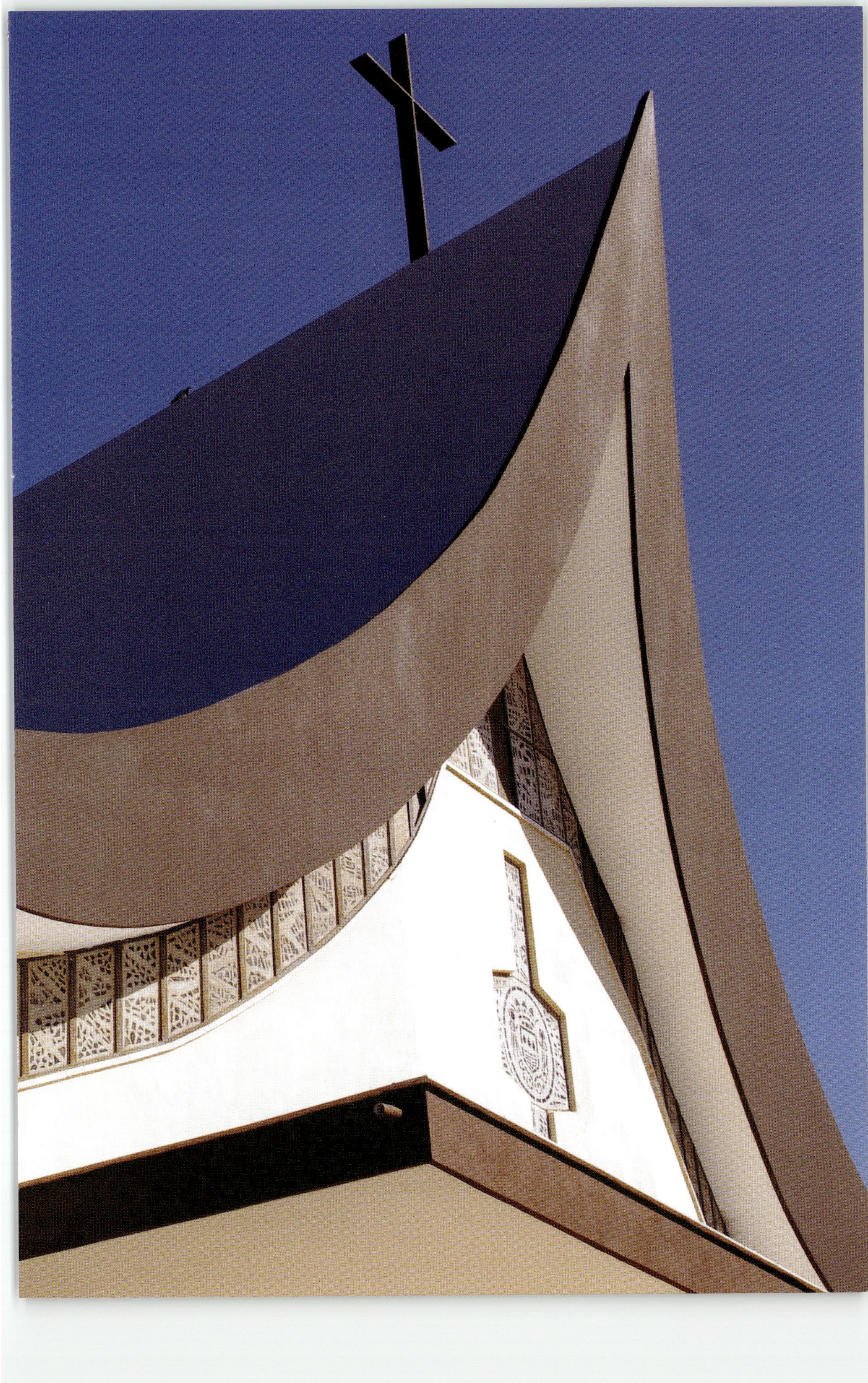

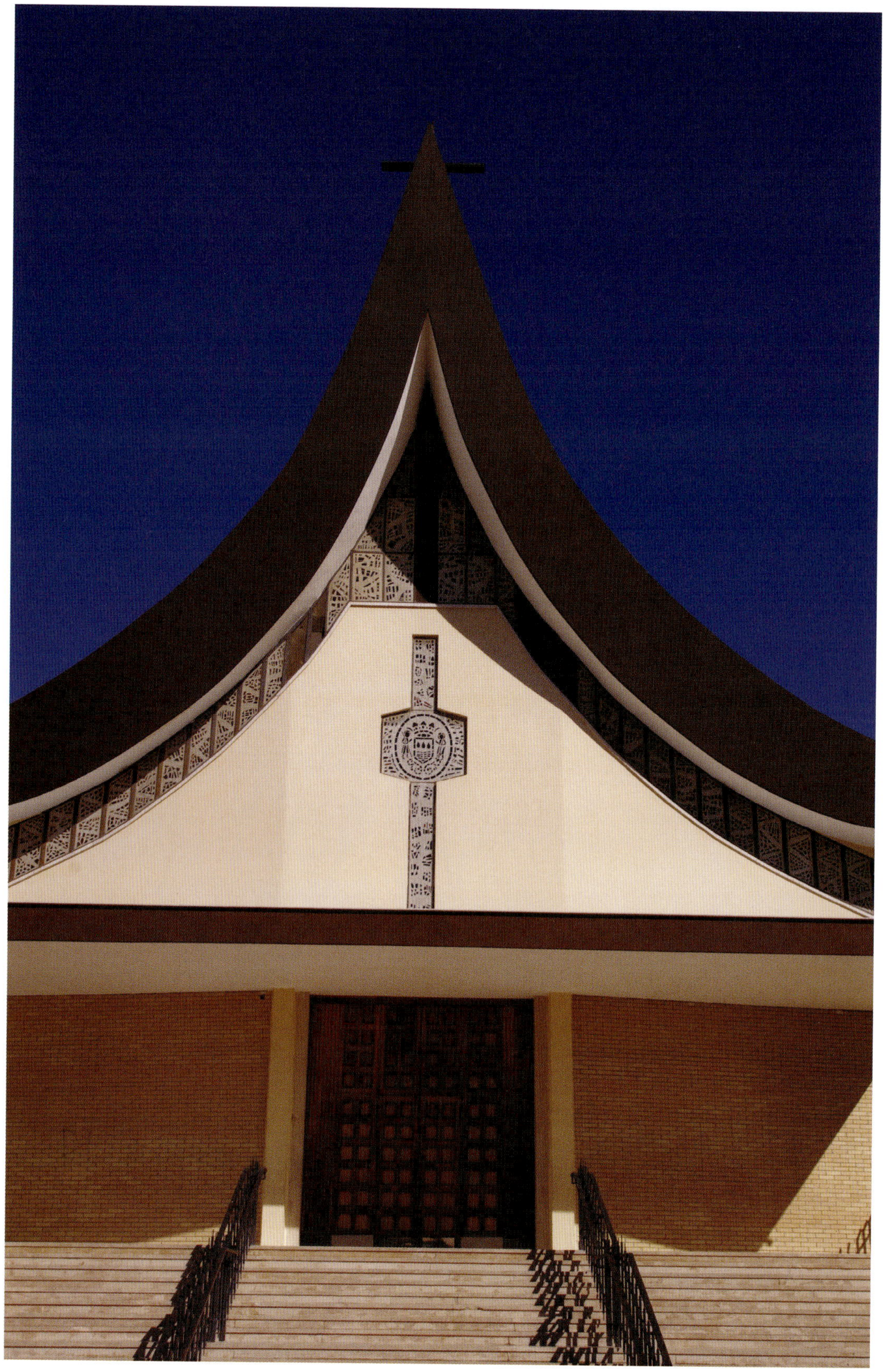

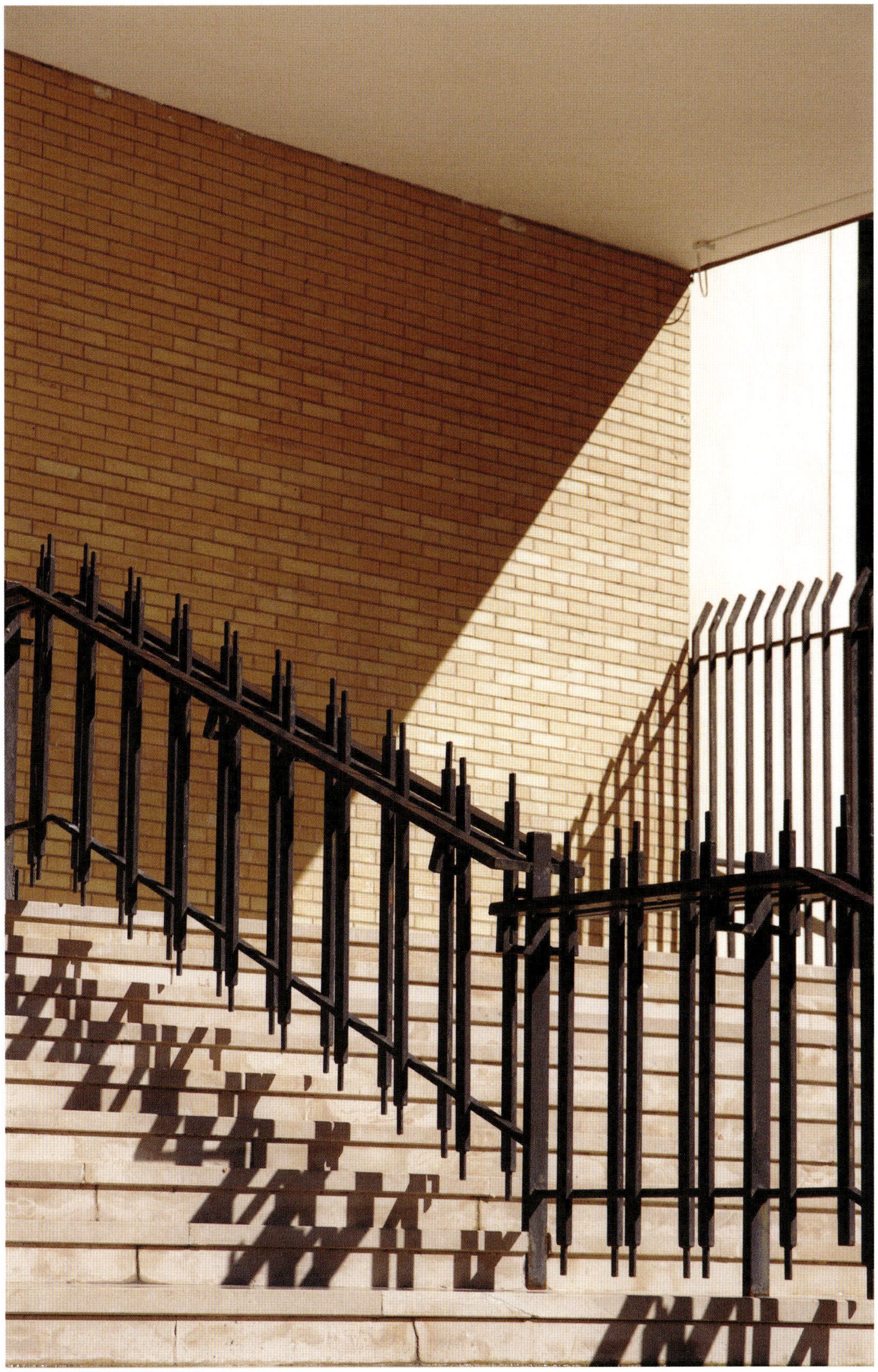

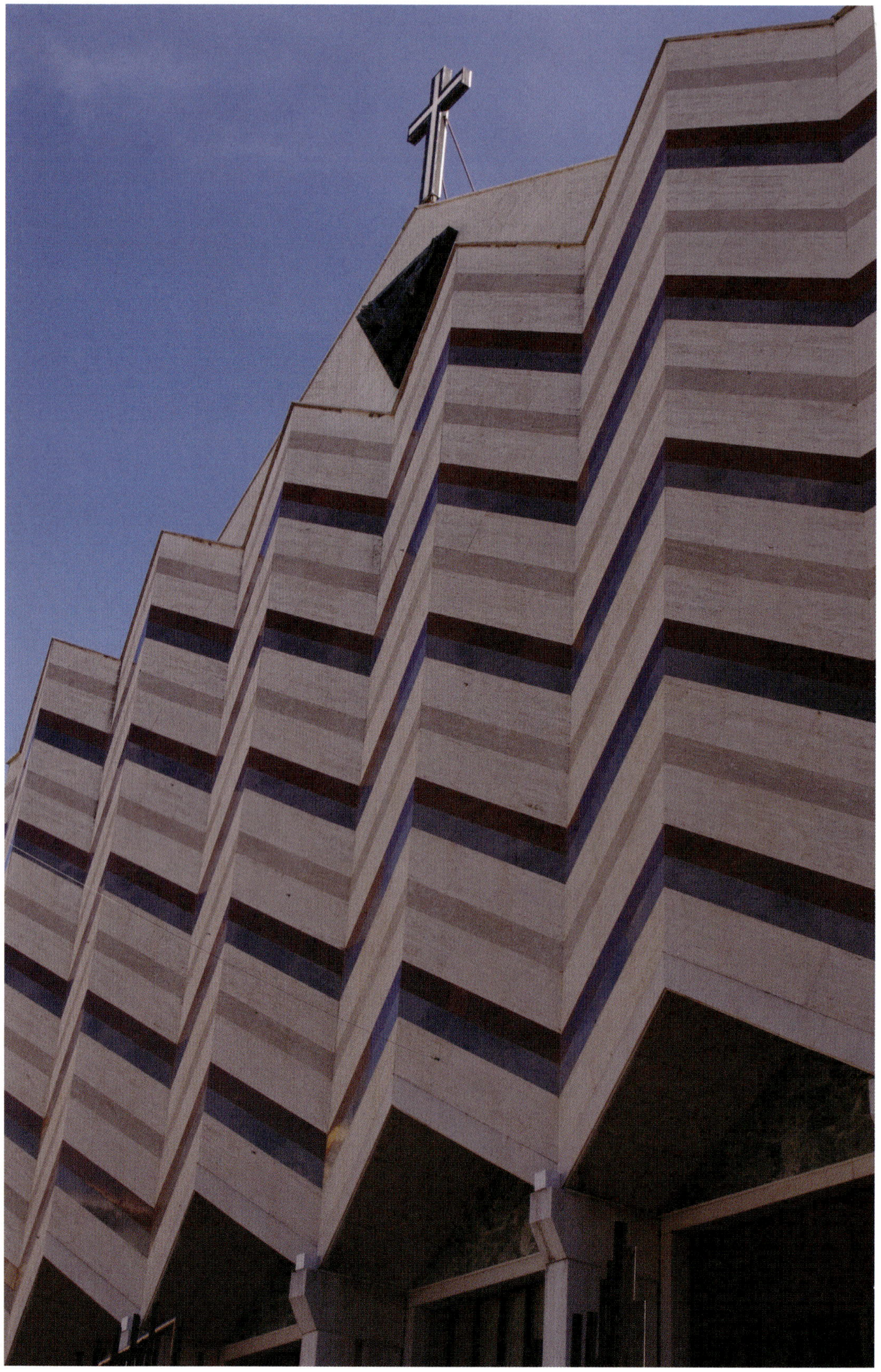

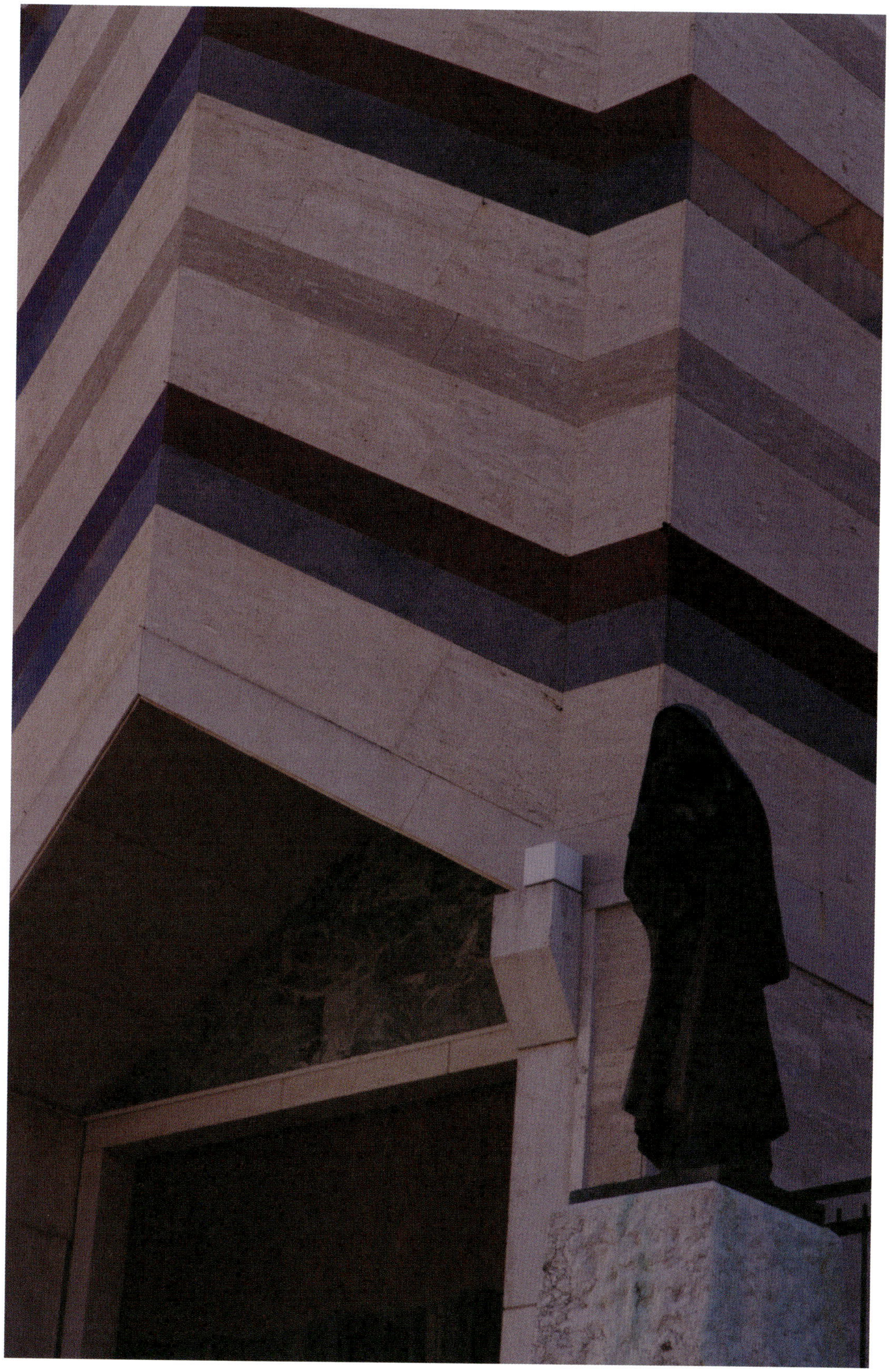

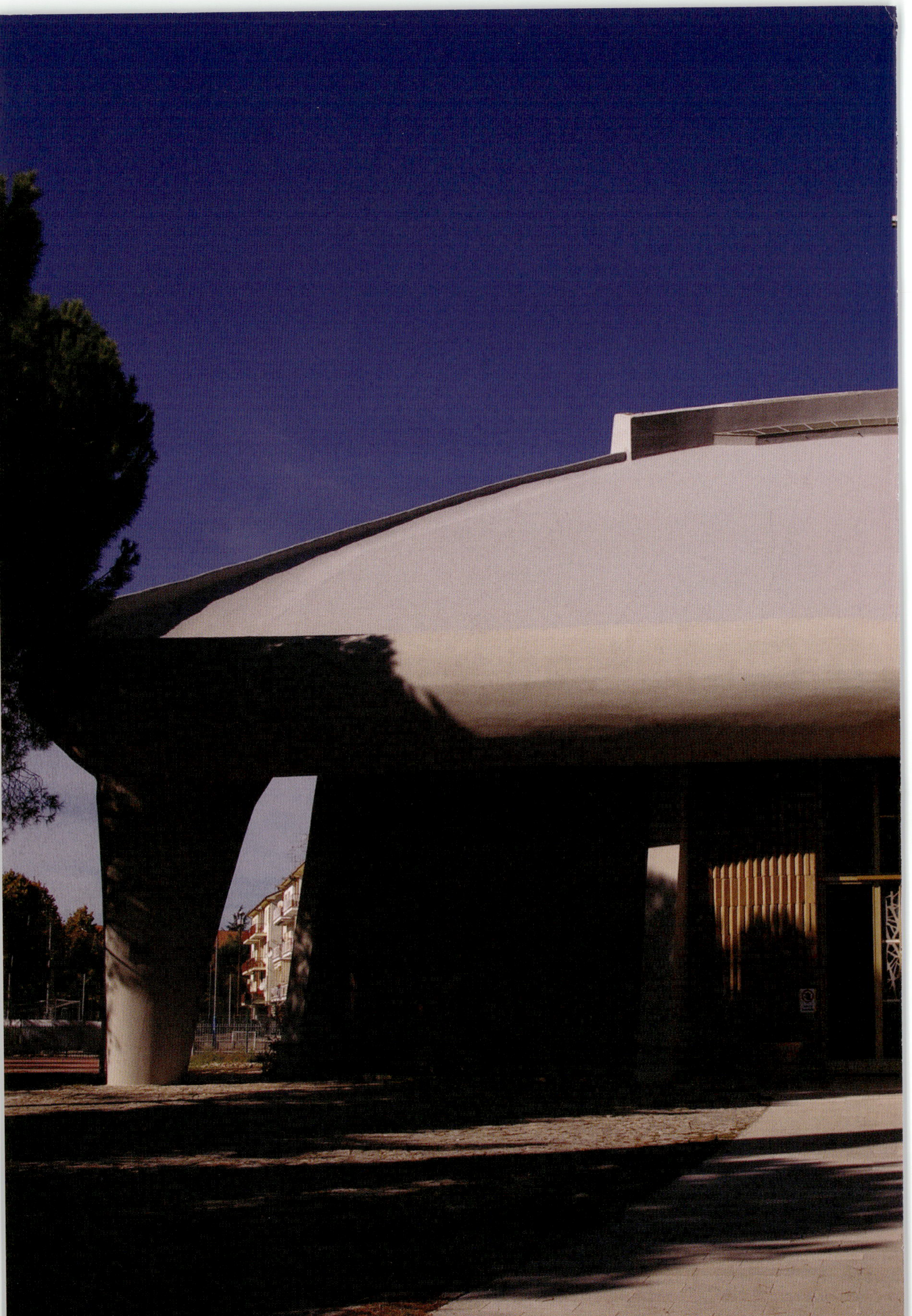

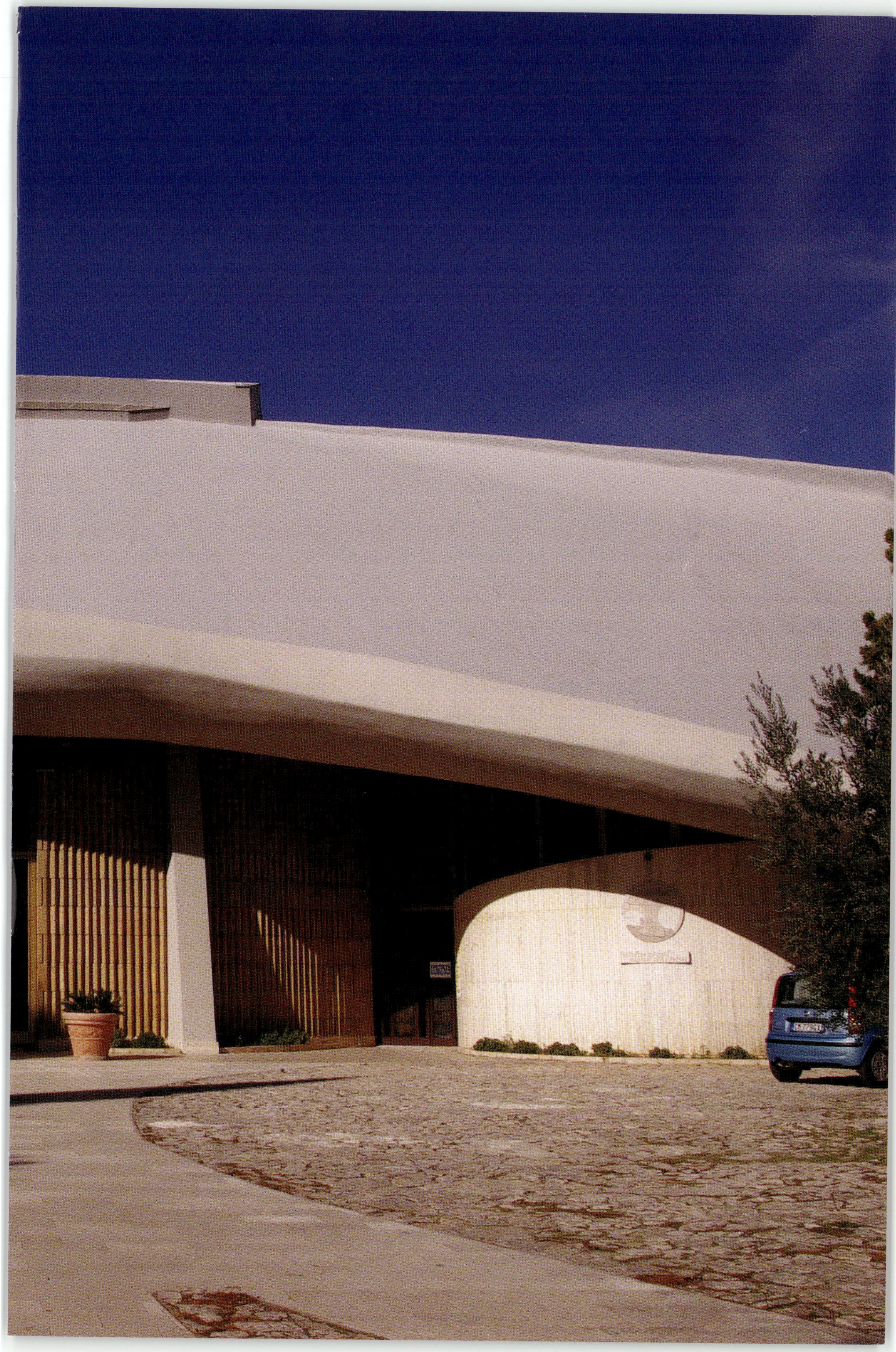

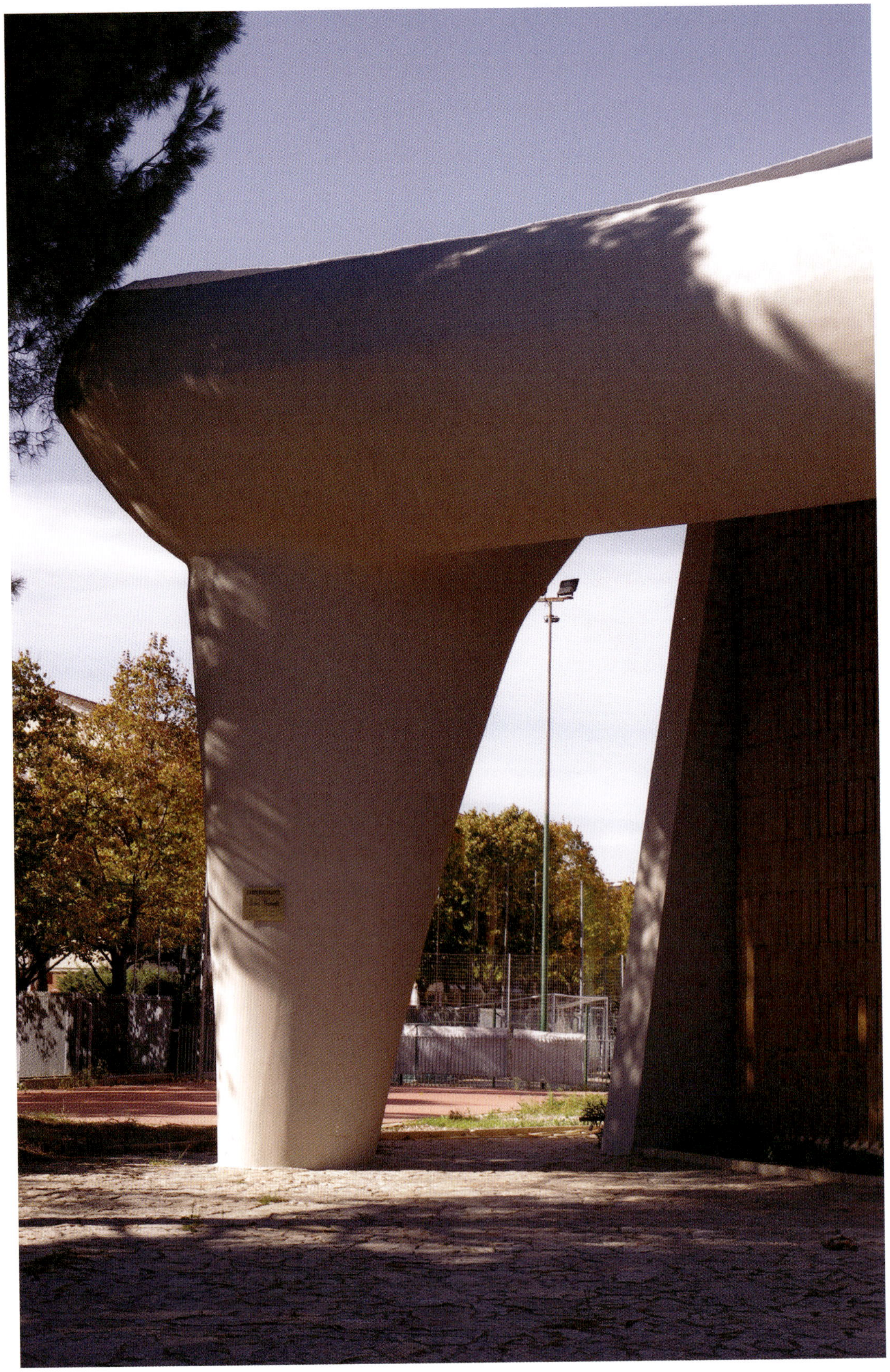

Published by Bureau Sepän, 2022

Special thanks to Alan Marzo, Zoe Macheret
& Miguel Almeida for their support.

www.olivierduport.fr